Common American Phrases

in Everyday Contexts

**A Detailed Guide to
Real-Life Conversation
and Small Talk**

Third Edition

RICHARD A. SPEARS, Ph.D.

New York Chicago San Francisco Lisbon London Madrid Mexico City
Milan New Delhi San Juan Seoul Singapore Sydney Toronto

The **McGraw·Hill** Companies

12 13 14 15 16   QFR   23 22 21 20 19

ISBN   978-0-07-177607-3
MHID   0-07-177607-9

e-ISBN 978-0-07-177608-0
e-MHID   0-07-177608-7

Library of Congress Cataloging-in-Publication Data

Spears, Richard A.
    Common American phrases in everyday contexts : a detailed guide to real-life
conversation and small talk / Richard A. Spears.—3rd ed.
        p.   cm.
    Includes index.
    ISBN-13: 978-0-07-177607-3 (alk. paper)
    ISBN-10: 0-07-177607-9 (alk. paper)
    ISBN-13: 978-0-07-177608-0 (eBook)
    ISBN-10: 0-07-177608-7 (eBook)
    1. Americanisms—Dictionaries.   2. English language—United States—
Conversation and phrase books.   3. English language—United States—Terms and
phrases.   4. English language—Spoken English—United States.   5. Figures of
speech—Dictionaries.   I. Title.

PE2839 .S627   2011
423'.1—dc23   2011038156

Interior design by Terry Stone

Also by the author
American Slang Dictionary
McGraw-Hill's American Idioms Dictionary
McGraw-Hill's Conversational American English
NTC's Dictionary of Everyday American English Expressions
Phrases and Idioms

Contents

About This Dictionary

This dictionary is a collection of more than 2,100 everyday sentences and utterances that Americans use over and over in their greetings, good-byes, and everyday small talk. The third edition has been enlarged and updated to include the latest contemporary, high-frequency conversational idioms. Whereas it is true that there is an infinite number of possible sentences in any language, it is also true that some of those sentences are used repeatedly from day to day. The effective use of language is not in being able to create and understand an infinite number of sentences but in knowing and using the right sentence in the right way in a given context. Nonnative speakers of English have found the first two editions extremely useful for unraveling the shortened sentences and sentence fragments that they hear in personal encounters, both formal and informal.

The kinds of expressions recorded in this collection include complete sentences as well as sentence fragments and phrases. In many instances, fragments are punctuated as complete sentences (initial capital letter and terminal punctuation) because such utterances can stand alone just like complete sentences. Phrases and fragments that are always included or imbedded in other sentences do not have initial and terminal punctuation. The utterances here are presented without profanity, swearing, or slang unless the latter is a necessary part of the utterance. Depending, on age, class, context, and personal choice, actual use of these entries may be replete with profanity, swearing, and slang.

The style of the typical entry and the examples is highly colloquial. Many of the examples express joking, anger, and sarcasm. In general, this is not the type of language that one would choose to write, unless one were writing dialogue for a script. It is the type of language that one hears every day and needs to understand, however.

This collection is not only a dictionary but also a resource for the learning of these expressions. The user is encouraged not only to use the dictionary as a reference book but also to read it from cover to cover. An index of key words is included that allows the user to find the full form of a phrase by looking up any major word in the phrase.

Guide to the Use of the Dictionary

1. Entry heads are alphabetized word by word.

2. Entry heads appear in **boldface type**. Cited entry heads appear in this type.

3. An entry head may have one or more alternative forms. The alternatives are printed in **boldface type** and are preceded by "AND." Alternative forms are separated by semicolons.

4. Definitions and descriptions are in roman type. Alternative or closely related definitions and paraphrases are separated by semicolons.

5. A definition or paraphrase may be followed by comments in parentheses. These comments give additional information about the expression, including cautions, notes on origins, or cross-referencing. Each numbered sense can have its own comments.

6. Many expressions have more than one major sense or meaning. These meanings are numbered with boldface numerals.

7. Sometimes a numbered sense will have an additional alternative form that does not belong to the other senses. In such cases the AND and the alternative form follow the numeral.

8. The definitions of some entries are preceded by information in square brackets. The information provides a context that narrows down the scope of the definition. E.g., [of truth] undeniable.

9. The first step in finding an expression is to try looking it up in the dictionary. Entries that consist of two or more words are entered in their normal order, such as **Act your age!** Phrases are never inverted or reordered like **age! Act your**.

10. The alphabetizing ignores *a*, *an*, and *the* at the beginning of an entry head. Look for expressions beginning with *a*, *an*, and *the* under the second word.

11. If you do not find the expression you want, or if you cannot decide what the form of the expression you seek is, look up any major word in the expression in the Key Word Index, which begins on page 241. Pick out the expression you want and look it up in the dictionary.

Terms and Symbols

☐ (a box) marks the beginning of an example.

AND indicates that an entry head has one or more variant forms that are the same or similar in meaning as the entry head.

catchphrase describes an expression meant to catch attention because of its cleverness or aptness.

cliché an expression that is overused and sounds trite.

compare to means to consult the entry indicated and look for similarities to the entry head containing the "compare to" instruction.

entry head is the first word or phrase, in boldface, of an entry; the word or phrase that the definition explains.

go to means to turn to the entry indicated.

see also means to consult the entry indicated for additional information or for expressions that are similar in form or meaning to the entry head containing the "see also" instruction.

an **A for effort** recognition for having tried to do something even if it was not successful. □ *The plan didn't work, but I'll give you an A for effort for trying.* □ *Bobby played his violin in the concert and got an A for effort. Tom said, "It sounded terrible!"*

Able to sit up and take (a little) nourishment. Go to (I'm) able to sit up and take (a little) nourishment.

About that time. Go to (It's) about that time.

Absolutely! a strong affirmation. □ MOTHER: *Do you want another piece of cake?* CHILD: *Absolutely!* □ *Q: Are you ready to go? A: Absolutely!*

Absolutely not! a strong denial or refusal. (Compare to Definitely not!) □ BOB: *Will you please slip this bottle into your pocket?* BILL: *Absolutely not!* □ BOB: *Can I please have the car again tonight?* FATHER: *Absolutely not! You can't have the car every night!*

Act your age! Behave more maturely! (A rebuke for someone who is acting childish. Often said to a child who is acting like an even younger child.) □ *Johnny was squirming around and pinching his sister. His mother finally said, "Johnny, act your age!"* □ CHILD: *Aw, come on! Let me see your book!* MARY: *Be quiet and act your age. Don't be such a baby.*

Adios. Good-bye. (From Spanish. Used in casual or familiar conversation.) □ BOB: *See you later, man.* BILL: *Yeah, man. Adios.* □ BOB: *Adios, my friend.* MARY: *See you, Bob.*

Afraid not. Go to (I'm) afraid not.

Afraid so. Go to (I'm) afraid so.

after all in addition; considering the fact that; thinking in retrospect. □ *You should really be nicer to him. After all, he is your brother.* □ *A: But he acts very rude sometimes, and he's so boring. B: But really, Sally, after all!*

After while(, crocodile). Good-bye till later.; See you later. (*Crocodile* is used only for the sake of the rhyme. This is the response to **See you later, alligator.**) □ *MARY: See you later. BILL: After while, crocodile.* □ *JANE: After while. MARY: Toodle-oo.*

After you. a polite way of encouraging someone to go ahead of oneself; a polite way of indicating that someone else should or can go first. □ *Bob stepped back and made a motion with his hand indicating that Mary should go first. "After you," smiled Bob.* □ *BOB: It's time to get in the food line. Who's going to go first? BILL: After you. BOB: Thanks.*

Afternoon. Go to (Good) afternoon.

Again(, please). Say it one more time, please. □ *The play director said, "Again, please. And speak more clearly this time."* □ *TOM: I need some money. I'll pay you back. BILL (pretending not to hear): Again, please. TOM: I said I need some money. How many times do I have to say it?*

Age before beauty. a comical and slightly rude way of encouraging someone to go ahead of oneself; a comical, teasing, and slightly grudging way of indicating that someone else should or can go first. □ *As they approached the door, Bob laughed and said to Bill, "Age before beauty."* □ *"No, no. Please, you take the next available seat," smiled Tom. "Age before beauty, you know."*

Ahem! Excuse me!; Look in this direction!; Give me your attention! (This is a way of spelling the sound of clearing one's throat to draw someone's attention.) □ *ANDY: Ahem! DON: Did somebody say something? ANDY: Ahem! DAVE: Oh, sorry, Andy. What do you want?* □ *DAVE: Ahem! Andy. ANDY: What? DAVE: There was a spider crawling up your pants leg, but I don't see it now.*

Ain't it the truth? Isn't that just the way it is?; I agree with you completely. (Informal.) □ *A: Things aren't the way they used to be in the good old days. B: Ain't it the truth?* □ *A: You just can't buy good shoes anymore. B: Ain't it the truth?*

alive and kicking Go to alive and well.

alive and well AND **alive and kicking; safe and sound** safe, healthy, and unharmed. □ *Q: How have you guys been? Haven't seen much of you. A: We're alive and well. Having a great time!* □ *Q: Have you heard from Tom and Jan? Did they go out of town? A: No, they're at home, safe and sound.*

all in all AND **all things considered; on balance** a transition indicating a summary, a generalization, or the announcement of a conclusion. □ *BILL: All in all, this was a fine evening. ALICE: I think so too.* □ *"Our time at the conference was well spent, all in all," thought Fred.* □ *BILL: How did it go? ALICE: On balance, it went quite well.* □ *BOB: Did the play turn a profit? FRED: I suppose that we made a nice profit, all things considered.*

All is not lost. Things are not totally bad.; This is not a total failure. □ *Don't worry. I'll help. All is not lost.* □ *All is not lost. Here comes Reggie with a jar of French mustard!*

all over 1. completed; done; finished. □ *Hooray. The play has ended, and it was it a huge success. Yippee! It's all over!* □ *It's all over for Fred. He was fired today, and two guards led him out of the building.* **2.** everywhere. □ *TOM: I think I shouldn't have mentioned Fred's problems. I hope it doesn't become gossip. ANN: You should have keep your mouth shut. It's all over now.* □ *The disease started out slowly, hitting only a few neighborhoods. Now it's all over.*

All right. 1. an indication of agreement or acquiescence. (Often pronounced *aright* in familiar conversation.) □ *FATHER: Do it now, before you forget. BILL: All right.* □ *TOM: Please remember to bring me back a pizza. SALLY: All right, but I get some of it.* **2.** (Usually **All right!**) a shout of agreement or encouragement. □ *ALICE: Come on, let's give Sally some encouragement. FRED: All right, Sally! Keep it up! You can do it!* □ *"That's the way to go! All right!" shouted various members of the audience.*

All right already! AND **All righty already!** an impatient way of indicating agreement or acquiescence. (The second version is more comical than rude. Dated but still used.) □ *ALICE: All right already! Stop pushing me! MARY: I didn't do anything!* □ *BILL: Come on! Get over here! BOB: All righty already! Don't rush me!*

All systems are go. an indication that everything is ready or that things are going along as planned. (Borrowed from the jargon used during America's early space exploration.) □ *BILL: Can we leave now? Is the car gassed up and ready? TOM: All systems are go. Let's get going.* □ *SALLY: Are you all rested up for the track meet? MARY: Yes. All systems are go.*

All the best to someone. Go to **Give my best to** someone.

all the more reason for doing something AND **all the more reason to** do something with even better reason or cause for doing something. (Can be included in a number of grammatical constructions.) □ BILL: *I don't do well in calculus because I don't like the stuff.* FATHER: *All the more reason for working harder at it.* □ BOB: *I'm tired of painting this fence. It's so old it's rotting!* SALLY: *All the more reason to paint it.*

all things considered Go to all in all.

Allow me. AND **Permit me.** a polite way of announcing that one is going to assist someone, unasked. (Typically said by a man assisting a woman by opening a door, lighting a cigarette, or providing support or aid in moving about. In **Allow me**, the stress is usually on *me*. In **Permit me**, the stress is usually on *mit*.) □ *Tom and Jane approached the door. "Allow me," said Tom, grabbing the doorknob.* □ *"Permit me," said Fred, pulling out a gold-plated lighter and lighting Jane's cigarette.*

almost lost it almost having lost one's temper, composure, or control. (Also literal.) □ *I was so mad, I almost lost it.* □ *When he saw the dent in his fender, he almost lost it.*

Aloha. 1. Hello. (Hawaiian. Used in casual or familiar conversation or in Hawaii.) □ *"Aloha. Welcome," smiled the hostess.* □ ALICE: *Hello. Can I come in?* SUE: *Come in. Aloha and welcome.* **2.** Goodbye. (Hawaiian. Used in casual or familiar conversation or in Hawaii.) □ MARY: *It's time we were going. Aloha.* JANE: *Aloha, Mary. Come again.* □ *All the family stood by the little plane, cried and cried, and called, "Aloha, aloha," long after my little plane took me away to the big island.*

Am I glad to see you! I am very glad to see you! (Not a question. There is a stress on *I* and another on *you*.) □ BILL: *Well, I finally got here!* JOHN: *Boy howdy! Am I glad to see you!* □ TOM *(as Bill opens the door): Here I am, Bill. What's wrong?* BILL: *Boy, am I glad to see you! Come on in. The hot water heater exploded.*

Am I right? Isn't that so?; Right? (A way of demanding a response and stimulating further conversation.) □ JOHN: *Now, this is the kind of thing we should be doing. Am I right?* SUE: *Well, sure. I guess.* □ FRED: *You don't want to do this for the rest of your life. Am I right?* BOB: *Yeah.* FRED: *You want to make something of yourself. Am I right?* BOB: *I suppose.*

And how! an enthusiastic indication of agreement. □ MARY: *Wasn't that a great game? Didn't you like it? SALLY: And how!* □ BOB: *Hey, man! Don't you just love this pizza? TOM: And how!*

and so forth AND **and so on** continuing the list (of things or people) in the same manner. (Both expressions can be used together for emphasis.) □ *I will require a room for one, a soft bed, a private bathroom, a mini bar, a balcony with a nice view, and so forth.* □ *She has requested a deluxe room with bath, balcony, and so on.* □ *She wants a private bath, a good view, and everything else she can think of, and so on and so forth.*

and so on Go to and so forth.

and then some and even more. □ *He demands all of our best products and lowest prices and then some.* □ *In order to get there by midnight, you will be on the road all day and then some.*

And you? AND **Yourself?** a way of redirecting a previously asked question to the asker or someone else. □ BILL: *Do you want some more cake? MARY: Yes, thanks. Yourself? BILL: I've had enough.* □ JANE: *Are you enjoying yourself? BILL: Oh, yes, and you?*

Any friend of someone('s) **(is a friend of mine).** I am pleased to meet a friend of the person named. (Said when meeting or being introduced to a friend of a friend.) □ FRED: *Well, nice to meet you Tom. Any friend of my brother is a friend of mine. TOM: Thanks, Fred. Nice to meet you too.* □ JOHN: *Thank you so much for helping me. SALLY: You're welcome. Any friend of Sue's.*

Anybody I know? Go to Anyone I know?

anyhow Go to anyway.

Anyone I know? AND **Anybody I know?** a coy way of asking who someone is. □ SALLY: *Where were you last night? JANE: I had a date. SALLY: Anyone I know?* □ BILL: *I've got a date for the formal next month. HENRY: Anybody I know?*

Anything else? Go to (Will there be) anything else?

Anything going on? Go to (Is) anything going on?

Anything new down your way? Has any interesting event happened where you live? (Rural and familiar.) □ BILL: *Anything new down your way? BOB: Nothing worth talking about.* □ MARY: *Hi, Sally. Anything new down your way? SALLY: No, what's new with you? MARY: Nothing.*

Anything you say. Yes.; I agree. □ MARY: *Will you please take this over to the cleaners? BILL: Sure, anything you say.* □ SALLY: *You're going to finish this before you leave tonight, aren't you? MARY: Anything you say.*

Anytime. 1. an indication that one is available to be called upon, visited, or invited at any time in the future. □ MARY: *I'm so glad you invited me for tea. JANE: Anytime. Delighted to have you.* □ SALLY: *We really enjoyed our visit. Hope to see you again. BILL: Anytime. Please feel free to come back.* **2.** a polite but casual way of saying **You're welcome.** □ MARY: *Thanks for driving me home. BOB: Anytime.* □ SALLY: *We were grateful for your help after the fire last week. JANE: Anytime.*

Anytime you are ready. an indication that the speaker is waiting for the person spoken to to make the appropriate move. □ MARY: *I think it's about time to go. BILL: Anytime you're ready. DOCTOR: Shall we begin the operation? TOM: Anytime you're ready.*

anyway AND **anyhow** in spite of all this; regardless. (Words such as this often use intonation to convey the connotation of the sentence that is to follow. The brief intonation pattern accompanying the word may indicate sarcasm, disagreement, caution, consolation, sternness, etc.) □ JOHN: *I just don't know what's going to happen. MARY: Things look very bleak. JOHN: Anyway, we'll all end up dead in the long run.* □ BOB: *Let's stop this silly argument. FRED: I agree. Anyhow, it's time to go home, so none of this argument really matters, does it? BOB: Not a bit.*

(Are) things getting you down? Are things bothering you? □ JANE: *Gee, Mary, you look sad. Are things getting you down? MARY: Yeah. JANE: Cheer up! MARY: Sure.* □ TOM: *What's the matter, Bob? Things getting you down? BOB: No, I'm just a little tired.*

Are you (all) set? 1. Do you have everything you need? □ DON: *Are you all set? Do you have enough staples, glue, and paint to do the project? IDA: Yeah. We're set.* □ *Are you set? Do you have what you need?* **2.** Have you finished eating, and are you ready for the bill? □ WAITER: *Hope you enjoyed your meal. Are you all set? DON: Yes, we're ready for the check.* □ *You guys don't look hungry anymore. Are you set?*

(Are you) doing okay? AND **You doing okay? 1.** How are you? □ MARY: *Doing okay? BILL: You bet! How are you?* □ BILL: *Hey, man!*

Are you doing okay? Tom: Sure thing! And you? **2.** How are you surviving this situation or ordeal? □ *Mary: You doing okay? Bill: Sure. What about you? Mary: I'm cool.* □ *Tom: Wow, that was some gust of wind! Are you doing okay? Mary: I'm still a little frightened, but alive.*

(Are you) feeling okay? Do you feel well? (More than a greeting inquiry.) □ *Tom: Are you feeling okay? Bill: Oh, fair to middling.* □ *Mary: Are you feeling okay? Mary: I'm still a little dizzy, but it will pass.*

(Are you) going my way? If you are traveling in the direction of my destination, could I please go with you or can I have a ride in your car? □ *Mary: Are you going my way? Sally: Sure. Get in.* □ *"Going my way?" asked Tom as he saw Mary get into her car.*

Are you in? Do you intend to participate?; Are you on the team? □ *Hanna: Okay, that's the deal. Are you in? Andrew: I'm in.* □ *Don: Are you part of this deal? You have to decide. Are you in?*

(Are you) leaving so soon? AND **You leaving so soon?** a polite inquiry made to a guest who has announced a departure. (Appropriate only for the first few guests to leave. It would seem sarcastic to say this to the last guest to leave or one who is leaving very late at night.) □ *Sue: We really must go. Sally: Leaving so soon? Sue: Fred has to catch a plane at five in the morning.* □ *John (seeing Tom at the door): You leaving so soon? Tom: Yes, thanks for inviting me. I really have to go. John: Well, good night, then.*

Are you leveling with me? Are you telling me the truth? □ *Max: Come on, Sammy. You know I wouldn't kid around. Sammy: Are you leveling with me? Max: You know I am.* □ *Are you leveling with me? If you're not, you are dead meat.*

Are you on board? Are you in agreement?; Are you part of the team? □ *Q: We've talked to you about this project before, John. You haven't given us a straight answer yet. We need to know now. Are you on board? A: Well, I guess so.* □ *Are you on board? It will require a substantial commitment of time, but the potential rewards are great.*

(Are you) ready for this? a way of presenting a piece of news or information that is expected to excite or surprise the person spoken to. □ *Tom: Boy, do I have something to tell you! Are you ready* *for this?* MARY: *Sure. Let me have it!* □ TOM: *Now, here's a great joke! Are you ready for this? It is so funny!* ALICE: *I can hardly wait.*

(Are you) ready to order? Would you care to tell me what you want to order to eat? (A standard phrase used in eating establishments to find out what a customer wants to eat.) □ *The waitress came over and asked, "Are you ready to order?"* □ TOM: *I know what I want. What about you, Sally? Are you ready to order?* SALLY: *Don't rush me!*

(Are you) sorry you asked? Now that you have heard the unpleasant answer, do you regret having asked the question? (Compare to You'll be sorry you asked.) □ FATHER: *How are you doing in school?* BILL: *I'm flunking out. Sorry you asked?* □ MOTHER: *You've been looking a little down lately. Is there anything wrong?* BILL: *I probably have mono. Are you sorry you asked?*

(as) far as I know AND **to the best of my knowledge** a signal of basic but not well-informed agreement, with an indication that the speaker's knowledge may not be adequate. □ TOM: *Is this brand of computer any good?* CLERK: *This is the very best one there is, as far as I know.* □ FRED: *Are the trains on time?* CLERK: *To the best of my knowledge, all the trains are on time today.* □ BILL: *Are we just about there?* TOM: *Far as I know.* BILL: *I thought you'd been there before.* TOM: *Never.*

(as) far as I'm concerned 1. from my point of view; as concerns my interests. □ BOB: *Isn't this cake good?* ALICE: *Yes, indeed. This is the best cake I have ever eaten as far as I'm concerned.* □ TOM: *I think I'd better go.* BOB: *As far as I'm concerned, you all can leave now.* **2.** Okay, as it concerns my interests. □ ALICE: *Can I send this package on to your sister?* JOHN: *As far as I'm concerned.* □ JANE: *Do you mind if I put this coat in the closet?* JOHN: *Far as I'm concerned. It's not mine.*

as for someone or something Go to **as to** someone or something.

As I expected. Go to **(Just) as I expected.**

as I see it AND **in my opinion; in my view** the way I think about it. □ TOM: *This matter is not as bad as some would make it out to be.* ALICE: *Yes. This whole affair has been overblown, as I see it.* □ BOB: *You're as wrong as can be.* JOHN: *In my view, you are wrong.*

as I was saying AND **like I was saying** to repeat what I've been saying; to continue with what I was saying. (The first form is appropriate in any conversation. The second form is colloquial, informal, and familiar. In addition, this use of *like* for *as*, as in the second form, is objected to by many people.) □ *BILL: Now, Mary, this is one of the round ones that attaches to the wire here. BOB (passing through the room): Hello, you two! Catch you later. BILL: Yeah, see you around. Now, as I was saying, this goes here on this wire.* □ *TOM: I hate to interrupt, but someone's car is being broken into down on the street. FRED: As I was saying, these illegal practices must stop.*

As if (I cared)! Go to Like I care!

as it is the way things are; the way it is now. □ *"I wish I could get a better job," remarked Tom. "I'm just getting by as it is."* □ *MARY: Can we afford a new refrigerator? FRED: As it is, it would have to be a very small one.*

(as) like(ly) as not equally likely and not likely. □ *Like as not, John will not be here for the meeting.* □ *Q: Do you think she'll be on time? A: As likely as not, because she has to stop by the candy store.*

as such authentic; in the way just mentioned; as one would expect. □ *ALICE: Did you have a good vacation? JOHN: Well, sort of. It wasn't a vacation, as such. We just went and visited Mary's parents. ALICE: That sounds nice. JOHN: Doesn't it.* □ *ANDREW: Someone said you bought a beach house. HENRY: Well, it's certainly not a beach house, as such. More like a duck blind, in fact.*

as to someone or something AND **as for** someone or something regarding someone or something; having to do with someone or something. □ *As for Charles, someone needs to explain to him how important it is that we all work together.* □ *As for dessert, would apple pie with ice cream be okay?*

as we speak just now; at this very moment. (This has almost reached cliché status.) □ *"I'm sorry, sir," consoled the agent at the gate, "the plane is taking off as we speak."* □ *TOM: Waiter, where is my steak? It's taking a long time. WAITER: It is being grilled as we speak, sir— just as you requested.*

as you say 1. AND **like you say** a phrase indicating (patronizing) agreement with someone. (The *like* is used colloquially only.) □ *JOHN: Things are not going well for me today. What should I do? BOB: Some days are like that. As you say, it's just not going well for you, that's all.* □ *JOHN: This arrangement is not really good. There's not enough room for both of us. MARY: I guess you're right. It is* *crowded, and, like you say, there's not enough room.* **2.** (usually **As you say.**) a polite and formal way of indicating agreement or acquiescence. (Literally, I will do as you say.) □ *JOHN: Please take this to the post office. BUTLER: As you say, sir.* □ *BUTLER: There is a Mr. Franklin at the door. MARY: Thank you, James. Tell him I've gone to Egypt for the winter. BUTLER: As you say, madam.*

at best at most; according to the highest estimate. □ *A: I hope things went well for your reception. B: We were hoping for a large crowd, but there were only a dozen there at best.* □ *What a lousy team. Only half the players at best are major-league quality!*

at that considering what has been mentioned; after you have thought about it. □ *Now that you mention it, his talents are pretty valuable at that.* □ *FATHER: Despite her caustic manner, Mary has been very helpful to us. MOTHER: I guess she has been pretty helpful at that.*

at the end of the day when everything is over. (Also literal.) □ *We all try to do the right thing in our business deals, and at the end of the day, it ought to be appreciated by our customers.* □ *Don't sweat the small stuff. At the end of the day, it will all come out in the wash. You better believe it!*

at the present time now. (Almost a cliché.) □ *"We are very sorry to report that we are unable to fill your order at the present time," stated the little note on the order form.* □ *MARY: How long will it be until we can be seated? WAITER: There are no tables available at the present time, madam. MARY: But, how long?*

aw 1. an interjection indicating dissent. □ *BILL: Put the film in the fridge. BOB: Aw, that's stupid! It'll just get cold!* □ *TOM: The new cars are all unsafe. BILL: Aw, you don't know what you're talking about!* **2.** an interjection indicating pleading. □ *TOM: No! FRED: Aw, come on! Please!* □ *MARY: Get away from my door! JOHN: Aw, come on! Let me in!* □ *FRED: You hurt my feelings. BOB: Aw, I didn't mean it.*

B

bar none with no exceptions. (Here, *bar* is a preposition with the same meaning as *except*.) □ *She is absolutely the best there is, bar none!* □ *We had many dishes to choose from. The menu is quite extensive. Everything looked really good, but we chose the pineapple, radish, and asparagus pizza. It was the worst pizza I've ever had in my life, bar none!*

Batter up! The first person should get ready to start now! (Also literal in baseball.) □ *Okay, everyone has to make a three-minute presentation today. Let's get started with the first one. Batter up!* □ *Somebody has to start. Who wants to be first? Come on. Batter up!*

Be careful. 1. an instruction to take care in a particular situation. □ BILL: *I'm going to the beach tomorrow.* SALLY: *Be careful. Use lots of sunscreen!* □ JANE: *Well, we're off to the Amazon.* MARY: *Heavens! Be careful!* **2.** a way of saying *good-bye* while cautioning the hearer to take care. □ JOHN: *See you around, Fred.* FRED: *Be careful.* □ ALICE: *Well, I'm off.* JOHN: *Bye, Alice. Be careful.*

Be good. a departure response meaning "Good-bye and behave yourself." □ JANE: *Well, we're off. Be back in a week.* MARY: *Okay, have fun. Be good.* JANE: *Do I have to?* □ TOM: *Bye. Be good.* BILL: *See ya.*

Be happy to (do something**).** Go to **(I'd be) happy to (**do something**).**

Be my guest. Help yourself.; After you. (A polite way of indicating that one should go first, help oneself, or take the last bit of something.) □ MARY: *I would just love to have some more cake, but there is only one piece left.* SALLY: *Be my guest.* MARY: *Wow! Thanks!* □ JANE: *Here's the door. Who should go in first?* BILL: *Be my guest. I'll wait out here.* JANE: *Why don't you go first?*

Be quiet! Stop talking or making noise. (Made polite with *please*.) □ BILL *(entering the room)*: *Hey, Tom!* TOM: *Please be quiet! I'm on* *the phone.* □ Tom: *Hey, Bill!* Bill: *Be quiet! You're too noisy.* Tom: *Sorry.*

Be right there. Go to (I'll) be right there.

Be right with you. Go to (I'll) be right with you.

Be seeing you. Go to (I'll) be seeing you.

Be thankful for small blessings. Be grateful for any small benefits or advantages one has, especially in a generally difficult situation. □ *We have very little money, but we must be thankful for small blessings. At least we have enough food.* □ *Bob was badly injured in the accident, but at least he's still alive. Let's be thankful for small blessings.*

Be that as it may even though that may be true. □ Sue: *I'm sorry that I am late for the test. I overslept.* Rachel: *Be that as it may, you have missed the test and will have to petition for a makeup examination.* □ Henry: *I lost my job, so I couldn't make the car payment on time.* Rachel: *Be that as it may, the payment is overdue, and we'll have to take the car back.*

be the case to be true, describing an actual situation. □ *I think Bill is a vegetarian, and if that is the case, we should not serve him meat.* □ *Susie believes trees can talk, but that is not the case.*

Be there or be square. You really must come to the event. (Older slang. Still heard. *Square* = uncool.) □ *There is a gathering this evening at the boss's house. Sure to be a joyous occasion. Be there or be square.* □ *There is a big concert in the park tonight. Some local rock star will perform. Be there or be square.*

Be with you in a minute. Go to (Someone will) be with you in a minute.

Bear up! Be brave!; Show courage! □ *Bear up, Fred! You can do it. It will all be over in a few days.* □ *I know that things are going badly just now, but bear up! We are all standing behind you.*

Beat it! Go away!; Get out! (Slang.) □ Bill: *Sorry I broke your radio.* Bob: *Get out of here! Beat it!* □ *"Beat it, you kids! Go play somewhere else!" yelled the storekeeper.*

Beats me. Go to (It) beats me.

Been a long time. Go to (It's) been a long time.

Been a pleasure. Go to (It's) been a pleasure.

Been getting by. Go to (I've) been getting by.

Been keeping busy. Go to (I've) been keeping busy. See also (Have you) been keeping busy?

Been keeping cool. Go to (I've) been keeping cool. See also (Have you) been keeping cool?

Been keeping out of trouble. Go to (I've) been keeping out of trouble. See also (Have you) been keeping out of trouble?

Been okay. Go to (I've) been okay. See also (Have you) been okay?

Been under the weather. Go to (I've) been under the weather.

Been up to no good. Go to (I've) been up to no good.

Beg pardon. Go to (I) beg your pardon.

beg the question 1. to evade the issue; to carry on a false argument in which one assumes as proved the very point that is being argued. □ *Stop arguing in circles. You're begging the question.* □ *It's hopeless to argue with Sally. She always begs the question.* **2.** to invite the asking of the following question. (A completely incorrect reinterpretation of the phrase. Very popular in the last few years.) □ *His behavior begs the question: Is he basically rude or just dull?* □ *This letter begs the question: "How much money should I charge?"*

Beg your pardon. Go to (I) beg your pardon.

beg your pardon, but Go to (I) beg your pardon, but.

begging your pardon, but Go to (I) beg your pardon, but.

Behind you! Look behind you!; There is danger behind you! □ *"Behind you!" shouted Tom just as a car raced past and nearly knocked Mary over.* □ *Alice shouted, "Behind you!" just as the pickpocket made off with Fred's wallet.*

believe it or not an expression indicating that a previous statement is true whether or not the hearer believes it. □ *Tom: Well, Fred really saved the day. Sue: Believe it or not, I'm the one who saved the day.* □ *Bill: How good is this one? Clerk: This is the best one we have, believe it or not.*

Believe you me! You really should believe me!; You'd better take my word for it! □ *Alice: Is it hot in that room? Fred: It really is. Believe you me!* □ *Sue: How do you like my cake? John: Believe you me, this is the best cake I've ever eaten!*

(The) best of luck (to you). I wish you good luck. □ ALICE: *Good-bye, Bill.* BILL: *Goodbye, Alice. Best of luck.* ALICE: *Thanks. Bye.* □ *"Good-bye, and the best of luck to you," shouted Mary, waving and crying at the same time.*

Better be going. Go to (I'd) better be going.

Better be off. Go to (I'd) better be going.

Better get moving. Go to (I'd) better get moving. See also (You'd) better get moving.

Better get on my horse. Go to (I'd) better get on my horse.

Better hit the road. Go to (It's) time to hit the road.

Better keep quiet about it. Go to (Someone had) better keep still about it.

Better keep still about it. Go to (Someone had) better keep still about it.

Better late than never. a catchphrase said when someone arrives late or when something happens or is done late. □ MARY: *Hi, Tom. Sorry I'm late.* BILL: *Fret not! Better late than never.* □ *When Fred showed up at the doctor's office three days after his appointment, the receptionist said, "Well, better late than never."*

better left unsaid [of a topic that] should not be discussed; [of a thought that] everyone is thinking, but would cause difficulty if talked about in public. (Typically follows *It is . . . , That is . . . , The details are . . . ,* or even *Some things are . . .*) □ MARY: *I really don't know how to tell you this.* BOB: *Then don't. Maybe it's better left unsaid.* □ BILL: *I had a such a terrible fight with Sally last night. I can't believe what I said.* BOB: *I don't need to hear all about it. Some things are better left unsaid.*

Better luck next time. 1. an expression that comforts someone for a minor failure. (Said with a pleasant tone of voice.) □ BILL: *That does it! I can't run any farther. I lose!* BOB: *Too bad. Better luck next time.* □ MARY: *Well, that's the end of my brand-new weight-lifting career.* JANE: *Better luck next time.* **2.** an expression that ridicules someone for a failure. (Said with rudeness or sarcasm. The tone of voice distinguishes sense 2 from sense 1.) □ SALLY: *I lost out to Sue, but I think she cheated.* MARY: *Better luck next time.* □ SUE: *You thought you could get ahead of me, you twit! Better luck next time!* SALLY: *I still think you cheated.*

Better mind your Ps and Qs. Go to (You'd) better mind your Ps and Qs.

Better safe than sorry. It's better to take extra precautions than to take risks and suffer the consequences. □ *I know I probably don't need an umbrella today, but better safe than sorry.* □ *Q: Why do I have to buy all this car insurance? A: Better safe than sorry.*

Better than nothing. Go to (It's) better than nothing.

Better things to do. Go to (I've) (got) better things to do.

Bingo! That's it, just what I've been waiting for! (From the game Bingo, in which the word "Bingo!" is shouted by the first person to succeed in the game.) □ *Bob was looking in the button box for an old button to match the ones on his shirt. "Bingo!" he cried. "Here it is!"* □ *BILL: I've found it! Bingo! MARY: I guess you found your contact lens?*

bit by bit Go to little by little.

Bite your tongue! an expression said to someone who has just stated an unpleasant supposition that unfortunately may be true. □ *MARY: I'm afraid that we've missed the plane already. JANE: Bite your tongue! We still have time.* □ *MARY: Marry him? But you're older than he is! SALLY: Bite your tongue!*

Bottoms up. AND **Down the hatch!; Here's looking at you.; Here's mud in your eye.; Here's to you.; Skoal!** an expression said as a toast when people are drinking together. (The *bottoms* refers to the bottoms of the drinking glasses.) □ *BILL: Bottoms up. TOM: Here's mud in your eye. BILL: Care for another?* □ *"Well, down the hatch," said Fred, pouring the smooth and ancient brandy slowly across his tongue.*

Boy! AND **Boy, oh boy!** a sentence opener expressing surprise or emphasis. (This is not a term of address and can be used with either sex, although it is quite informal.) □ *JOHN: Hi, Bill. BILL: Boy! Am I glad to see you!* □ *BOB: What happened here? FRED: I don't know. BOB: Boy! This place is a mess!* □ *"Boy! I'm tired!" moaned Henry.* □ *"Boy, oh boy! This cake looks good," thought Jack.*

Boy howdy! an exclamation of excited surprise. (Colloquial and folksy.) □ *BOB: Well, I finally got here. FRED: Boy howdy! Am I glad to see you!* □ *BILL: How do you like my horse? FRED: That's one fine-looking filly! Boy howdy!*

Boy, oh boy! Go to Boy!

Boys will be boys. That's the kind of thing that boys seem to do.; That's the kind of silly behavior that boys and men exhibit. □ *They really messed up the living room, but boys will be boys.* □ *Boys will be boys, but they can be trained.*

Bravo! a cheer of praise for someone who has done something very well. □ *"Keep it up! Bravo!" cheered the audience.* □ *At the end of the tenor's aria, the members of the audience leapt to their feet and with one voice shouted, "Bravo!"*

Break a leg! a parting word of encouragement given to a performer before a performance. (It is traditionally viewed as bad luck to wish a performer good luck, so the performer is wished bad luck in hopes of causing good luck.) □ BILL: *The big show is tonight. I hope I don't forget my lines.* JANE: *Break a leg, Bill!* □ MARY: *I'm nervous about my solo.* BOB: *You'll do great. Don't worry. Break a leg!*

break a sweat to sweat; to break out in a sweat; to feel exhausted. (Can refer to physical, or figuratively, to mental activity. Often in the negative.) □ *What a lazy jerk. We work our butts off, and he never even breaks a sweat.* □ *It was nothing. I worked the crossword puzzle in four minutes and never broke a sweat.*

Break it up! Stop fighting!; Stop arguing! □ TOM: *I'm going to break your neck!* BILL: *I'm going to mash in your face!* BOB: *All right, you two, break it up!* □ *When the police officer saw the boys fighting, he came over and hollered, "Break it up! You want me to arrest you?"*

Bully for you! 1. an expression that praises someone or someone's courage. □ *The audience shouted, "Bravo! Bully for you!"* □ BOB: *I quit my job today.* SALLY: *Bully for you! Now what are you going to do?* BOB: *Well, I need a little loan to tide me over.* **2.** a sarcastic phrase ridiculing someone's statement or accomplishment. □ BOB: *I managed to save three dollars last week.* BILL: *Well, bully for you!* □ MARY: *I won a certificate good for a free meal!* SALLY: *Bully for you!*

Butt out! Go away and mind your own business! (Rude. Said to someone who has "butted in.") □ *Jane and Mary were talking when Bill came over and interrupted. "Butt out!" said Jane.* □ TOM: *Look, Mary, we've been going together for nearly a year.* JANE *(approaching): Hi, you guys!* TOM: *Butt out, Jane! We're talking.*

Buy you a drink? Go to (Could I) buy you a drink?

By all means. Yes.; Absolutely. □ *Q: Will you help me with this? A: By all means.* □ *ANN: Let's leave all the extra food with the janitor. JAN: By all means.*

by chance accidentally; randomly; without planning. □ *I found this book by chance at a book sale.* □ *We met by chance in a class in college.*

by the same token a phrase indicating that the speaker is introducing parallel or contrary information. □ *TOM: I really got cheated! BOB: You think they've cheated you, but, by the same token, they believe that you've cheated them.* □ *"By the same token, most people really want to be told what to do," counseled Henry.*

by the skin of someone's **teeth** just barely. □ *HENRY: I almost didn't make it. ANDREW: What happened? HENRY: I had to flag down a taxi. I just made it by the skin of my teeth.* □ *"Well, Bob, you passed the test by the skin of your teeth," said the teacher.*

by the way AND **incidentally 1.** a phrase indicating that the speaker is adding information. □ *TOM: Is this one any good? CLERK: This is the largest and, by the way, the most expensive one we have in stock.* □ *BILL: I'm a Realtor. Is your house for sale? ALICE: My house is not for sale, and, by the way, I too am a Realtor.* **2.** a phrase indicating that the speaker is casually opening a new subject. □ *BILL: Oh, by the way, Fred, do you still have that hammer you borrowed from me? FRED: I'll check. I thought I gave it back.* □ *JANE: By the way, don't you owe me some money? SUE: Who, me?*

Bye. Good-bye. (Friendly and familiar.) □ *TOM: Bye. MARY: Take care. Bye.* □ *SALLY: See you later. Bye. TOM: Bye.*

Bye-bye. Good-bye. (Very familiar.) □ *MARY: Bye-bye. ALICE: See you later. Bye-bye.* □ *TOM: Bye-bye. Remember me to your brother. BILL: I will. Bye.*

Call again. Please visit this shop again sometime. (Said by shopkeepers and clerks.) □ *"Thank you," said the clerk, smiling. "Call again."* □ *CLERK: Is that everything? JOHN: Yes. CLERK: That's ten dollars even. JOHN: Here you are. CLERK: Thanks. Call again.*

Call me name. Go to (You can) call me name.

Can do. I can do it. (The opposite of **No can do.**) □ *JANE: Will you be able to get this finished by quitting time today? ALICE: Can do. Leave it to me.* □ *BOB: Can you get this pack of papers over to the lawyer's office by noon? BILL: Can do. I'm leaving now. Bye.*

Can I speak to someone? Go to **Could I speak to** someone?

Can it! Be quiet!; Stop talking!; Drop the subject! (Slang and fairly rude.) □ *BOB: I'm tired of this place. Let's go. FRED: That's enough out of you! Can it!* □ *JOHN: Hey, Tom! What are you doing, man? TOM: Can it! I'm studying.*

Can too. Go to (I) can too.

Can you excuse us, please? Go to **Could you excuse us, please?**

Can you handle it? 1. Are you able to deal with this problem? (May be a personal problem or a work assignment.) □ *BILL: This file is a mess. Can you handle it?* □ *FATHER: This is a difficult situation, Son. Can you handle it? BOB: Yeah, Dad. Don't worry.* **2.** AND **Could you handle it?** Will you agree to deal with what I have described? □ *MARY: I need someone to work on the Jones account. Can you handle it? JANE: Sure.* □ *BILL: Someone is on the phone about the car payments. Could you handle it? FATHER: Yes.*

Can you hold? Go to **Could you hold?**

Can you imagine? Can you believe that?; Imagine that! □ *She wore jeans to the dance. Can you imagine?* □ *Billy was eating the houseplant! Can you imagine?*

Can't argue with that. Go to (I) can't argue with that.

Can't be helped. Go to (It) can't be helped.

Can't beat that. Go to (I) can't beat that. See also (You) can't beat that.

Can't complain. Go to (I) can't complain.

Can't fight city hall. Go to (You) can't fight city hall.

Can't get there from here. Go to (You) can't get there from here.

Can't help it. Go to (I) can't help it.

Can't make heads or tails of something. Go to (I) can't make heads or tails of something.

Can't rightly say. Go to (I) can't rightly say.

Can't say (as) I do. Go to (I) can't say that I do.

Can't say (as) I have. Go to (I) can't say that I have.

Can't say for sure. Go to (I) can't say for sure.

Can't say that I do. Go to (I) can't say that I do.

Can't say that I have. Go to (I) can't say that I have.

Can't say's I do. Go to (I) can't say that I do.

Can't take it with you. Go to (You) can't take it with you.

Can't thank you enough. Go to (I) can't thank you enough.

Can't top that. Go to (I) can't beat that. See also (You) can't beat that.

Can't unring the bell. Go to (I) can't unring the bell.

Can't win them all. Go to (You) can't win them all.

Capeesh? Do you understand? (From Italian.) □ TOM: *Do I have to stay here?* FRED: *That's the way it's going to be. Capeesh?* TOM: *Yeah.* □ MARY: *I will not tolerate any of this anymore. Capeesh?* BILL: *Sure. Gotcha!*

Care for another? Go to (Would you) care for another (one)?

Care if I join you? Go to Could I join you?

Care to dance? Go to (Would you) care to dance?

Care to (do something**)?** Go to (Would you) care to (do something)?

Care to join us? Go to (Would you) care to join us?

Cash or credit (card)? Do you wish to pay for your purchases with cash or a credit card? □ *Mary put all her packages on the counter. Then the clerk said, "Cash or credit card?"* □ CLERK: *Is that everything?* RACHEL: *Yes. That's all.* CLERK: *Cash or credit?*

Catch me later. AND **Catch me some other time.** Please try to talk to me later. □ BILL *(angry): Tom, look at this phone bill!* TOM: *Catch me later.* □ *"Catch me some other time," hollered Mr. Franklin over his shoulder. "I've got to go to the airport."*

Catch me some other time. Go to Catch me later.

Catch you later. Go to (I'll) catch you later.

Certainly! Go to Definitely!

Certainly not! Go to Definitely not!

a **change of scenery** a move to a different place, where the scenery is different or where things in general are different. □ *I thought I would go to the country for a change of scenery.* □ *A change of scenery would help me relax and organize my life.*

change something **out** AND **swap** something **out** to exchange something (for something else); to replace something. (The *out* makes the phrase colloquial or slang.) □ DON: *I had to change out the batteries, and now it works fine.* □ HANNA: *What should I do to brighten up this kitchen?* ISABEL: *Why don't you swap the cabinets out?*

Changed my mind. Go to (I) changed my mind.

Changed your mind? Go to (Have you) changed your mind?

channel someone to copy or imitate someone's actions or philosophy. □ *Every president wants to channel a former president who was successful.* □ *Our boss seems to be channeling his former boss who thought that we were all paid too much.*

Charmed(, I'm sure). an expression said after being introduced to someone. (Almost a parody. Would not be used in most everyday situations.) □ MARY: *I want you to meet my great-aunt Sarah.* SALLY: *Charmed, I'm sure.* □ MARY: *Bill, meet Sally. Sally, this is Bill.* BILL: *My pleasure.* SALLY: *Charmed.*

Check. That is correct.; That is accounted for. □ SUE: *Is the coffee ready yet?* JOHN: *Check.* □ MARY: *Let's go over the list. Flashlight?*

John: Check. Mary: Band-Aids? John: Check. Mary: Pencils?
John: Check. Mary: Matches? John: Check. Mary: Great!

Check, please. AND **Could I have the bill?; Could I have the**
check? Could I please have the bill for this food or drink? □
When they both had finished their dessert and coffee, Tom said to
the waiter, "Check, please." □ *Bill: That meal was really good. This*
is a fine place to eat. Tom: Waiter! Check, please. Waiter: Right
away, sir.

check something **at the door 1.** to leave something with an appointed
custodian near the entrance to a place. (Coats, parcels, umbrellas,
and hats are dealt with in this manner. In the Old West, guns were
likewise checked at the door.) □ *Please check your wraps at the*
door. □ *Will I be able to check my umbrella at the door?* **2.** to set
aside a thought or an attitude when undertaking serious thinking.
(Figurative.) □ *You need to check those old ideas at the door and*
look deeper for more relevant things. □ *Sorry you're in such a grouchy*
old mood. Next time, you can just check your frown at the door.

Cheer up! Don't worry!; Try to be happy! □ *Tom: Things are really*
looking bad for me financially. Mary: Cheer up! Things'll work out
for the best. □ *Sue: Cheer up! In no time at all, things will be peachy*
keen. Bob: In no time at all, they'll be a lot worse.

Cheerio. Good-bye. (Chiefly British.) □ *Bob: Bye. Tom: Cheerio.* □
"Cheerio," said Mary, skipping out of the room like a schoolgirl.

Chow. Go to Ciao.

Ciao. AND **Chow.** Good-bye. (Italian. **Chow** is not the Italian spelling.) □ *John: Ciao. Mary: Ciao, baby.* □ *"Ciao," said Mary Fran-*
cine as she swept from the room.

Clear the way! Please get out of the way, because someone or something is coming through and needs room. □ *The movers were*
shouting, "Clear the way!" because they needed room to take the
piano out of the house. □ *Tom: Clear the way! Clear the way! Mary:*
Who does he think he is? Bob: I don't know, but I'm getting out of
the way.

Close, but no cigar! Close, but not close enough to win! (Close in
a race, guessing, or predicting, as if a cigar were a prize for winning.) □ *She ran a good race but finished a little behind the winner.*

Too bad. Close, but no cigar! □ *Good guess, Chuck. Close, but no cigar!*

Close enough for government work. Go to (It's) close enough for government work.

Cold enough for you? Go to (Is it) cold enough for you?

Come again. 1. Please come back again sometime. □ MARY: *I had a lovely time. Thank you for asking me.* SALLY: *You're quite welcome. Come again.* □ *"Come again," said Mrs. Martin as she let Jimmy out the door.* **2.** (usually **Come again?**) I didn't hear what you said. Please repeat it. (A little dated and folksy.) □ SALLY: *Do you want some more carrots?* MARY: *Come again?* SALLY: *Carrots. Do you want some more carrots?* □ *Uncle Henry turned his good ear toward the clerk and said, "Come again?"*

Come and get it! Dinner's ready. Come eat! (Folksy and familiar.) □ *The camp cook shouted, "Soup's on! Come and get it!"* □ TOM: *Come and get it! Time to eat!* MARY: *What is it this time? More bean soup?* TOM: *Certainly not! Lentils.*

come as no surprise will not be surprising [for someone] to learn [something]. □ *It will come as no surprise for you to learn that the company is losing money this year.* □ *It came as no surprise that the president had been lying.*

Come back and see us. AND **Come back and see me.** Come visit us [or me] again. (Often said by a host or hostess to departing guests.) □ BILL: *Good night. Thanks for having me.* SALLY: *Oh, you're quite welcome. Come back and see us.* □ BOB: *I enjoyed my visit. Good-bye.* MARY: *It was very nice of you to pay me a visit. Come back and see me.*

Come back anytime. Please come and visit us again. You're always welcome. (Often said by a host or hostess to departing guests.) □ MARY: *So glad you could come.* BILL: *Thank you. I had a wonderful time.* MARY: *Come back anytime.* □ BOB: *Thanks for the coffee and cake. Bye.* MARY: *We're glad to have you. Please come back anytime.*

Come back when you can stay longer. Come back again sometime when your visit can be longer. (Often said by a host or hostess to departing guests.) □ JOHN: *I really must go.* SUE: *So glad you could come. Please come back when you can stay longer.* □ BILL:

Well, I hate to eat and run, but I have to get up early tomorrow.
MARY: *Well, come back when you can stay longer.*

Come in and make yourself at home. Please come into my home
and make yourself comfortable. □ SUE: *Oh, hello, Tom. Come in
and make yourself at home.* TOM: *Thanks. I will. (entering) Oh, it's
nice and warm in here.* □ *"Come in and make yourself at home,"
said Bob.*

Come in and sit a spell. AND **Come in and set a spell.; Come
in and sit down.; Come in and take a load off your feet.**
Please come in and have a seat so we can visit. (Colloquial and
folksy. *Set* is especially folksy.) □ *"Hi, Fred," smiled Tom, "Come
in and sit a spell."* □ TOM: *I hope I'm not intruding.* BILL: *Not at all.
Come in and set a spell.*

Come in and sit down. Go to Come in and sit a spell.

Come in and take a load off your feet. Go to Come in and sit a
spell.

Come off it! Don't act so haughty!; Stop acting that way! □ TOM:
This stuff just doesn't meet my requirements. BILL: *Come off it, Tom!
This is exactly what you've always bought.* TOM: *That doesn't mean
I like it.* □ MARY: *We are not amused by your childish antics.* SUE:
Come off it, Mary. Who do you think you're talking to?

Come on! 1. Stop it!; Stop doing or saying things like that! □ *Sally
was tickling Tom, and he was laughing like mad. Finally, he sputtered, "Come on!"* □ MARY: *Are you really going to sell your new
car?* SALLY: *Come on! How dumb do you think I am?* **2.** Please
oblige me! □ MOTHER: *Sorry. You can't go!* BILL: *Come on, let me
go to the picnic!* □ *"Come on," whined Jimmy, "I want some more!"*

Come (on) in. Enter.; Come into this place. (A polite invitation to
enter someone's home, office, room, etc. It is more emphatic with
on.) □ BOB: *Hello, you guys. Come on in. We're just about to start
the music.* MARY: *Great! Mmm! Something smells good!* TOM: *Yeah.
When do we eat?* BOB: *Just hold your horses. All in good time.* □
BILL: *Come in. Nice to see you.* MARY: *I hope we're not too early.*
BILL: *Not at all.*

come out of left field [for a problem or dilemma] to come from a
place that one would not expect. □ *This new problem came out of*

left field. We were really surprised. □ *Your remarks came out of left field. I can't understand your complaint.*

Come right in. Come in, please. □ *"Come right in and make yourself at home!" said the host.* □ FRED *(opening the door): Well, hi, Bill.* BILL: *Hello, Fred. Good to see you.* FRED: *Come right in.* BILL: *Thanks.*

Coming through(, please). Please let me pass through. (Often said by someone trying to get through a crowd of people, as in a passageway or an elevator. Compare to **Out, please.**) □ TOM: *Coming through, please.* SUE: *Give him some room. He wants to get by.* □ MARY *(as the elevator stops): Well, this is my floor. Coming through, please. I've got to get off.* JOHN: *Bye, Mary. It's been good talking to you.*

Could be better. Go to (Things) could be better.

Could be worse. Go to (Things) could be worse.

Could have fooled me. Go to (You) could have fooled me.

Could I be excused? Would you give me permission to leave?; Would you give me permission to leave the table? (Also used with *can* or *may* in place of *could*.) □ BILL: *I'm finished, Mom. Could I be excused?* MOTHER: *Yes, of course, when you use good manners like that.* □ *"Can I be excused?" asked Bill, with a big grin on his face and his broccoli hidden in his napkin.*

(Could I) buy you a drink? 1. Could I purchase a drink for you? (An offer by one person—usually in a bar—to buy a drink for another. Then the two will drink together. Also used with *can* or *may* in place of *could*.) □ *When Sally and Mary met at the agreed time in the hotel bar, Sally said to Mary, "Could I buy you a drink?"* □ *Then this strange man sat down and said, "Buy you a drink?" Well, I could have just died!* **2.** Could I make you a drink? (A slightly humorous way of offering to prepare and serve someone a drink, as in one's home. Also used with *can* or *may* in place of *could*.) □ BILL: *Come in, Fred. Can I buy you a drink?* FRED: *Sure. What are you having?* BILL: *I've got wine and beer.* □ MARY: *Can I buy you a drink? What do you have there now?* BOB: *Oh, sure. It's just gin and tonic.* MARY: *Great! I'll be right back with it.*

Could I call you? 1. I am too busy to talk to you now. Do you mind if I telephone you later on? (Usually in a business context. Also used with *can* in place of *could. May* is too polite here.) □ SALLY: *I can't talk to you right now. Could I call you?* TOM: *Sure, no problem.* □ BILL: *I've got to run. Sorry. Can I call you?* BOB: *No, I'm leaving town. I'll try to get in touch next week.* **2.** Do you mind if I call you and ask for another date sometime?; Do you mind if I call you sometime (in order to further our relationship)? (Usually in a romantic context. Also used with *can* or *may* in place of *could.*) □ MARY: *I had a marvelous time, Bob.* BOB: *Me, too. Can I call you?* MARY: *Sure.* □ BOB: *I had a marvelous time, Mary. May I call you?* MARY: *Maybe in a week or two. I have a very busy week ahead. I'll call you, in fact.*

Could I come in? Do you mind if I enter? (Also used with *can* or *may* in place of *could.*) □ TOM (standing in the doorway): *Hello, I'm with the Internal Revenue Service. Could I come in?* MARY: *Go ahead, make my day!* □ BILL: *Hi, Tom. What are you doing here?* TOM: *Could I come in? I have to talk to you.* BILL: *Sure. Come on in.*

Could I get by, please? Would you please allow me space to pass by? (Also used with *can* or *may* in place of *could. May* is almost too polite.) □ *Poor Bill, trapped at the back of the elevator behind a huge man, kept saying, "Could I get by, please?" But nobody moved.* □ *"Can I get by, please?" Jane said, squeezing between the wall and a wheelchair.*

(Could I) get you something (to drink)? a way of offering someone a drink, usually an alcoholic drink. (Compare to **(Could I) buy you a drink?** Also used with *can* or *may* in place of *could.*) □ BILL: *Hi, Alice! Come on in! Can I get you something to drink?* ALICE: *Just a little soda, if you don't mind.* □ WAITER: *Get you something to drink?* JOHN: *No, thanks. I'll just order now.*

(Could I) give you a lift? Can I offer you a ride to some place? (Also used with *can* or *may* in place of *could.*) □ *Bill stopped his car at the side of the road where Tom stood. "Can I give you a lift?" asked Bill.* □ JOHN: *Well, I've got to leave.* ALICE: *Me, too.* JOHN: *Give you a lift?* ALICE: *Sure. Thanks.*

Could I have a lift? AND **How about a lift?** Would you please give me a ride (in your car)? (This usually refers to a destination that is the same as the driver's or on the way to the driver's destination. Also used with *can* or *may* in place of *could.*) □ BOB: *Going north? Could I have a lift?* BILL: *Sure. Hop in.* BOB: *Thanks. That's such a* *long walk to the north end of campus.* □ SUE: *Can I have a lift? I'm late.* MARY: *Sure, if you're going somewhere on Maple Street.*

Could I have a word with you? Go to I'd like (to have) a word with you.

Could I have someone **call you?** a question asked by a telephone answerer when the person the caller is seeking is not available. (The *someone* can be a person's name or a pronoun, or even the word *someone*. Also used with *can* or *may* in place of *could*.) □ TOM: *Bill's not here now. Could I have him call you?* BILL: *Yeah. Ask him to leave a message on my machine.* TOM: *Sure.* □ *"Could I have her call you?" asked Mrs. Wilson's secretary.*

Could I have the bill? Go to Check, please.

Could I have the check? Go to Check, please.

Could I help you? Could I assist you? (Said by shopkeepers, clerks, food service workers, and telephone answerers. Also used with *can* or *may* in place of *could*.) □ *The clerk came over and said, "Could I help you?"* □ CLERK: *May I help you?* MARY: *No, thanks. I'm just looking.*

Could I join you? AND **(Do you) care if I join you?; (Do you) mind if I join you?** Will you permit me to sit with you? (An inquiry seeking permission to sit at someone's table or join someone else in some activity. Also used with *can* or *may* in place of *could*.) □ *Tom came into the café and saw Fred and Sally sitting in a booth by the window. Coming up to them, Tom said, "Could I join you?"* □ *"Do you mind if I join you?" asked the lady. "There are no other seats."*

Could I leave a message? the phrase used on the telephone to request that a message be written down for a person who is not available to come to the telephone. (Also with *can* or *may*.) □ BILL: *Can I talk to Fred?* MARY: *He's not here.* BILL: *Could I leave a message?* MARY: *Sure. What is it?* □ *"May I leave a message?" asked Mary politely.*

Could I see you again? Could we go out on another date sometime? (Also with *can* or *may*.) □ TOM: *I had a wonderful time, Mary. Can I see you again?* MARY: *Call me tomorrow, Tom. Good night.* □ *"Could I see you again?" muttered Tom, dizzy with the magic of her kiss.*

Could I see you in my office? I want to talk to you in the privacy of my office. (Typically said by the boss to an employee. Also used with *can* or *may* in place of *could*.) □ *"Mr. Franklin," said Bill's boss sort of sternly, "could I see you in my office for a minute? We need to talk about something."* □ SUE: *Could I see you in my office?* JOHN: *Sure. What's cooking?*

Could I speak to someone**?** AND **Can I speak to** someone**?; May I speak to** someone**?** the phrase used to request to talk to a particular person, usually on the telephone. (The *someone* stands for a person's name. Also used with *talk* in place of *speak*.) □ TOM *(answering the phone): Good morning, Acme Air Products. With whom do you wish to speak?* BILL: *Can I speak to Mr. Wilson?* TOM: *One moment.* □ SALLY: *May I speak to the manager, please?* CLERK: *Certainly, madam. I'm the manager.*

Could I take a message? the phrase used on the telephone to offer to take a message and give it to the person the caller is seeking. (Also with *can* or *may*.) □ BILL: *Can I talk to Fred?* MARY: *He's not here. Could I take a message?* □ *"May I take a message?" asked Mary politely.*

Could I take your order (now)? an expression used by food service personnel to determine if the customer is ready to order food. (Also with *can* or *may*.) □ WAITER: *May I take your order now?* MARY: *Of course. Jane, what are you going to have?* JANE: *I'm having what you're having.* MARY: *Oh.* WAITER: *I'll be back in a minute.* □ MARY: *This is a nice place.* BILL: *Yes, it is.* WAITER: *Can I take your order?* MARY: *Yes, we're ready.*

Could I tell someone **who's calling?** a question asked by telephone answerers to find out politely who is asking for someone. (*Someone* is replaced by a person's name or by a pronoun. Also used with *can* or *may* in place of *could*.) □ MARY *(on the phone): Hello. Could I speak to Bill Franklin?* SALLY: *Could I tell him who's calling?* □ BILL *(speaking on the phone): Is Tom there?* MARY: *May I tell him who's calling?* BILL: *It's Bill.* MARY: *Just a minute.*

Could I use your powder room? AND **Where is your powder room?** a polite way to ask to use the bathroom in someone's home. (Refers to powdering one's nose. Also used with *can* or *may* in place of *could*.) □ MARY: *Oh, Sally, could I use your powder room?* SALLY: *Of course. It's just off the kitchen, on the left.* □ TOM:

Nice place you've got here. Uh, where is your powder room? BETH: *At the top of the stairs.*

Could we continue this later? Could we go on with this conversation at a later time? (Also used with *can* or *may* in place of *could*.) □ BOB: *After that, we both ended up going out for a pizza.* SUE: *Could we continue this later? I have some work I have to get done.* BOB: *Sure. No problem.* □ As Mary and John were discussing something private, Bob entered the room. *"Could we continue this later?"* whispered John. *"Yes, of course,"* answered Mary.

Could you excuse us, please? AND **Would you excuse us, please?; Will you excuse us, please?** We must leave. I hope you will forgive us. (A polite way of announcing a departure. Also with *can* in place of *could*.) □ BILL: *Will you excuse us, please? We really must leave now.* BOB: *Oh, sure. Nice to see you.* □ BILL: *Could you excuse us, please? We simply must rush off.* ALICE: *So sorry you have to go. Come back when you can stay longer.*

Could you handle it? Go to Can you handle it?

Could you hold? AND **Will you hold?** Do you mind if I put your telephone call on hold? (Also with *can* in place of *could*.) □ *"Could you hold?" asked the operator.* □ SUE *(answering the telephone): Hello. Acme Motors. Can you hold?* BOB: *I guess.* SUE *(after a while): Hello. Thank you for holding. Can I help you?*

Could you keep a secret? I am going to tell you something that I hope you will keep a secret. (Also used with *can* in place of *could*.) □ TOM: *Could you keep a secret?* MARY: *Sure.* TOM: *Don't tell anybody, but I'm going to be a daddy.* □ SUE: *Can you keep a secret?* ALICE: *Of course.* SUE: *We're moving to Atlanta.*

Couldn't ask for more. Go to (I) couldn't ask for more.

Couldn't be better. Go to (It) couldn't be better. See also (I) couldn't be better.

couldn't be happier totally happy. □ *We are delighted. Couldn't be happier.* □ *They both couldn't be happier since they got married.*

Couldn't be helped. Go to (It) can't be helped.

Could(n't) care less. Go to (I) could(n't) care less.

Couldn't help it. Go to (I) couldn't help it.

curdle someone's **blood** to frighten or disgust someone severely. □ *The story was scary enough to curdle your blood.* □ *The terrible scream was enough to curdle my blood.*

Cut it out! Stop doing that!; Stop saying that! (Colloquial and familiar.) □ SUE: *Why, I think you have a crush on Mary!* TOM: *Cut it out!* □ *"Cut it out!" yelled Tommy as Billy hit him again.*

Cut me a little slack. AND **Cut me some slack.** Please give me a little leeway.; Allow me some flexibility in meeting the requirements. □ *Come on, man. I'm sorry, but I didn't see you. Don't be so angry. Cut me a little slack.* □ *I tried to get my landlord to cut me some slack, but all he could say was: "You must pay the rent!"*

Cut me some slack. Go to Cut me a little slack.

Cut the comedy! AND **Cut the funny stuff!** Stop acting silly and telling jokes!; Be serious! □ JOHN: *All right, you guys! Cut the comedy and get to work!* BILL: *Can't we ever have any fun?* JOHN: *No.* □ BILL: *Come on, Mary, let's throw Tom in the pool!* MARY: *Yeah, let's drag him over and give him a good dunking!* TOM: *Okay, you clowns, cut the funny stuff! I'll throw both of you in!* BILL: *You and what army?*

Cut the funny stuff! Go to Cut the comedy!

cut to the chase to get to the important matters. □ *Let's stop all this chatter and cut to the chase.* □ *I like the way you cut to the chase and don't waste my time.*

dance on someone's **grave** to celebrate someone's misfortune. □ *I don't know which one of us will get the promotion, but I hope that we can be noble about it. Maybe we can agree that the winner will not dance on the loser's grave.* □ *I don't mind losing the house as much as I will hate to see the bank dancing on my grave when it finally forecloses.*

a **day late and a dollar short** unprepared; unfortunately inadequate. (A slightly humorous expression of despair at failure.) □ *It's the story of my life. A day late and a dollar short.* □ *Here is old Chuck again. Unprepared and ill equipped. A day late and a dollar short.*

deal someone **in 1.** to bring someone into a card game (poker) by dealing that person a hand of cards. □ *I want to play. Deal me in.* □ *ISABEL (sitting down at the table): Can you deal me in?* **2.** to allow someone to join in. □ *If it's not too late to participate in the negotiations, please deal me in.* □ *Q: Can I still buy some of this stock? A: Sure. Shall I deal you in?*

Dear me! an expression of mild dismay or regret. □ *SUE: Dear me, is this all there is? MARY: There's more in the kitchen.* □ *"Oh, dear me!" fretted John, "I'm late again."*

Definitely! AND **Certainly!** Yes, of course! □ *BILL: Will you be there Saturday? MARY: Definitely!* □ *SUE: Would you be so kind as to carry this up the stairs? BILL: Certainly!*

Definitely not! AND **Certainly not!** No, without any doubt at all. (Compare to **Absolutely not!**) □ *BILL: Will you lend me some money? BOB: No way! Definitely not!* □ *BOB: Have you ever stolen anything? FRED: Certainly not!*

Delighted to have you. Go to (I'm) delighted to have you (here).

Delighted to make your acquaintance. Go to (I'm) delighted to make your acquaintance.

did you hear? Go to have you heard?

Did you order all this weather? Are you responsible for this weather? (A jocular way of starting a conversation. No assumption of causality. The *weather* can be more specific, such as *rain, sun, heat, cold, snow,* etc.) □ *Don: How's it going? Hey, Andy, did you order all this snow? Andy: Sure, Don, I do snow in the winter and rain in the fall.* □ *Hello, friend. Nice day, isn't it? Did you order all this sunshine?*

Dig in! Please start eating your meal (heartily). □ *When we were all seated at the table, Grandfather said, "Dig in!" and we all did.* □ *Sue: Sit down, everybody. Bob: Wow, this stuff looks good! Alice: It sure does. Sue: Dig in!*

Dig up! Listen carefully! (Slang.) □ *John: All right, you guys! Dig up! You're going to hear this one time and one time only! Bill: Get quiet, you guys!* □ *Bill: Dig up! I'm only going to say this once. Bob: What was that? Bill: I said listen!*

Dinner is served. It is time to eat dinner. Please come to the table. (Formal, as if announced by a butler.) □ *Sue: Dinner is served. Mary (aside): Aren't we fancy tonight?* □ *"Dinner is served," said Bob, rather formally for a barbecue.*

(Do) have some more. an invitation to take more of something, usually food or drink. □ *Bill: Wow, Mrs. Franklin, this scampi is great! Sally: Thank you, Bill. Do have some more.* □ *Jane: What a lovely, light cake. Mary: Oh, have some more. Otherwise the boys will just wolf it down.*

Do I have to paint (you) a picture? Go to Do I have to spell it out (for you)?

Do I have to spell it out (for you)? AND **Do I have to paint (you) a picture?** What do I have to do to make this clear enough for you to understand? (Shows impatience.) □ *Mary: I don't think I understand what you're trying to tell me, Fred. Fred: Do I have to spell it out for you? Mary: I guess so. Fred: We're through, Mary.* □ *Sally: Would you please go over the part about the square root again? Mary: Do I have to paint you a picture? Pay attention!*

Do I make myself (perfectly) clear? Do you understand exactly what I mean? (Very stern.) □ MOTHER: *You're going to sit right here and finish that homework. Do I make myself perfectly clear?* CHILD: *Yes, ma'am.* □ SUE: *No, the answer is no! Do I make myself clear?* BILL: *Are you sure?*

do pretty well for oneself to make a good salary; to hold a well-paying job. (*Oneself* can be replaced by any of the reflexives: *myself, himself, herself, itself, ourselves, yourself, themselves.*) □ *Q: Have you seen Don's new car? He traded in last year's model. A: I guess he's doing pretty well for himself.* □ *Our company is doing pretty well for itself, considering the recession.*

Do sit down. Don't stand on ceremony.; Please sit down. (A polite phrase encouraging people to resume their seats after rising for an introduction or out of deference.) □ *Tom rose when Mary approached the table, but she said graciously, "Do sit down. I just wanted to thank you again for the lovely gift."* □ *TOM (entering the room): Hello, Bill. BILL (rising): Hi, Tom. TOM (still standing): Do sit down. I just wanted to say hello.*

do someone **one better** Go to go someone one better.

do something **in a heartbeat** to do something almost immediately. □ *If I had the money, I would go back to college in a heartbeat.* □ *Just tell me that you need me, and I'll come there in a heartbeat.*

Do tell. a response to one of a series of statements by another person. (The expression can indicate disinterest. Each word has equal stress. See also **You don't say.**) □ *BILL: The Amazon basin is about ten times the size of France. MARY: Do tell.* □ *FRED: Most large ships produce their own fresh water. SUE: Do tell. Say, Fred, has anyone ever told you how interesting you are? FRED: No. SUE: I suspected as much.*

Do we have to go through all that again? Do we have to discuss that matter again? (Compare to **Let's not go through all that again.**) □ *BILL: Now, I still have more to say about what happened last night. SALLY: Do we have to go through all that again?* □ *SALLY: I can't get over the way you treated me at our own dinner table. FRED: I was irritated at something else. I said I was sorry. Do we have to go through all that again?*

(Do you) care if I join you? Go to Could I join you?

Do you expect me to believe that? That is so unbelievable that you do not expect me to believe it, do you? (A bit impatient. Compare to You can't expect me to believe that.) □ *BILL: I'm going to quit my job and open a restaurant. MARY: That's silly. Do you expect me to believe that? BILL: I guess not.* □ *MARY: Wow! I just got selected to be an astronaut! SALLY: Do you expect me to believe that? MARY: Here's the letter! Now do you believe me?*

Do you follow? Do you understand what I am saying?; Do you understand my explanation? □ *MARY: Keep to the right past the fork in the road, then turn right at the crossroads. Do you follow? JANE: No. Run it by me again.* □ *JOHN: Take a large bowl and break two eggs into it and beat them. Do you follow? SUE: Sure.*

(Do you) get my drift? AND **(Do you) get the message?** Do you understand what I mean?; Do you understand what I am getting at? (Slang.) □ *FATHER: I want you to settle down and start studying. Get my drift? BOB: Sure, Pop. Whatever you say.* □ *MARY: Get out of my way and stop following me around. Get the message? JOHN: I guess so.*

(Do you) get the message? Go to (Do you) get my drift?

(Do you) get the picture? Do you understand the situation?; Do you know what this means you have to do? □ *BILL: I want to get this project wrapped up before midnight. Do you get the picture? TOM: I'm afraid I do. BILL: Well, then, get to work.* □ *FRED: I'm really tired of all this. I want you to straighten up and get moving. Get the picture? BILL: I got it.*

Do you have any issues with that? Do you object to that?; Do you have any problems with that? □ *Q: I am going to ask you to work late this Friday. Do you have any issues with that? A: My problem is that I am leaving on a plane at 7:00.* □ *I am going to wear my hair however I want! Do you have any issues with that?*

(Do) you hear? Do you hear and understand what I said? (Typically Southern.) □ *JOHN: I want you to clean up this room this instant! Do you hear? SUE: Okay. I'll get right on it.* □ *BOB: Come over here, Sue. I want to show you something, you hear? SUE: Sure. What is it?*

(Do you) know what? AND **You know what?** an expression used to open a conversation or switch to a new topic. □ *BOB: You know what? MARY: No, what? BOB: I think this milk is spoiled.* □ *BOB:*

Know what? BILL: Tell me. BOB: Your hair needs cutting. BILL: So what?

(Do you) know what I mean? Go to (Do you) know what I'm saying?

(Do you) know what I'm saying? AND **You know (what I'm saying)?; (Do you) know what I mean?; You know what I mean?; You know?** Do you understand me?; Do you agree? (See also **you know**.) □ *JOHN: This is really great for me and the whole group. You know? SUE: Yes, I know.* □ *SUE: This is, like, really great! Do you know what I'm saying? MARY: Yeah, I've been there. It's great.* □ *It's really, really, really hot today. You know?*

(Do) you mean to say something? AND **(Do) you mean to tell me** something? Do you really mean what you just said? (A way of giving someone an opportunity to alter a comment. The *something* represents a paraphrase.) □ *MARY: I'm leaving tomorrow. SALLY: Do you mean to say you're leaving school for good? MARY: Yes.* □ *BOB: Do you mean to tell me that this is all you've accomplished in two weeks? BILL: I guess so. BOB: I expected more.*

(Do) you mean to tell me something? Go to (Do) you mean to say something?

Do you mind? 1. You are intruding on my space!; You are bothering me! (Impatient or incensed. Essentially, "Do you mind stopping what you are doing?" See also **If you don't mind.**) □ *The lady in line behind Sue kept pushing against her every time the line moved. Finally, Sue turned and said sternly, "Do you mind?"* □ *All through the first part of the movie, two people in the row behind John kept up a running conversation. Finally, as the din grew loud enough to cause a number of people to go "shhh," John rose and turned, leaned over into their faces, and shouted, "Do you mind?"* **2.** Do you object to what I am poised to do? □ *Mary had her hand on the lovely silver cake knife that would carry the very last piece of cake to her plate. She looked at Tom, who stood next to her, eyeing the cake. "Do you mind?" she asked coyly.* □ *"Do you mind?" asked John as he raced by Sally through the door.*

(Do you) mind if I do something? a polite way of seeking someone's permission or agreement to do something. (See also **(Do you) mind if I join you?**) □ *MARY: Do you mind if I sit here? JANE: No,* *help yourself.* □ Tom: *Mind if I smoke?* BILL: *I certainly do.* Tom: *Then I'll go outside.*

(Do you) mind if I join you? Go to Could I join you?

Do you read me? 1. an expression used by someone communicating by radio, asking if the hearer understands the transmission clearly. (See also **(I) read you loud and clear.**) □ CONTROLLER: *This is Aurora Center, do you read me?* PILOT: *Yes, I read you loud and clear.* □ CONTROLLER: *Left two degrees. Do you read me?* PILOT: *Roger.* **2.** Do you understand what I am telling you? (Used in general conversation, not in radio communication.) □ MARY: *I want you to pull yourself together and go out and get a job. Do you read me?* BILL: *Sure. Anything you say.* □ MOTHER: *Get this place picked up immediately. Do you read me?* CHILD: *Yes, ma'am.*

(Do you) want to know something? AND **(You want to) know something?** an expression used to open a conversation or switch to a new topic. □ JOHN: *Want to know something?* SUE: *What?* JOHN: *Your hem is torn.* □ BILL: *Hey, Tom! Know something?* TOM: *What is it?* BILL: *It's really hot today.* TOM: *Don't I know it!*

(Do you) want to make something of it? AND **You want to make something of it?** Do you want to start a fight about it? (Rude and contentious.) □ TOM: *You're really bugging me. It's not fair to pick on me all the time.* BILL: *You want to make something of it?* □ BOB: *Please be quiet. You're making too much noise.* FRED: *Do you want to make something of it?* BOB: *Just be quiet.*

(Do) you want to step outside? an expression inviting someone to go out-of-doors to settle an argument by fighting. □ JOHN: *Drop dead!* BOB: *All right, I've had enough out of you. You want to step outside?* □ BILL: *So, you're mad at me! What else is new? You've been building up to this for a long time.* BOB: *Do you want to step outside and settle this once and for all?* BILL: *Why not?*

Does it work for you? Is this all right with you?; Do you agree? (Colloquial. Can be answered by **(It) works for me.**) □ BILL: *I'll be there at noon. Does it work for you?* BOB: *Works for me.* □ MARY: *We're having dinner at eight. Does it work for you?* JANE: *Sounds just fine.*

Doesn't bother me any. Go to (It) doesn't bother me any.

Doesn't bother me at all. Go to (It) doesn't bother me any.

Doesn't hurt to ask. Go to (It) doesn't hurt to ask.

Doesn't matter to me. Go to (It) (really) doesn't matter to me.

Doing okay. Go to (I'm) doing okay. See also (Are you) doing okay?

Don't ask. You would not like the answer you would get, so do not ask.; It is so bad, I do not wish to be reminded about it, so do not ask about it. □ JOHN: *How was your class reunion?* ALICE: *Oh, heavens! Don't ask.* □ TOM: *What was your calculus final exam like?* MARY: *Don't ask.* □ SUE: *How old were you on your last birthday?* FRED: *Don't ask.*

Don't ask me. Go to How should I know?

Don't be a stranger! AND **Don't make yourself a stranger!** Please come back to visit often. □ *It was really good to see you, Fred. Don't be a stranger. Come back and see us.* □ Q: *Don't be a stranger, you hear?* A: *Thanks, I look forward to seeing you again.* □ *Don't make yourself a stranger. Drop by the house more often. We're always open.*

Don't be gone (too) long. Good-bye. Hurry back here. □ TOM: *I've got to go to the drugstore to get some medicine.* SUE: *Don't be gone too long.* TOM: *I'll be right back.* □ *"Don't be gone long," said Bill's uncle. "It's about time to eat."*

Don't be so picky! Don't be so choosy!; Don't always hold out for something or someone better! □ IDA: *I'd like a piece of chicken with no skin on it and no sauce. I'll have some broccoli if it's not overcooked. A little mashed potatoes would be fine, but only a small portion and not if there's butter in it.* HANNA: *Sakes alive! Don't be so picky!* □ IDA: *Yuck. My apple is bruised.* MOTHER: *Don't be so picky!* □ A: *There's a little hole in my sock.* B: *Don't be so picky!*

Don't be too sure. I think you are wrong, so do not sound so certain.; You may be wrong, you know. (Compare to **Don't speak too soon.**) □ BILL: *Ah, it's sure great being home and safe—secure in one's castle.* MARY: *Don't be too sure. I just heard glass breaking downstairs.* □ BILL: *I think I've finally saved up enough money to retire.* JOHN: *Don't be too sure. Inflation can ruin your savings.*

Don't believe I've had the pleasure. Go to (I) don't believe I've had the pleasure.

Don't believe so. Go to (I) don't believe so.

Don't bet on it! Don't assume anything!; It isn't happening! (See also (I) wouldn't bet on it.) □ HANNA: *I expect that you will be* *going to the mountains again this year. IDA: Don't bet on it. This has been a bad year financially.* □ *A: I expect to see you at the office bright and early tomorrow morning. B: Don't bet on it! Tomorrow is Sunday.*

Don't bother. Please don't do it. It is not necessary, and it is too much trouble. □ *MARY: Should I put these in the box with the others? BILL: No, don't bother.* □ *SUE: Do you want me to save this spoonful of mashed potatoes? JANE: No, don't bother. It isn't worth it. SUE: I hate to waste it.*

Don't bother me! Go away!; Leave me alone! □ *TOM: Hey, Bill! BILL: Don't bother me! I'm busy. Can't you see?* □ *"Don't bother me! Leave me alone!" the child shouted at the dog.*

Don't bother me none. Go to (It) makes no difference to me.

Don't breathe a word of this to anyone. This is a secret or secret gossip. Do not tell it to anyone. □ *MARY: Can you keep a secret? JOHN: Sure. MARY: Don't breathe a word of this to anyone, but Tom is in jail.* □ *BILL: Have you heard about Mary and her friends? SALLY: No. Tell me! Tell me! BILL: Well, they all went secretly to Mexico for the weekend. Everyone thinks they are at Mary's, except Mary's mother, who thinks they are at Sue's. Now, don't breathe a word of this to anyone. SALLY: Of course not! You know me!*

Don't call us, we'll call you. We will let you know if we wish to talk to you further.; We will let you know if you got the job, so don't bother calling and asking. (Often a dismissal.) □ *SALLY: Thank you for coming by for the interview. We'll let you know. BILL: How soon do you think Mr. Franklin will decide? SALLY: Don't call us, we'll call you.* □ *"Don't call us, we'll call you," said the assistant director, as if he had said it a hundred times already today, which he probably had.*

Don't do anything I wouldn't do. an expression said when two friends are parting. (Familiar and colloquial.) □ *BILL: See you tomorrow, Tom. TOM: Yeah, man. Don't do anything I wouldn't do. BILL: What wouldn't you do?* □ *MARY: Where are you going, Bill? BILL: Oh, just around. MARY: Sure, you're spinning. Well, don't do anything I wouldn't do. BILL: Okay, but what wouldn't you do? MARY: Beat it, you clown! BILL: I'm off.*

Don't even look like something**!** Do not even appear to be doing something! (The *something* can be thinking about something or actually doing something.) □ *MARY: Are you thinking about taking that last piece of cake? BOB: Of course not. MARY: Well, don't even look like you're doing it!* □ *JOHN: You weren't going to try to sneak into the theater, were you? BOB: No. JOHN: Well, don't even look like it, if you know what's good for you.*

Don't even think about (doing) it. Do not do it, and do not even think about doing it. □ *John reached into his jacket for his wallet. The cop, thinking John was about to draw a gun, said, "Don't even think about it."* □ *MARY: Look at that diver! It must be forty feet down to the water. BOB: Don't even think about doing it yourself.*

Don't even think about it (happening). Do not even think about something terrible actually happening. (Compare to **Don't even think about (doing) it.**) □ *MARY: Oh, those cars almost crashed! How horrible! FRED: Don't even think about it.* □ *SALLY: If the banks fail, we'll lose everything we have. SUE: Don't even think about it!*

Don't forget to write. Go to Remember to write.

Don't get up. Please, there is no need to rise to greet me or in deference to me. □ *Mary approached the table to speak to Bill. Bill started to push his chair back as if to rise. Mary said, "Don't get up. I just want to say hello."* □ *TOM (rising): Hello, Fred. Good to see you. FRED (standing): Don't get up. How are you?*

Don't get your bowels in an uproar! Do not get so excited! (Slang.) □ *BILL: What have you done to my car? Where's the bumper? The side window is cracked! BOB: Calm down! Don't get your bowels in an uproar!* □ *FATHER: Now, Son, we need to talk a little bit about you and your pet snake. Where is it? JOHN: I don't know. FATHER (outraged): What! JOHN: Don't get your bowels in an uproar! It always turns up.*

Don't give it a (second) thought. Go to Think nothing of it.

Don't give it another thought. Go to Think nothing of it.

Don't give up! Do not stop trying!; Keep trying! □ *JOHN: Get in there and give it another try. Don't give up! BILL: Okay. Okay. But it's hopeless.* □ *JANE: I asked the boss for a raise, but he said no. TOM: Don't give up. Try again later.*

Don't give up the ship! Do not give up yet!; Do not yield the entire enterprise! (From a naval expression.) □ *BILL: I'm having a devil* *of a time with calculus. I think I want to drop the course.* SALLY: *Keep trying. Don't give up the ship!* □ BILL: *Every time we get enough money saved up to make a down payment on a house, the price of houses skyrockets. I'm about ready to stop trying.* SUE: *We'll manage. Don't give up the ship!*

Don't give up too eas(il)y! AND **Don't give up without a fight!** Do not yield so easily.; Keep struggling and you may win. Do not give up too soon. □ SUE: *She says no every time I ask her for a raise.* MARY: *Well, don't give up too easily. Keep after her.* □ JOHN: *I know it's my discovery, not hers, but she won't admit it.* SALLY: *Don't give up without a fight.*

Don't give up without a fight! Go to Don't give up too eas(il)y!

Don't hold your breath. Do not stop breathing while you are waiting for something to happen. (Meaning that it will take longer for it to happen than you can possibly hold your breath.) □ TOM: *The front yard is such a mess.* BOB: *Bill's supposed to rake the leaves.* TOM: *Don't hold your breath. He never does his share of the work.* □ SALLY: *Someone said that gasoline prices would go down.* BOB: *Oh, yeah? Don't hold your breath.*

Don't I know it! I know that very well! □ MARY: *Goodness gracious! It's hot today.* BOB: *Don't I know it!* □ SUE: *You seem to be putting on a little weight.* JOHN: *Don't I know it!*

Don't I know you from somewhere? a way of starting a conversation with a stranger, usually at a party or other gathering. □ BILL: *Don't I know you from somewhere?* MARY: *I don't think so. Where did you go to school?* □ HENRY: *Don't I know you from somewhere?* ALICE: *No, and let's keep it that way.*

Don't let someone or something **get you down.** Don't let some person or situation bother you. □ TOM: *I'm so mad at her, I could scream!* SUE: *Don't let her get you down.* □ JOHN: *This project at work is getting to be a real mess.* JANE: *Don't let it get you down. It will be over with soon.*

Don't let the bastards wear you down. Don't let those people get the best of you. (Exercise caution with *bastard*.) □ BILL: *The place I work at is really rough. Everybody is rude and jealous of each other.* TOM: *Don't let the bastards wear you down.* □ JANE: *I have to go down to the county clerk's office and figure out what this silly bureau-*

cratic letter means. SUE: *You might call them on the phone. In any case, don't let the bastards wear you down.*

Don't make me laugh! Do not make such ridiculous statements—they only make me laugh. (Compare to **You make me laugh!**) □ MARY: *I'll be a millionaire by the time I'm thirty.* TOM: *Don't make me laugh!* MARY: *I will! I will!* □ MARY: *I'm trying out for cheerleader.* SUE: *You, a cheerleader? Don't make me laugh!*

Don't make me no nevermind. Go to (It) makes no difference to me.

Don't make me say it again! AND **Don't make me tell you again!** I have told you once, and now I'm mad, and I'll be madder if I have to tell you again. (Typically said to a child who will not mind.) □ MOTHER: *I told you thirty minutes ago to clean up this room! Don't make me tell you again!* CHILD: *Okay. I'll do it.* □ BILL: *No, Sue, I will not buy you a beach house. Don't make me say it again!* SUE: *Are you sure?*

Don't make me tell you again! Go to Don't make me say it again!

Don't make yourself a stranger! Go to Don't be a stranger!

Don't mind if I do. Go to (I) don't mind if I do.

Don't mind me. Don't pay any attention to me.; Just ignore me. (Sometimes sarcastic.) □ *Bill and Jane were watching television when Jane's mother walked through the room, grabbing the newspaper on the way. "Don't mind me," she said.* □ *Bob was sitting at the table when Mary and Bill started up a quiet and personal conversation. Bob stared off into space and said, "Don't mind me." Bill and Mary didn't even notice.*

Don't push (me)! Don't put pressure on me to do something! (Also a literal meaning.) □ SUE: *You really must go to the dentist, you know.* JOHN: *Don't push me. I'll go when I'm good and ready.* □ BOB: *Come on! You can finish. Keep trying.* BILL: *Don't push me! I have to do it under my own steam!*

Don't quit trying. Go to Keep (on) trying.

Don't quit your day job. You are not very good at what you are doing, and clearly you only do this on a part-time or temporary basis, so don't quit your regular job in hopes that you can support yourself doing this task that you do not do very well. □ *I saw your* *comedy act at the nightclub. Don't quit your day job!* □ *So, you laid the bricks in this wall. Well, don't quit your day job.*

Don't rush me! Don't try to hurry me! □ *BILL: Hurry up! Make up your mind! BOB: Don't rush me! BILL: I want to get out of here before midnight.* □ *BILL: The waiter wants to take your order. What do you want? JANE: Don't rush me! I can't make up my mind. WAITER: I'll come back in a minute.*

Don't say it! I don't want to hear it!; I know, so you don't have to say it. □ *JOHN (joking): What is that huge pile of stuff on your head? BILL: Don't say it! I know I need a haircut.* □ *FRED: And then I'll trade that car in on a bigger one, and then I'll buy a bigger house. BOB: Fred! FRED: Oh, don't say it! BOB: You're a dreamer, Fred. FRED: I had hoped you wouldn't say that.*

Don't see you much around here anymore. Go to (We) don't see you much around here anymore.

Don't speak too soon. I think you may be wrong. Don't speak before you know the facts. (Compare to **Don't be too sure.**) □ *BILL: It looks like it'll be a nice day. MARY: Don't speak too soon. I just felt a raindrop.* □ *TOM: It looks like we made it home without any problems. BILL: Don't speak too soon, there's a cop behind us in the driveway.*

Don't spend it all in one place. a catchphrase said after giving someone some money, especially a small amount. □ *FRED: Dad, can I have a dollar? FATHER: Sure. Here. Don't spend it all in one place.* □ *"Here's a quarter, kid," said Tom, flipping Fred a quarter. "Don't spend it all in one place."* □ *ALICE: Here's the five hundred dollars I owe you. TOM: Oh, thanks. I need this. ALICE: Don't spend it all in one place. TOM: I have to or they'll take my car back.*

Don't stand on ceremony. Do not wait for a formal invitation.; Please be at ease and make yourself at home. □ *JOHN: Come in, Tom. Don't stand on ceremony. Get yourself a drink and something to eat and mingle with the other guests. TOM: Okay, but I can only stay for a few minutes.* □ *"Don't stand on ceremony, Fred," urged Sally. "Go around and introduce yourself to everyone."*

Don't stay away so long. Please visit more often. (Said upon the arrival or departure of a guest.) □ *JOHN: Hi, Bill! Long time no see. Don't stay away so long! BILL: Thanks, John. Good to see you.* □

MARY: I had a nice time. Thanks for inviting me. SALLY: Good to see you, Mary. Next time, don't stay away so long.

Don't sweat it! Don't worry about it. (Slang.) □ *BILL: I think I'm flunking algebra! BOB: Don't sweat it! Everybody's having a rough time.* □ *MARY: Good grief! I just stepped on the cat's tail, but I guess you heard. SUE: Don't sweat it! The cat's got to learn to keep out of the way.*

Don't sweat the small stuff. Don't worry about the little problems that have minor consequences. □ *IDA: I just can't seem to get comfortable in my office chair. I'm too far from the network printer, and my own printer is too slow. HANNA: Don't sweat the small stuff. You're also a week late on your time-and-effort report.* □ *Relax, Tom. Don't sweat the small stuff. Save your energy for the really serious problems.*

Don't tell a soul. Please do not tell anyone this gossip. □ *BILL: Is your brother getting married? SALLY: Yes, but don't tell a soul. It's a secret.* □ *MARY: Can you keep a secret? JOHN: Sure. MARY: Don't tell a soul, but Tom is in jail.*

Don't tell me what to do! Do not give me orders. □ *BOB: Get over there and pick up those papers before they blow away. SALLY: Don't tell me what to do! BOB: Better hurry. One of those papers is your paycheck. But it's no skin off my nose if you don't.* □ *SUE: Next, you should get a haircut, then get some new clothes. You really need to fix yourself up. SALLY: Don't tell me what to do! Maybe I like me the way I am!*

Don't think so. Go to I guess not.

Don't waste my time. Do not take up my valuable time with a poor presentation.; Do not waste my time trying to get me to do something. □ *BOB: I'd like to show you our new line of industrial-strength vacuum cleaners. BILL: Beat it! Don't waste my time.* □ *"Don't waste my time!" said the manager when Jane made her fourth appeal for a raise.*

Don't waste your breath. You will not get a positive response to what you have to say, so don't even say it.; Talking will get you nowhere. □ *ALICE: I'll go in there and try to convince her otherwise. FRED: Don't waste your breath. I already tried it.* □ *SALLY: No, I won't agree! Don't waste your breath. BILL: Aw, come on.*

Don't waste your time. You will not get anywhere with it, so don't waste time trying. □ MARY: *Should I ask Tom if he wants to go to the convention, or is he still in a bad mood?* SALLY: *Don't waste your time.* MARY: *Bad mood, huh?* □ JANE: *I'm having trouble fixing this doorknob.* MARY: *Don't waste your time. I've ordered a new one.*

Don't work too hard. an expression said at the end of a conversation after or in place of *good-bye.* □ MARY: *Bye, Tom.* TOM: *Bye, Mary. Don't work too hard.* □ SUE: *Don't work too hard!* MARY: *I never do.*

Don't worry. Do not become anxious—everything will be all right. □ *"Don't worry, Fred," said Bill, "everything will be all right."* □ BILL: *I think I left the car windows open.* SUE: *Don't worry, I closed them.*

Don't worry about a thing. Everything will be taken care of. Do not be anxious. □ MARY: *This has been such an ordeal.* SUE: *I'll help. Don't worry about a thing.* □ *"Don't worry about a thing," the tax collector had said. "We'll take care of everything." Or was it "We'll take everything?"*

(Don't you) get it? Don't you understand the point or the joke? □ *Q: It's very simple. Don't you get it? A: Sorry, I just don't understand.* □ ISABEL: *I've explained it as well as I can. Get it?*

Don't you just love it? Don't you agree that it is great? (Also used sarcastically.) □ HANNA: *What a cool little computer!* IDA: *Yes. Don't you just love it?* □ DON: *Yuck. It looks like it's going to rain all day again today.* ANDY: *Don't you just love it?*

Don't you know? 1. Don't you know the answer?; I don't know—I thought you did. □ MARY: *How do I get to the Morris Building? Where do I turn?* JANE: *Don't you know? I have no idea!* □ SUE: *We're supposed to either sign these contracts or rewrite them. Which is it?* JOHN: *Don't you know?* **2.** AND **(Don't you) see?** Do you understand?; Do you see? (Usually pronounced *doan-cha know,* often without rising question intonation. Typically, nothing more than a call for some quick response from the person being talked to.) □ JOHN: *This whole thing can be straightened out with hardly any trouble at all, don't you know?* SUE: *What makes you so sure?* JOHN: *I've had this same problem before.* □ BILL: *Why are you stopping the car?* JOHN: *We usually stop here for the night, don't you know?* BILL: *I know a better place down the road.*

Don't you know it! You can be absolutely sure about that!; You're exactly right, and I agree with you. (This is not a question.) □ ALICE: *Man, is it hot!* FRED: *Don't you know it!* □ BOB: *This is the best cake I have ever eaten. The cook is the best in the world!* BILL: *Don't you know it!*

(Don't you) see? Go to Don't you know?

(Don't) you wish! Don't you wish that what you have just said were really true? □ MARY: *I'm going to get a job that lets me travel a lot.* SALLY: *Don't you wish!* □ SALLY: *Sorry you lost the chess game. It was close, but your opponent was top-notch.* BOB: *Next time, I'll do it! I'll win the next round.* SALLY: *Don't you wish!*

down the drain lost forever; wasted. □ *I just hate to see all that money go down the drain.* □ *Well, there goes the whole project, right down the drain.*

Down the hatch! Go to Bottoms up.

down to the wire at the very last minute; up to the very last instant. □ *I have to turn this in tomorrow, and I'll be working down to the wire.* □ *When we get down to the wire, we'll know better what to do.*

Dream on. What you are expecting or wanting to happen is nothing but fantasy, so enjoy yourself and create as many fantasies as you want. □ *You want to get promoted to general manager? Dream on.* □ *You, an opera singer? Dream on.*

drinking the Kool-Aid accepting flawed arguments that have bad consequences. (From an incident in 1978 in which about 900 people died from willingly drinking poisoned Flavor Aid, a fruit-flavored drink. The expression almost always uses the name of a more widely known drink, Kool-Aid. Both Kool-Aid and Flavor Aid are protected trade names.) □ *Those jerks in the Mossback Party are still drinking the Kool-Aid. They'll believe anything their leaders tell them.* □ *You're just drinking the Kool-Aid if you think any political party is going to level with you.*

Drive safely. an expression used to advise a departing person to be careful while driving. □ MARY: *Good-bye, Sally. Drive safely.* SALLY: *Good-bye. I will.* □ *"Drive safely!" everyone shouted as we left on our trip.*

drive something **home** to make something very definite; to make something clearly understood energetically. (As if one were driving a nail solidly into wood.) □ *Your speech needs some more work. You need to be more enthusiastic if you want to drive each point home.* □ *These are the three things that you really want to get across in the ad campaign. You have to drive them home using highly stimulating art and clever graphics. Let me see it again tomorrow morning.*

Drop by for a drink (sometime). a casual invitation for someone to pay a visit. □ *Bob: Good to see you, Mary. Drop by for a drink sometime. Mary: Love to. Bye.* □ *"Drop by for a drink sometime, stranger," said Bill to his old friend, Sally.*

Drop by sometime. Go to Drop in sometime.

drop everything to stop doing everything. □ *Drop everything and go outside. The house is on fire.* □ *Do you expect me to drop everything and come and pick you up at school?*

Drop in sometime. AND **Drop over sometime.; Drop by sometime.** Visit my home or office sometime when you are nearby. □ *Bob: Bye, Bill, nice seeing you. Bill: Hey, drop in sometime. Bob: Okay. Bill: Great! Bye.* □ *"Drop in sometime," said Bob to his uncle.*

Drop it! Go to Drop the subject!

Drop me a line. Communicate with me by mail and tell me your news. □ *John: If you get into our area, drop me a line. Fred: I sure will, John. John: Bye.* □ *Mary: I'm going to Cleveland for a few months. Sue: Drop me a line when you get there. Mary: I will. Bye.*

Drop me a note. Communicate with me by mail, and let me know what is going on with you. □ *Mary: I'm off for Brazil. Good-bye. Sally: Have a good time. Drop me a note.* □ *"Drop me a note from France," said Bill, waving good-bye.*

drop names to mention the names of important or famous people as if they were personal friends. □ *Mary always tries to impress people by dropping the names of well-known film stars.* □ *Bill's such a snob. Leave it to him to drop the names of all the local gentry.*

Drop over sometime. Go to Drop in sometime.

Drop the subject! AND **Drop it!** Do not discuss it further! □ *Bill: Yes, you're gaining a little weight. I thought you were on a diet. Sally: That's enough! Drop the subject!* □ *Bill: That house looks expensive. What do you think it's worth? Mary: That's my aunt's house. Just what did you want to know about it? Bill: Oh, drop it! Sorry I asked.*

Easy does it. 1. Move slowly and carefully. □ *BILL (holding one end of a large crate): It's really tight in this doorway. BOB (holding the other end): Easy does it. Take your time.* □ *NURSE (holding Sue's arm): Easy does it. These first few steps are the hardest. SUE: I didn't know I was so weak.* **2.** Calm down.; Don't lose your temper. □ *JOHN: I'm so mad I could scream. BOB: Easy does it, John. No need to get so worked up. JOHN: I'm still mad!* □ *SUE (frantic): Where is my camera? My passport is gone too! FRED: Easy does it, Sue. I think you have someone else's purse.*

Enjoy! I hope you enjoy what you are going to do.; I hope you enjoy what I have served you to eat.; I hope you enjoy life in general. □ *"Here's your coffee, dear," said Fred. "Enjoy!"* □ *SUE: What a beautiful day! Good-bye. TOM: Good-bye. Enjoy!*

Enjoy your meal. an expression used by food service personnel after the food has been served. □ *The waiter set the plates on the table, smiled, and said, "Enjoy your meal."* □ *WAITER: Here's your dinner. JANE: Oh, this lobster looks lovely! TOM: My steak looks just perfect. WAITER: Enjoy your meal.*

Enough is enough! That is enough! I won't stand for any more! □ *SUE: That color of lipstick is all wrong for you, Sally. SALLY: Enough is enough! Sue, get lost! SUE: I was just trying to help.* □ *BOB: Enough is enough! I'm leaving! BILL: What on earth did I do? BOB: Good-bye.*

Enough (of this) foolishness! Go to (That's) enough (of this) foolishness!

Evening. Go to (Good) evening.

every other person or thing every second person or thing; alternating. □ *The magician turned every other card over.* □ *Every other table had an ashtray on it.*

Everyone is (standing) behind you. Go to We're all (standing) behind you.

everything humanly possible everything that is in the range of human powers. □ *The rescuers did everything humanly possible to find the lost campers.* □ *The doctor tried everything humanly possible to save the patient.*

Everything okay? Go to (Is) everything okay?

Everything will work out (all right). Go to Things will work out (all right).

Everything will work out for the best. Go to Things will work out (all right).

Everything's coming up roses. Everything is really just excellent. □ *Life is wonderful. Everything's coming up roses.* □ *Q: How are things going? A: Everything's coming up roses.*

Everything's going to be all right. AND **Everything will be all right.** Do not worry—everything will be okay. (A number of other expressions can be substituted for *all right,* such as *okay, just fine, great,* etc.) □ *"Don't worry, Fred," said Bill. "Everything will be all right."* □ *MARY: I just don't know if I can go on! BOB: Now, now. Everything will be just fine.*

Excellent! Great!; Fine! □ *BOB: What's happening? FRED: Hi! I'm getting a new car. BOB: Excellent!* □ *BOB: All the players are here and ready to go. SUE: Excellent! BOB: When do we start the game?*

Excuse me. AND **Excuse, please.; Pardon (me).; 'Scuse (me).; 'Scuse, please.** ('Scuse is colloquial.) **1.** an expression asking forgiveness for some minor social violation, such as belching or bumping into someone. □ *JOHN: Ouch! BOB: Excuse me. I didn't see you there.* □ *MARY: Oh! Ow! SUE: Pardon me. I didn't mean to bump into you.* □ *TOM: Ouch! MARY: Oh, dear! What happened? TOM: You stepped on my toe. MARY: Excuse me. I'm sorry.* **2.** Please let me through.; Please let me by. □ *TOM: Excuse me. I need to get past. BOB: Oh, sorry. I didn't know I was in the way.* □ *MARY: Pardon me. SUE: What? MARY: Pardon me. I want to get past you.*

Excuse me? AND **Pardon (me)?; 'Scuse me?** What do you mean by that last remark?; I beg your pardon? (Shows amazement at someone's rudeness.) □ *MARY: Your policies seem quite inflexible to me. BILL: Excuse me?* □ *BOB: These silly people are getting on my nerves. MARY: Pardon me?*

Excuse, please. Go to Excuse me.

Fair to middling. a response to a greeting inquiry into the state of one's health. (Colloquial and folksy.) □ JOHN: *How are you doing?* BOB: *Oh, fair to middling, I guess. And you?* JOHN: *Things could be worse.* □ BILL: *How are you feeling?* JANE: *Oh, fair to middling, thanks.* BILL: *Still a little under the weather, huh?* JANE: *Just a little.*

Fancy meeting you here! I am very surprised to meet you here! □ TOM: *Hi, Sue! Fancy meeting you here!* SUE: *Hi, Tom. I was thinking the same thing about you.* □ *"Fancy meeting you here," said Mr. Franklin when he bumped into Mrs. Franklin at the racetrack.*

Fancy that! AND **Imagine that!** I am very surprised to hear that.; That is hard to imagine or believe. □ MARY: *My father was elected president of the board.* SALLY: *Fancy that!* □ SUE: *This computer is ten times faster than the one we had before.* JANE: *Imagine that! Is it easy to operate?* SUE: *Of course not.*

far as I know Go to (as) far as I know.

far as I'm concerned Go to (as) far as I'm concerned.

Farewell. Good-bye. □ MARY: *See you later, Bill.* BILL: *Farewell, my dear.* MARY: *Take care.* □ BOB: *Have a good trip.* SUE: *Farewell, Bob.* BOB: *Don't do anything I wouldn't do.*

fat chance very little likelihood. □ *Fat chance he has of getting the promotion.* □ *You think she'll lend you the money? Fat chance!*

Feeling okay. Go to (I'm) feeling okay. See also (Are you) feeling okay?

field questions to answer a series of questions, especially from reporters. □ *After her speech, Jane fielded questions from reporters.* □ *The president's press agents field questions from the newspaper.*

Fill in the blanks. You can figure out the rest.; You can draw a conclusion from that. □ MARY: *What happened at Fred's house last night?* BILL: *There was a big fight, then the neighbors called the* *police. MARY: Then what happened? BILL: Fill in the blanks. What do you think?* □ *JOHN: They had been lost for two days, then the wolves came, and the rest is history. JANE: Yes, I think I can fill in the blanks.*

Fine by me. Go to (That's) fine with me.

Fine with me. Go to (That's) fine with me.

first of all first and perhaps most important. □ *"First of all, let me say how happy I am to be here," said Fred, beginning his speech.* □ *HENRY: How much is all this going to cost, Doctor? DOCTOR: First of all, do you have any insurance?*

Fire away! Start doing something, especially to ask questions! (As if giving soldiers the instructions to start firing.) □ *ANDY: Dad, do you mind if I ask you a few questions? FATHER: Fire away!* □ *IDA: The mayor will now take a few questions from reporters. MAYOR: Fire away!*

Flattery will get you nowhere. You can praise me, but I'm not going to give you what you want. □ *A: You are beautiful and talented. B: Flattery will get you nowhere, but keep talking.* □ *Flattery will get you nowhere, but that doesn't mean you should stop flattering me!*

Floor it! Go to Punch it!

for all intents and purposes seeming as if; looking as if. □ *Tom stood there, looking, for all intents and purposes, as if he were going to strangle Sally, but, being the gentleman that he is, he just glowered.* □ *MARY: Is this finished now? JOHN: For all intents and purposes, yes.*

For crying in a bucket! Go to For crying out loud!

For crying out loud! AND **For crying in a bucket!** an exclamation of shock, anger, or surprise. □ *FRED: For crying out loud! Answer the telephone! BOB: But it's always for you!* □ *JOHN: Good grief! What am I going to do? This is the end! SUE: For crying in a bucket! What's wrong?*

for free for no charge or cost; free of any cost. □ *They let us into the movie for free.* □ *I will let you have a sample of the candy for free.*

(For) goodness sake(s)! Go to (Goodness) sakes alive!

for instance for example. □ *I've lived in many cities, for instance, Boston, Chicago, and Detroit.* □ *Jane is very generous. For instance, she volunteers her time and gives money to charities.*

for nothing for no purpose at all. □ *Bob: You sure put a lot of work into this project. It's too bad it didn't work out as planned. Jan: Yes, all that work for nothing.* □ *I worried all day about the dinner tonight, and it turned out to be a lovely event. All that worry for nothing.*

for openers AND **for starters** to begin with. □ *For openers, let's discuss our plans for the coming year.* □ *Now, I want to talk about binomials today. Let's look at the first paragraph on page 12 for starters.*

For Pete('s) sake(s)! Go to For pity('s) sake(s)!

For pity('s) sake(s)! AND **For Pete('s) sake(s)!** a mild exclamation of surprise or shock. (The extra *(s)* is colloquial.) □ *Fred: For pity's sake. What on earth is this? Alice: It's just a kitten.* □ *John: Good grief! What am I going to do? This is the end! Sue: What is it now, for Pete's sake?*

For shame! That is shameful! □ *Sue: Did you hear that Tom was in jail? Fred: For shame! What did he do? Sue: Nobody knows.* □ *Mary: I've decided not to go to the conference. John: For shame! Who will represent us?*

for starters Go to for openers.

For sure. Yes.; Certainly. (Colloquial.) □ *Sally: Are you ready to go? Bob: For sure. Sally: Then, let's go.* □ *Jane: Are you coming with us? John: For sure. I wouldn't miss this for the world.*

For two cents I would do something! With a little encouragement, I would do something. □ *For two cents I'd bust him right in the mouth!* □ *I'm so tired of being treated like a servant rather than an employee. For two cents I would quit right now!*

for what it's worth a phrase added to a piece of information suggesting that the information may or may not be useful. □ *Mary: What do you think about it, Fred? Fred: Well, let me tell you something, for what it's worth.* □ *John: For what it's worth, you're doing great! Sue: Thanks! It's worth a lot!*

for your information a phrase that introduces or follows a piece of information. (Can be spoken with considerable impatience.) □

MARY: *What is this one?* SUE: *For your information, it is exactly the same as the one you just asked about.* □ BOB: *How long do I have to wait here?* BILL: *For your information, we will be here until the bus driver feels that it is safe to travel.*

Forget (about) it! 1. Drop the subject!; Never mind!; Don't bother me with it. □ JANE: *Then, there's this matter of the unpaid bills.* BILL: *Forget it!* □ SALLY: *What's this I hear about you and Tom?* SUE: *Forget about it!* **2.** Nothing. □ SUE: *What did you say?* MARY: *Forget it!* □ TOM: *Now I'm ready to go.* SUE: *Excuse me?* TOM: *Oh, nothing. Just forget it.* **3.** You're welcome.; It was nothing. □ JOHN: *Thank you so much for helping me!* BILL: *Oh, forget it!* □ BOB: *We're all very grateful to you for coming into work today.* MARY: *Forget about it! No problem!*

'Fraid not. Go to (I'm) afraid not.

'Fraid so. Go to (I'm) afraid so.

frankly Go to (Speaking) (quite) frankly.

Fret not! Don't worry!; Do not fret about it! □ MARY: *Oh, look at the clock! I'm going to be late for my appointment!* BOB: *Fret not! I'll drive you.* □ *"Fret not!" said Sally. "We're almost there!"*

from day one since the beginning; since the first day. □ *From day one, she was a very calm and happy child.* □ *He has been a nuisance from day one. Someone needs to tell him to cool it.*

from my perspective AND **from where I stand; from my point of view; the way I see it** a phrase used to introduce one's own opinion. □ MARY: *What do you think of all this?* TOM: *From my perspective, it is just terrible.* □ BOB: *From my point of view, this looks like a very good deal.* BILL: *That's good for you. I stand to lose money on it.* □ ALICE: *From where I stand, it appears that you're going to have to pay a lot of money to get this matter settled.* SUE: *I'll pay anything. I just want to get all this behind me.*

from my point of view Go to from my perspective.

from now on at all times in the future; from now until well into the future. □ *From now on, you will do exactly as I tell you.* □ Q: *Do you think you can change your way of doing this?* A: *Sure. I'll do it your way from now on.*

from the get-go AND **from the git-go** from the beginning; from the very first. (*Git* is a spelling of a frequently heard pronunciation.) □ *ANDY: Fred just doesn't seem to be catching on to the job. HANNA: Yes, we had our doubts about him from the git-go.* □ *This is the last time I'll buy a used car. This one's been trouble since the get-go.*

from the old school holding attitudes or ideas that were popular and important in the past but which are no longer considered relevant or in line with modern trends. □ *Grammar was not taught much in my son's school, but fortunately he had a teacher from the old school.* □ *Aunt Jane is from the old school. She never goes out without wearing a hat and gloves.*

from where I stand Go to from my perspective.

Gangway! Clear the way!; Get out of the way! □ *"Gangway!" cried Fred. "Here comes the band!"* □ *TOM: Please move so we can get by. BOB: You'll never get anywhere with that. Gangway! Gangway! Gangway!*

gee an expression of disappointment, disagreement, surprise, or other emotions. (Words such as this often use intonation to convey the connotation of the sentence that is to follow. The brief intonation pattern accompanying the word may indicate sarcasm, disagreement, caution, consolation, sternness, etc.) □ *"Gee, why not?" whined Billy.* □ *BILL: Gee, I really want to go. JANE: Well then, go ahead and go!* □ *JOHN: Gee, Tom, I'm sort of surprised. TOM: You shouldn't be.* □ *ALICE: Gee, I thought you were gone. BOB: No, I'm still here.*

Get back to me (on this). Report back to me. (Often a deadline is added.) □ *TOM: Here's a contract for you to go over. Get back to me on this by Monday morning. MARY: Sure thing, Tom.* □ *ALICE: When you have this thing figured out, get back to me, and we'll talk. TOM: Righto.*

Get it? Go to (Don't you) get it?

Get lost! Go away!; Stop bothering me! □ *BILL: I'm still real mad at you. TOM: Bill! Bill! I'm sorry about it. Let's talk. BILL: Get lost!* □ *Fred kicked his foot at the dog behind him and shouted, "Get lost, you worthless mutt!"*

Get my drift? Go to (Do you) get my drift?

Get off my back! Stop harassing me!; Leave me alone about this matter! (Slang.) □ *TOM: You'd better get your paper written. BILL: I'll do it when I'm good and ready. Get off my back!* □ *ALICE: I'm tired of your constant criticism! Get off my back! JANE: I was just trying to help.*

Get off my tail! 1. Stop following me!; Stop following me so closely! (Slang.) □ *There was a car following too close, and Tom shouted into the rearview mirror, "Get off my tail!"* □ Tom: *Look, Bill, don't you have something else to do? Quit following me around! Get off my tail!* Bill: *Can I help it if we both go to the same places?* **2.** Get off my back! □ Tom: *You'd better get your laundry done.* Bill: *I'll do it when I'm good and ready. Get off my tail!* □ Bill: *Get off my tail! I don't need a watchdog!* Jane: *You do too.*

get off scot-free to end up not having to pay the penalty. (*Scot* [old] = tax or burden.) □ *Do you really think you can pull a trick like that and get off scot-free? You're lucky you're not in jail!* □ *I explained to the judge about how I was out of a job, and my kids were sick, and my wife left me, and my mother needed an operation, and I thought I would get off scot-free. He threw the book at me!*

Get out of here! Go away!; Leave this place! □ John: *I've heard enough of this! Get out of here!* Bill: *I'm going! I'm going!* □ Bill: *Where have you been? You smell like a sewer! Get out of here!* Fred: *I can't imagine what you smell.*

Get out of my face! Go away and stop bothering me!; Get yourself away from me! □ Alice: *Beat it! Get out of my face! Go away and stop bothering me!* Fred: *What on earth did I do?* □ Bill: *You really think I'll buy something that has been copied?* Bob: *I want you to give my proposal some thought.* Bill: *Get out of my face! I'll never buy something that's stolen!*

Get over it! Forget about it!; Don't think about it! □ Don: *So he broke up with you. Get over it!* □ *I'm really broken up about it. I keep saying to myself, "Get over it!"*

Get over yourself! Don't be so conceited!; Stop being the center of your life! □ Isabel: *I said to him, "You're your own hobby. Get over yourself!"* □ Andy: *You think you're so smart! Get over yourself!*

Get the lead out! AND **Shake the lead out!** Hurry up! (Slang. As if slowed down by lead in one's pockets or somewhere else.) □ *"Move it, you guys!" hollered the coach. "Shake the lead out!"* □ Bob: *Get the lead out, you loafer!* Bill: *Don't rush me!*

Get the message? Go to (Do you) get my drift?

Get the picture? Go to (Do you) get the picture?

Get well soon. I hope you get well soon. (Literal and formulaic.) □ *Inside the card, it said, "Sorry you've been sick. Get well soon."* □ *Ted, I'm sorry to hear that your arthritis is kicking up again. Try to get well soon, old buddy.*

Get you something (to drink)? Go to (Could I) get you something (to drink)?

Get your nose out of my business. Go to Mind your own business.

Getting any? Go to (You) getting any?

Give it a rest. AND **Give** something **a rest. 1.** Stop talking about a particular subject. □ *I'm tired of hearing about it. Give it a rest!* □ *You've said everything that can be said. Give it a rest.* **2.** Stop using one's mouth to talk incessantly. □ *I've been listening to your constant jabber for the entire afternoon! Now, shut up! Give it a rest!* □ *Aren't you ever quiet? Give it a rest!*

Give it time. Be patient.; In time, things will change for the better or for the worse. □ *Things will get better. Don't worry. Give it time.* □ *Of course, things will improve. Give it time.*

Give it up! Stop trying. You are wasting your time. (Informal.) □ *BOB: Today was too much! I just can't do calculus! BILL: Give it up! Get out of that course and get into something less cruel. BOB: I think I will.* □ *TOM: I'm just not a very good singer, I guess. SUE: It's no good, Tom. Give it up! TOM: Don't you think I'm doing better, though? SUE: Give it up, Tom!*

Give it your best shot. Make a good try at doing something. □ *I know it is a difficult assignment, but give it your best shot.* □ *Go into the meeting relaxed and well prepared. Give it your best shot, and I just know you'll make the sale.*

Give me a break! 1. Please give me a chance!; Please give me another chance! □ *BOB: I know I can do it. Let me try again. MARY: Well, I don't know. BOB: Give me a break! MARY: Well, okay.* □ *"Give me a break!" cried Mary to the assistant director. "I know I can handle the part."* **2.** I have had enough! Drop this matter!; Stop bothering me! □ *TOM: Now I'm going to sing a song about the hill people in my country. MARY: Give me a break! Sing something I know!* □ *"Give me a break!" shouted Bob. "Go away and stop bothering me!"*

Give me a call. AND **Give me a ring.** Please call me (later) on the telephone. □ *MARY: See you later, Fred. FRED: Give me a call if you* *get a chance.* □ *"When you're in town again, Sue, give me a call," said John.* □ *BOB: When should we talk about this again? BILL: Next week is soon enough. Give me a ring.*

Give me a chance! 1. Please give me an opportunity to do this! □ *MARY: I just know I can do it. Oh, please give me a chance! SUE: All right. Just one more chance.* □ *BOB: Do you think you can do it? JANE: Oh, I know I can. Just give me a chance!* **2.** Please give me a fair chance and enough time to complete the task. □ *ALICE: Come on! I need more time. Give me a chance! JANE: Would another ten minutes help?* □ *BOB: You missed that one! BILL: You moved it! There was no way I could hit it. Give me a chance! Hold it still!*

Give me a ring. Go to Give me a call.

Give me five! AND **Give me (some) skin!; Skin me!; Slip me five!; Slip me some skin!** Shake my hand!; Slap my hand in greeting! (Slang.) □ *"Yo, Tom! Give me five!" shouted Henry, raising his hand.* □ *BOB: Hey, man! Skin me! BILL: How you doing, Bob?*

Give me (some) skin! Go to Give me five!

Give my best to someone. AND **All the best to** someone. Please convey my good wishes to a particular person. (The *someone* can be a person's name or a pronoun. See also **Say hello to** someone **(for me).**) □ *ALICE: Good-bye, Fred. Give my best to your mother. FRED: Sure, Alice. Good-bye.* □ *TOM: See you, Bob. BOB: Give my best to Jane. TOM: I sure will. Bye.* □ *BILL: Bye, Rachel. All the best to your family. RACHEL: Thanks. Bye.*

Give one **an inch, and** one **will take a mile.** AND **Give** some people **an inch, and they will take a mile.** Allow someone a little leeway, and that person will take even more liberty. (The *people* can be *them, some people,* or a specific group of people.) □ *A: I told John he could use my ladder, but then he came back and helped himself to my lawnmower, and he hasn't brought either one back. B: Give him an inch, and he'll take a mile.* □ *First they wanted to wear funny hats to school. Now they want to bring their cell phones. Give them an inch, and they'll take a mile.*

Give some people **an inch, and they will take a mile.** Go to Give one **an inch, and** one **will take a mile.**

give someone **an earful** to tell someone a great amount of information or make a lot of complaints to someone. □ *She was really mad* *about something and gave me an earful.* □ *I needed to talk to someone, so I gave poor Mary an earful.*

Give something **a rest.** Go to Give it a rest.

Give you a lift? Go to (Could I) give you a lift?

Glad to hear it. Go to (I'm) glad to hear it.

Glad to meet you. Go to (I'm) (very) glad to meet you.

Glad you could come. Go to (I'm) glad you could come.

Glad you could drop by. Go to (I'm) glad you could drop by.

Glad you could stop by. Go to (I'm) glad you could drop by.

Go ahead. Please do it.; You have my permission and encouragement to do it. □ ALICE: *I'm leaving.* JOHN: *Go ahead. See if I care.* □ JANE: *Can I put this one in the refrigerator?* JANE: *Sure. Go ahead.*

(Go ahead,) make my day! 1. Just try to do me harm or disobey me. I will enjoy punishing you. (From a phrase said in a movie where the person saying the phrase is holding a gun on a villain and would really like the villain to do something that would justify firing the gun. Now a cliché. Compare to Keep it up!) □ *The crook reached into his jacket for his wallet. The cop, thinking the crook was about to draw a gun, said, "Go ahead, make my day!"* □ *As Bill pulled back his clenched fist to strike Tom, who is much bigger and stronger than Bill, Tom said, "Make my day!"* **2.** Go ahead, ruin my day!; Go ahead, give me the bad news. (A sarcastic version of sense 1.) □ TOM *(standing in the doorway): Hello, I'm with the Internal Revenue Service. Could I come in?* MARY: *Go ahead, make my day!* □ SALLY: *I've got some bad news for you.* JOHN: *Go ahead, make my day!*

Go away! Leave me!; Get away from me! □ MARY: *You're such a pest, Sue. Go away!* SUE: *I was just trying to help.* □ *"Go away!" the child yelled at the bee.*

Go chase yourself! AND **Go climb a tree!; Go fly a kite!; Go jump in the lake!** Go away and stop bothering me! □ BOB: *Get out of here! You're driving me crazy! Go chase yourself!* BILL: *What did I do to you?* BOB: *You're just in the way. Go!* □ BILL: *Dad, can I have ten bucks?* FATHER: *Go climb a tree!* □ FRED: *Stop pestering me. Go jump in the lake!* JOHN: *What did I do?* □ BOB: *Well, Bill, don't you owe me some money?* BILL: *Go fly a kite!*

Go climb a tree! Go to Go chase yourself!

Go figure! It doesn't make sense! Just try to explain it! □ ANN: *John quit his job and ran away with his secretary.* BOB: *He's got to be crazy!* ANN: *Then he came back and asked his wife's forgiveness.* BOB: *Go figure!* □ A: *We did everything we could to please him. He didn't want the prime rib, and he turned up his nose at the wine. He said all he wanted was a hamburger and a beer.* B: *Go Figure!*

Go fly a kite! Go to Go chase yourself!

Go for it! Go ahead! Give it a good try! □ SALLY: *I'm going to try out for the basketball team. Do you think I'm tall enough?* BOB: *Sure you are! Go for it!* □ BOB: *Mary can't quit now! She's almost at the finish line!* BILL: *Go for it, Mary!* ALICE: *Come on, Mary!*

go great guns to do something enthusiastically. □ A: *We have a lot of work to do today, folks. You're going to have to go great guns to get it all done, but I know I can count on you.* B: *Yeah, sure.* □ A: *Things sure look busy around here. Is the boss watching or something?* B: *No, we're always going great guns around here.*

Go jump in the lake! Go to Go chase yourself!

Go on. 1. (Usually **Go on!**) That's silly!; You don't mean that! □ JOHN: *Go on! You're making that up!* BILL: *I am not. It's the truth!* □ BILL: *Gee, that looks like a snake there in the path.* BOB: *Go on! That isn't a snake. No snake is that big.* **2.** Please continue. □ ALICE: *I guess I should stop here.* TOM: *No. Don't stop talking. I'm very interested. Go on.* □ BILL: *Don't turn here. Go on. It's the next corner.* BOB: *Thanks. I didn't think that was where we should turn.*

go someone **one better** AND **do** someone **one better** to do better than someone else; to top or beat someone at one thing. □ *That is quite an experience, but I can go you one better.* □ Q: *Who could possibly throw the ball farther than I did?* A: *I think I can do you one better.*

go the extra mile to try harder to please someone or to get the task done correctly; to do more than one is required to do to reach a goal. □ *I like doing business with that company. They always go the extra mile.* □ *My teacher goes the extra mile to help us.*

God forbid! a phrase expressing a desire that God should prevent the situation that the speaker has just mentioned from ever happening. □ TOM: *It looks like taxes are going up again.* BOB: *God forbid!* □ BOB: *Bill was in a car wreck. I hope he wasn't hurt!* SUE: *God forbid!*

God only knows! No one knows but God. □ *Tom: How long is all this going to take? Alice: God only knows!* □ *Bob: Where are we going to find one hundred thousand dollars? Mary: God only knows!*

God willing. an expression indicating that there is a high certainty that something will happen, so high that only God could prevent it. □ *John: Please try to be on time. Alice: I'll be there on time, God willing.* □ *Bob: Will I see you after your vacation? Mary: Of course, God willing.*

Going my way? Go to (Are you) going my way?

Golly! an expression of surprise or interest. □ *Alice: Golly, is it real? Mary: Of course it's real!* □ *Jane: Look at the size of that fish! Sue: Golly!*

(Good) afternoon. 1. the appropriate polite greeting for use between noon and supper time. □ *Sally: How are you today? Jane: Good afternoon. How are you? Sally: Fine, thank you.* □ *Bob: Afternoon. Nice to see you. Bill: Good afternoon. How are you? Bob: Fine, thanks.* **2.** an expression used on departure or for dismissal between noon and supper time. (Meaning "I wish you a good afternoon.") □ *Sally: See you later, Bill. Bill: Afternoon. See you later.* □ *Mary: Nice to see you. Tom: Good afternoon. Take care.*

Good call! AND **Nice call!** That's a good exercise of judgment.; That's good spotting of a potential problem! (See also **Good catch!**) □ *Jane noticed a clause in the contract that would cost us a lot of money if bad weather interrupted shipping. John smiled and said, "Good call, Jane! That might get you a promotion!"* □ *Good call! No one else saw that car coming.*

Good catch! AND **Nice catch!; Nice save!** It's good that you saw the problem in advance and did something about it! (As if someone had caught a ball just in time. See also **Good call!**) □ *Andrew: Nice catch, Bob! You saved the company a lot of money. Hanna: I didn't see that clause in the contract. Nice catch, Bob.*

Good enough. That's good.; That's adequate. □ *Bill: Well, now. How's that? Bob: Good enough.* □ *Bob: I'll be there about noon. Bob: Good enough. I'll see you then.*

(Good) evening. 1. the appropriate polite greeting for use between supper time and the time of taking leave for the night or by midnight. (Compare to **Good night.**) □ *Bob: Good evening, Mary. How are you? Mary: Evening, Bob. Nice to see you.* □ *"Good evening,"* *said each of the guests as they passed by Mr. and Mrs. Franklin.* **2.** the appropriate polite phrase used for leave-taking between supper time and before the time of final leave-taking to go to bed. □ MARY: *Let's call it a day. See you tomorrow, Bill.* BILL: *Yes, it's been a long and productive day. Good evening, Mary.* □ BOB: *Nice seeing you, Mr. Wilson.* MR. WILSON: *Good evening, Bob.*

Good for you! a complimentary expression of encouragement for something that someone has done. □ SUE: *I just got a raise.* BILL: *Good for you!* □ JANE: *I really told him what I thought of his rotten behavior.* SUE: *Good for you! He needs it.*

Good grief! an exclamation of surprise, disgust, shock, or amazement. □ ALICE: *Good grief! I'm late!* MARY: *That clock's fast. You're probably okay on time.* □ BILL: *There are seven newborn kittens under the sofa!* JANE: *Good grief!*

(Good) heavens! an exclamation of surprise, shock, or amazement. (See also **(My) heavens!**) □ JOHN: *Good heavens! A diamond ring!* BILL: *I bet it's not real.* □ JANE: *Ouch!* JOHN: *Good heavens! What happened?* JANE: *I just stubbed my toe.*

Good job! Go to **Nice going!**

Good luck! **1.** a wish of good luck to someone. □ MARY: *I have my recital tonight.* JANE: *I know you'll do well. Good luck!* □ SALLY: *I hear you're leaving for your new job tomorrow morning.* BOB: *That's right.* SALLY: *Well, good luck!* **2.** You will certainly need luck, but it probably will not work. (Sarcastic.) □ BILL: *I'm going to try to get this tax bill lowered.* SUE: *Good luck!* □ BILL: *I'm sure I can get this cheaper at another store.* CLERK: *Good luck!*

(Good) morning. the standard greeting phrase used anytime between midnight and noon. □ BOB: *Good morning.* BILL: *Good morning, Bob. You sure get up early!*

Good night. **1.** (also **Night.**) the appropriate departure phrase for leave-taking after dark. (This assumes that the speakers will not see one another until morning at the earliest.) □ JOHN: *Bye, Alice.* ALICE: *Night. See you tomorrow.* □ BILL: *Good night, Mary.* MARY: *Night, Bill.* **2.** the appropriate phrase for wishing someone a good night's sleep. □ FATHER: *Good night, Bill.* BILL: *Night, Pop.* □ FATHER: *Good night.* MOTHER: *Good night.* **3.** (usually **Good Night!**) a mild exclamation. □ JANE: *Good night! It's dark! What* *time is it?* MARY: *It's 2:00 A.M.* JANE: *In that case, good morning.* □ *"Good night!" cried Fred. "Look at this mess!"*

the **good old days** back in an earlier time that everyone remembers as a better time, even if it really wasn't. □ *Back in the good old days, during WWII, they used real cactus needles in record players.* □ *The good old days didn't start until they had indoor bathrooms.*

Good talking to you. Go to (It's been) good talking to you.

Good to be here. Go to (It's) good to be here.

good to go all ready to go; all checked and pronounced ready to go. □ *I've checked everything, and we are good to go.* □ *Everything's good to go, and we will start immediately.*

Good to have you here. Go to (It's) good to have you here.

Good to hear your voice. Go to (It's) good to hear your voice.

Good to see you (again). Go to (It's) good to see you (again).

Good to talk to you. Go to (It's been) good talking to you.

Good-bye and good riddance. a phrase marking the departure of someone or something unwanted. □ FRED: *Supposing I was to just walk out of here, just like that?* MARY: *I'd say good-bye and good riddance.* □ *As the garbage truck drove away, carrying the drab old chair that Mary hated so much, she said, "Good-bye and good riddance."*

Good-bye for now. AND **(Good-bye) until next time.; Till next time.; Till we meet again.; Until we meet again.** Good-bye, I'll see you soon.; Good-bye, I'll see you next time. (Often said by the host at the end of a radio or television program.) □ ALICE: *See you later. Good-bye for now.* JOHN: *Bye, Alice.* □ MARY: *See you later.* BOB: *Good-bye for now.* □ *The host of the talk show always closed by saying, "Good-bye until next time. This is Wally Ott, signing off."*

(Good-bye) until next time. Go to Good-bye for now.

(Good-bye) until then. AND **(Good-bye) till then.; (Good-bye) till later.; (Good-bye) until later.** Good-bye until sometime in the future. □ SALLY: *See you tomorrow. Good-bye until then.* SUE: *Sure thing. See you.* □ MARY: *See you later.* BOB: *Until later.* □ *The announcer always ended by saying, "Be with us again next week at this time. Good-bye until then."*

Goodness! Go to (My) goodness (gracious)!

Goodness sake(s)! Go to (Goodness) sakes alive!

(Goodness) sakes alive! AND **(For) goodness sake(s)!; Sakes alive!** My goodness! (Folksy. A mild oath or exclamation.) □ *"Goodness sakes alive!" cried Grandma, "The deer ate my tulips!"* □ *A: Look at the size of that watermelon! B: Sakes alive! I'm sure I couldn't possibly lift it.*

the **gospel truth** [of truth] undeniable. □ *The witness swore he was telling the gospel truth.* □ *I told my parents the gospel truth about how the vase broke.*

Got better things to do. Go to (I've) (got) better things to do.

Got it? Do you understand (it)? □ *Q: I've gone over it with you a dozen times. It should be clear by now. Got it? A: Sure.* □ *BOB: Once again, this one, not that one. Got it? TOM: Could you go over it one more time?*

Got me beat. Go to (It) beats me.

Got me stumped. Go to (You've) got me stumped.

Got to be shoving off. Go to (I) have to shove off.

Got to fly. Go to (I've) got to fly.

Got to get moving. Go to (I've) got to get moving.

Got to go. Go to (I've) got to go.

Got to go home and get my beauty sleep. Go to (I've) got to go home and get my beauty sleep.

Got to hit the road. Go to (It's) time to hit the road.

Got to run. Go to (I've) got to run.

Got to shove off. Go to (I) have to shove off.

Got to split. Go to (I've) got to split.

Got to take off. Go to (I've) got to take off.

Gotcha! 1. I understand what you said or what you want. □ *JOHN: I want this done now! Understand? ALICE: Gotcha!* □ *BILL: Now, this kind of thing can't continue. We must do anything to prevent it from happening again. Do you understand what I'm saying to you? BOB: Gotcha!* **2.** I've caught you at your little game. □ *Mary was standing by the hall table, going through the mail very slowly. Fred came through and saw her. "Gotcha!" said Fred to an embarrassed Mary.* □ *BILL: My flight was nearly six hours late. BOB: Gotcha! I just heard you tell Mary it was three hours late.*

Gotta love it! Go to (You) (just) gotta love it!

grab a bite (to eat) to get something to eat; to get food that can be eaten quickly. □ *I need a few minutes to grab a bite to eat.* □ *Bob often tries to grab a bite between meetings.*

Great! That is wonderful!; I am pleased to hear it. □ *JANE: I'm getting a new job. BILL: Great!* □ *MARY: I'm done now. SALLY: Great! We can leave right away.*

Great Scott! an exclamation of shock or surprise. □ *"Great Scott! You bought a truck!" shrieked Mary.* □ *FRED: The water heater just exploded! BILL: Great Scott! What do we do now? FRED: Looks like cold showers for a while.*

Greetings. Hello. □ *SALLY: Greetings, my friend. BOB: Hello, Sally.* □ *MARY: Hi, Tom. TOM: Greetings, Mary. How are things? MARY: Just great, thanks. What about you? TOM: I'm cool.*

Greetings and felicitations! AND **Greetings and salutations!** Hello and good wishes. (A bit stilted.) □ *"Greetings and felicitations! Welcome to our talent show!" said the master of ceremonies.* □ *BILL: Greetings and salutations, Bob! BOB: Come off it, Bill. Can't you just say "Hi" or something?*

Greetings and salutations! Go to Greetings and felicitations!

Guess what! a way of starting a conversation; a way of forcing someone into a conversation. □ *ALICE: Guess what! BOB: I don't know. What? ALICE: I'm going to Europe this summer. BOB: That's very nice.* □ *JOHN: Guess what! JANE: What? JOHN: Mary is going to have a baby. JANE: Oh, that's great!*

Had a nice time. Go to (I) had a nice time.

Had it on the tip of my tongue. Go to (I) had it on the tip of my tongue.

Hand it over. Give it to me. (Informal.) □ *It's mine. Hand it over!* □ *Come on. Give me the box of jewels. Hand it over!*

Hand to God! Go to (My) hand to God!

Hang in there. Be patient, things will work out. □ Bob: *Everything is in such a mess. I can't seem to get things done right.* Jane: *Hang in there, Bob. Things will work out.* □ Mary: *Sometimes I just don't think I can go on.* Sue: *Hang in there, Mary. Things will work out.*

Hang on (a minute). and **Hang on a moment.; Hang on a second.** Please wait a minute. □ Mary: *Hang on a minute.* Tom: *What do you want?* Mary: *I want to ask you something.* □ Jane *(entering the room): Oh, Bill.* Bill *(covering the telephone receiver): Hang on a second. I'm on the phone.*

Hang on a moment. Go to Hang on (a minute).

Hang on a second. Go to Hang on (a minute).

Happy to (do something**).** Go to (I'd be) happy to (do something).

Hasn't been easy. Go to (It) hasn't been easy.

Hate to eat and run. Go to (I) hate to eat and run.

Have a ball! Enjoy yourself! (Informal.) □ Bill: *Well, we're off to the party.* Jane: *Okay. Have a ball!* □ *"Have a ball!" said Mary as her roommate went out the door.*

have a chair at the table Go to have some skin in the game.

have a chip in the game Go to have some skin in the game.

Have a go at it. Give it a try.; Try your hand at it. □ Alice: *Wow! This is fun!* Bob: *Can I have a go at it?* □ Tom: *I am having a good* *time painting this fence. It takes a lot of skill. HENRY: It does look challenging. TOM: Here, have a go at it. HENRY: Thanks!*

Have a good day. Go to Have a nice day.

Have a good one. Go to Have a nice day.

Have a good time. Enjoy yourself in what you are about to do. □ *BILL: I'm leaving for the party now. FATHER: Have a good time.* □ *SUE: Tonight is the formal dance at the Palmer House, and I'm going. MARY: Have a good time. I'm watching television right here.*

Have a good trip. AND **Have a nice trip.** Have a pleasant journey. (Compare to Have a safe trip. This phrase avoids references to safety.) □ *As Sue stepped onto the plane, someone in a uniform said, "Have a nice trip."* □ *"Have a good trip," said Bill, waving his good-byes.*

Have a heart! Please be kind and compassionate. □ *TEACHER: Things are looking bad for your grade in this class, Bill. BILL: Gee, have a heart! I work hard.* □ *"Have a heart, officer. I wasn't going all that fast," pleaded Alice.*

Have a nice day. AND **Have a good day.; Have a good one.** an expression said when parting or saying good-bye. (This is now quite hackneyed, and many people do not like to hear it.) □ *CLERK: Thank you. TOM: Thank you. CLERK: Have a nice day.* □ *BOB: See you, man! JOHN: Bye, Bob. Have a good one!*

Have a nice flight. I hope you enjoy your airplane flight. (Said when wishing someone well on an airplane trip. Often said by airline personnel to their passengers.) □ *CLERK: Here's your ticket, sir. Have a nice flight. FRED: Thanks.* □ *As Mary boarded the plane, almost everyone said, "Have a nice flight."*

Have a nice trip. Go to Have a good trip.

Have a safe journey. Go to Have a safe trip.

Have a safe trip. AND **Have a safe journey.** I hope that your journey is safe.; Be careful and assure that your journey is safe. □ *BILL: Well, we're off for London. SALLY: Have a safe trip.* □ *BILL: You're driving all the way to San Francisco? BOB: Yes, indeed. BILL: Well, have a safe trip.*

Have at it. Start doing it.; Start eating it. *JOHN: Here's your hamburger. Have at it. JANE: Thanks. Where's the mustard?* □ *JOHN: Did* *you notice? The driveway needs sweeping.* JANE: *Here's the broom. Have at it.*

Have fun. Have a good time.; Have an enjoyable time. □ BILL: *I'm leaving for the picnic now.* MOTHER: *Have fun.* □ BILL: *Good-bye.* BOB: *Good-bye, Bill.* FRED: *Bye, Bill. Have fun.*

Have I got something **for you!** I have something really exciting for you! □ *Have I got some news for you! Wait'll you hear about it!* □ *Have I got a deal for you! You're gonna love it.*

Have I made myself clear? Do you understand exactly what I am telling you? (Indicates anger or dominance.) □ *I don't intend to warn you again. Have I made myself clear?* □ *A: Please let me go to the top.* B: *I do not want you to go there! Have I made myself clear?*

Have it your way. It will be done your way.; You will get your way. (Usually shows irritation on the part of the speaker.) □ TOM: *I would like to do this room in blue.* SUE: *I prefer yellow. I really do.* TOM: *Okay. Have it your way.* □ JANE: *Let's get a pie. Apple would be good.* BOB: *No, if we are going to buy a whole pie, I want a cherry pie, not apple.* JANE: *Oh, have it your way!*

have one's **finger in too many pies** to be involved in too many things; to have too many tasks going to be able to do any of them well. □ *I'm too busy. I have my finger in too many pies.* □ *She never gets anything done because she has her finger in too many pies.*

have some face time with someone to have a period of time when one is dealing with another person face to face and not over the telephone or by e-mail. (See also **spend (some) quality time with** someone.) □ *As soon as I have some face time with Tom, I'll be able to tell you what his reaction is to your proposal.* □ *Thank you all for coming today. I would prefer to have some face time with each of you individually, and maybe we will do that some day.*

have (some**) issues (with** someone or something**)** to have problems with someone or something. □ *I have a lot of issues with Ted, and it is hard even to talk to him.* □ *Is there a problem with my choice of color? Do you have issues with bright orange?*

Have some more. Go to (Do) have some more.

have some skin in the game AND **have a chip in the game; have a chair at the table** to be a participant in an enterprise where one actually has something to lose if things do not go as planned. □ *If you had a chip in the game, I would take your advice more seriously.* □ *Listen to me! I don't need any smart-aleck outsider to tell me how to run my business! If you had some skin in the game, that would be one thing, but you don't have the slightest idea about what goes on around here.*

Have to be moving along. Go to (I) have to be moving along.

Have to go now. Go to (I) have to go now.

Have to move along. Go to (I) have to be moving along.

Have to run along. Go to (I) have to run along.

Have to shove off. Go to (I) have to shove off.

(Have you) been keeping busy? AND **(Have you been) keeping busy?; You been keeping busy?** a vague greeting that inquires about how someone has been occupied. (Also reflexive: *keeping yourself.*) □ TOM: *Been keeping busy?* BILL: *Yeah. Too busy.* □ SUE: *Hi, Fred. Have you been keeping busy?* FRED: *Not really. Just doing what I have to.*

(Have you) been keeping cool? AND **(Have you been) keeping cool?; You been keeping cool?** an inquiry about how someone is surviving very hot weather. (Also reflexive: *keeping yourself.*) □ TOM: *What do you think of this hot weather? Been keeping cool?* SUE: *No, I like this weather just as it is.* □ MARY: *Keeping cool?* BILL: *Yup. Run the air-conditioning all the time.*

(Have you) been keeping out of trouble? AND **(Have you been) keeping out of trouble?; You been keeping out of trouble?** a vague greeting asking one what one has been doing. (Also reflexive: *keeping yourself.*) □ BOB: *Hi, Mary. Have you been keeping out of trouble?* MARY: *Yeah. And you?* BOB: *Oh, I'm getting by.* □ TOM: *Hey, man! Been keeping out of trouble?* BOB: *Hell, no! What are you up to?* TOM: *Nothing.*

(Have you) been okay? AND **You been okay?** a vague greeting asking if one has been well. □ TOM: *Hey, man. How you doing?* BOB: *I'm okay. You been okay?* TOM: *Sure. See you!* □ MARY: *I heard you were sick.* SALLY: *Yes, but I'm better. Have you been okay?* MARY: *Oh, sure. Healthy as an ox.*

(Have you) changed your mind? AND **You changed your mind?** Have you decided to alter your decision? □ SALLY: *As of last week, they said you are leaving. Changed your mind?* BILL: *No. I'm leaving* *for sure.* □ TOM: *Well, have you changed your mind?* SALLY: *Absolutely not!*

have you heard? AND **did you hear?** a question used to introduce a piece of news or gossip. □ SALLY: *Hi, Mary.* MARY: *Hi. Have you heard about Tom and Sue?* SALLY: *No, what happened?* MARY: *I'll let one of them tell you.* SALLY: *Oh, come on! Tell me!* □ BOB: *Hi, Tom. What's new?* TOM: *Did you hear that they're raising taxes again?* BOB: *That's not new.*

Have you met someone**?** a question asked when introducing someone to someone else. (The question need not be answered. The *someone* is usually a person's name.) □ TOM: *Hello, Mary. Have you met Fred?* MARY: *Hello, Fred. Glad to meet you.* FRED: *Glad to meet you, Mary.* □ TOM: *Hey, Mary! Good to see you. Have you met Fred?* MARY: *No, I don't believe I have. Hello, Fred. Glad to meet you.* FRED: *Hello, Mary.*

Haven't got all day. Go to (I) haven't got all day.

Haven't I seen you somewhere before? AND **Haven't we met before?** a polite way of trying to meet someone. □ BOB: *Hi. Haven't I seen you somewhere before?* MARY: *I hardly think so.* □ BILL (*moving toward Jane*): *Haven't we met before?* JANE (*moving away from Bill*): *No way!*

Haven't seen you in a long time. Go to (I) haven't seen you in a long time.

Haven't seen you in a month of Sundays. Go to (I) haven't seen you in a month of Sundays.

Haven't we met before? Go to Haven't I seen you somewhere before?

Having a wonderful time; wish you were here. Go to (I'm) having a wonderful time; wish you were here.

Having quite a time. Go to I'm having quite a time.

Having the time of my life. Go to (I'm) having the time of my life.

Heads up! Look around! There is danger! □ *The load the crane was lifting swung over near the foreman. "Heads up!" shouted one of the workers, and the foreman just missed getting bonked on the head.* □ *Boxes were falling everywhere as the boat rolled back and forth in the storm. "Heads up!" called a sailor, and a big case of marmalade just missed my left shoulder.*

Heavens! Go to (Good) heavens! See also (My) heavens!

hell on earth a very unpleasant situation, as if one were in hell. □ *That man made my life hell on earth!* □ *The whole time I was there was just hell on earth.*

Hell with that! Go to (To) hell with that!

Hello! Just a minute!; What's this here? (A way of verbally responding to a surprise. The first syllable is higher in pitch than the second.) □ *Hello! Why is this rotten apple still in the refrigerator?* □ *What do I smell. Hello! There's a dead mouse here in the closet.*

Hell's bells (and buckets of blood)! an exclamation of anger or surprise. □ ALICE: *Your pants are torn in back.* JOHN: *Oh, hell's bells! What will happen next?* □ BILL: *Congratulations, you just flunked calculus.* JANE: *Hell's bells and buckets of blood! What do I do now?*

Help me (out) with this. AND **Help me understand this.** Please explain this further because it isn't clear or because it seems senseless. (Also literal.) □ *Now, help me out with this. When you say that the bridge is wobbly, do you mean it's dangerous or just a little scary?* □ *Help me understand this, if you don't mind. If I agree to pay your tax bill, you will supply me with a dozen fresh eggs per week for three years. What's the guarantee?*

Help me understand this. Go to Help me (out) with this.

Help yourself. Please take what you want without asking permission. □ SALLY: *Can I have one of these doughnuts?* BILL: *Help yourself.* □ *Mother led the little troop of my friends to the kitchen table, which was covered with cups of juice and plates of cookies. "Help yourself," she said.*

Here! Stop that!; No more of that! □ BOB: *You say that again and I'll bash you one.* BILL: *You and what army?* FATHER: *Here! That's enough!* □ *"Here! Stop that fighting, you two," shouted the school principal.*

Here goes nothing. I am going to do something difficult or important that may end up failing and therefore be worth nothing. □ *Q: Are you ready? Have you done your safety check? It's your turn to jump! Do it now! A: Okay. Here goes nothing!* □ *Opening the door of his new boss's office, Wallace muttered to himself, "Here goes nothing."*

Here we go again. We are going to experience the same thing again.; We are going to hear about or discuss the same thing again. □ *JOHN: Now, I would like to discuss your behavior in class yesterday. BILL (to himself): Here we go again.* □ *FRED: We must continue our discussion of the Wilson project. SUE: Here we go again. FRED: What's that? SUE: Nothing.*

Here's looking at you. Go to Bottoms up.

Here's mud in your eye. Go to Bottoms up.

Here's to you. Go to Bottoms up.

He's having issues. He's having problems. (Also in other persons.) □ *MOTHER: What's the matter with the baby? She's been cranky all day long. FATHER: Oh, she's just having issues, I guess.* □ *Our car won't start this morning. It's having issues with the weather, I guess.*

hey 1. a word used to get someone's attention; a sentence opener that catches someone's attention. (Informal. Words such as this often use intonation to convey the connotation of the sentence that is to follow. The brief intonation pattern accompanying the word may indicate sarcasm, disagreement, caution, consolation, sternness, etc. See also **say**. Often **Hey!** when used alone.) □ *BILL: Hey, Tom. Over here. I'm over here by the tree. TOM: Hi, Bill. What's up?* □ *TOM: Hey, who are you? MARY: Who do you think, Tom?* □ *"Hey, let's go for a ride!" cried little Billy.* □ *BOB: Hey, stop that! ALICE: Gee! What did I do?* □ *"Hey, look out!" warned Henry.* □ *FRED: Hey, come over here. BOB: What do you want?* □ *FRED: Hey, come here, Bob! BOB: What's up?* **2. Hello!** (A Southern U.S. greeting.) □ *MARY: Hey, Bill. BILL: Hey, Mary. What's up?* □ *JANE: Hey! MARY: Hey! JANE: You okay? MARY: Wonderful!*

Hi! Hello! (Very common.) □ *"Hi! What's cooking?" asked Tom.* □ *BILL: Hi, Tom. How are you? TOM: Fine. How are you doing?* □ *FRED: Hi, old buddy. Give me some skin. TOM: Good to see you, man.*

Hiya! Hello! (Very informal. From *Hi to you.*) □ *HENRY: Hiya, chum. What are you doing? BILL: Nothing.* □ *JOHN: Hey, man! How's by you? BOB: Hiya! Nothing much.*

Hold everything! Stop everything!; Everyone, stop! □ *"Hold everything!" cried Mary. "There's a squirrel loose in the kitchen!"* □ *BILL: Hold everything! Let's try this part again. BOB: But we've already rehearsed it four times.*

Hold it! Stop right there. □ *Tom: Hold it! Mary: What's wrong? Tom: You almost stepped on my contact lens.* □ *Bill: Hold it! Bob: What is it? Bill: Sorry. For a minute, that stick looked like a snake.*

Hold on (a minute)! AND **Hold on for a minute!** Stop right there!; Wait a minute! (*Minute* can be replaced by *moment, second,* or other time periods.) □ *Bob: Hold on, Tom. Tom: What? Bob: I want to talk to you.* □ *"Hold on!" hollered Tom. "You're running off with my shopping cart!"*

Hold, please. Go to Hold the wire(, please).

Hold the line(, please). Go to Hold the wire(, please).

Hold the wire(, please). AND **Hold, please.; Hold the line(, please).; Please hold.** Please wait on the telephone and do not hang up. (A phrase in use before telephone "hold" circuitry was in wide use.) □ *Bill: Hold the wire, please. (turning to Tom) Tom, the phone's for you. Tom: Be right there.* □ *Rachel: Do you wish to speak to Mr. Jones or Mr. Franklin? Henry: Jones. Rachel: Thank you. Hold the line, please.* □ *Sue: Good afternoon, Acme Motors, hold please. (click) Bill (hanging up): That makes me so mad!*

Hold your horses! Slow down! Don't be so eager! □ *Mary: Come on, Sally, let's get going! Sally: Oh, hold your horses! Don't be in such a rush!* □ *"Hold your horses!" said Fred to the herd of small boys trying to get into the station wagon.*

Hold your tongue! You have said enough!; You have said enough rude things. □ *Bill: You're seeing Tom a lot, aren't you? You must be in love. Jane: Hold your tongue, Bill Franklin!* □ *After listening to the tirade against him for nearly four minutes, Tom cried, "Hold your tongue!"*

Honestly? Go to Seriously?

hook up with someone to meet someone (somewhere); to meet or pick someone up (somewhere) for a sexual encounter. □ *I spent many evenings at a bar, hoping I could hook up with someone interesting. Actually, I became very close with the bartender.* □ *She's running around with some guy she hooked up with in a bar.*

Hop to it! Get started right now! □ *Bill: I have to get these things stacked up before I go home. Bob: Then hop to it! You won't get it done standing around here talking.* □ *"Hurry up! Hop to it!" urged Bill. "We've got to get this done!"*

Hope not. Go to (I) hope not.

Hope so. Go to (I) hope so.

Hope to see you again (sometime). Go to (I) hope to see you again (sometime).

hopefully it is to be hoped that. (Many people object to this usage.) □ HENRY: *Hopefully, this plane will get in on time so I can make my connection.* RACHEL: *I hope so too.* □ RACHEL: *Hopefully, all the problems are solved.* HENRY: *Don't be too sure.*

Horsefeathers! Nonsense! □ FRED: *I'm too old to walk that far.* SUE: *Horsefeathers!* □ *"Horsefeathers!" said Jane. "You're totally wrong!"*

Hot diggety (dog)! AND **Hot dog!; Hot ziggety!** an expression of excitement and delight. (These expressions have no meaning and no relationship to dogs.) □ RACHEL: *I got an A! Hot diggety dog!* HENRY: *Good for you!* □ BILL: *Look, here's the check! We're rich!* JANE: *Hot dog!* BILL: *What'll we spend it on?* JANE: *How about saving it?* □ TOM: *You won first place!* MARY: *Hot ziggety!*

Hot dog! Go to Hot diggety (dog)!

Hot enough for you? Go to (Is it) hot enough for you?

Hot ziggety! Go to Hot diggety (dog)!

How about a lift? Go to Could I have a lift?

How about you? What do you think?; What is your choice?; **What about you?** □ BOB: *How are you, Bill?* BILL: *I'm okay. How about you?* BOB: *Fine, fine. Let's do lunch sometime.* □ WAITER: *Can I take your order?* BILL: *I'll have the chef's salad and ice tea.* WAITER *(turning to Sue): How about you?* SUE: *I'll have the same.*

How (are) you doing? a standard greeting inquiry. (The entry without *are* is informal and usually pronounced "How ya doin'?") □ JANE: *How are you doing?* MARY: *I'm okay. What about you?* JANE: *Likewise.* □ SALLY: *Sue, this is my little brother, Bill.* SUE: *How are you, Bill?* BILL: *Okay. How you doing?*

How (are) you feeling? an inquiry into the state of someone's health. □ SALLY: *How are you feeling?* BILL: *Oh, better, thanks.* SALLY: *That's good.* □ BILL: *Hey, Jane! You been sick?* JANE: *Yeah.* BILL: *How you feeling?* JANE: *Not very well.*

How are you getting on? How are you managing?; How are you doing? □ JANE: *Well, Mary, how are you getting on?* MARY: *Things* *couldn't be better.* □ SUE: *Hey, John! How are you getting on? What's it like with all the kids out of the house?* JOHN: *Things are great, Sue!*

How 'bout them team players**?** What do you think of the way the named sports team has been playing? (A formulaic conversation starter.) □ *Poor Darrell. His only greetings are "How 'bout them Cubs?" or "Getting any?"* □ FATHER: *Well, how did you like our office party?* MOTHER: *Can't any of those guys say hello? What does all this "How 'bout them Dolphins?" mean?*

How 'bout this weather? Isn't this strange weather? (A formulaic conversation starter.) □ *Old dull Fred stands around quietly with a drink in his hand for a long time. Then he walks up to a real gorgeous blonde and says, "How 'bout this weather?" She looks at him for a few seconds and bursts out laughing.* □ Q: *Gee, it's hot! How 'bout this weather?* A: *Heat getting you down?*

How can I help you? Go to How may I help you?

How can I serve you? Go to How may I help you?

How come? How did that come about?; Why? □ SALLY: *I have to go to the doctor.* MARY: *How come?* SALLY: *I'm sick, silly.* □ JOHN: *I have to leave now.* BILL: *How come?* JOHN: *I just have to, that's all.* □ HENRY: *How come you always put your right shoe on first?* RACHEL: *Do I have to have a reason for something like that?*

How could you (do something)**?** How could you bring yourself to do a thing like that? (No answer is expected.) □ *Looking first at the broken lamp and then at the cat, Mary shouted, "How could you do that?"* □ TOM: *Then I punched him in the nose.* RACHEL: *Oh, how could you?*

How do you do. a standard greeting inquiry and response. (This expression never has rising question intonation, but the first instance of its use calls for a response. Sometimes the response does, in fact, explain how one is.) □ SALLY: *Hello. How do you do.* BOB: *How do you do.* □ MARY: *How do you do. So glad to meet you, Tom.* TOM: *Thank you. How are you?* MARY: *Just fine. Your brother tells me you like camping.* TOM: *Yes. Are you a camper?* MARY: *Sort of.*

How do you know? 1. How did you get that information? (A straightforward question. The stress is on *know*.) □ BILL: *The train is about to pull into the station.* SUE: *How do you know?* BILL: *I hear it.* □ FRED: *I have to apologize for the coffee. It probably isn't very* good. JANE: *How do you know?* FRED: *Well, I made it.* **2.** What makes you think you are correct? Why do you think you have enough information to make this judgment? (Contentious. The heaviest stress is on *you*.) □ BILL: *This is the best recording made all year.* BOB: *How do you know?* BILL: *Well, I guess it's just my opinion.* □ TOM: *Having a baby can be quite an ordeal.* MARY: *How do you know?* TOM: *I read a lot.*

How do you know someone**?** How did you make the acquaintance of someone?; How is it that you know someone? □ Q: *How do you know Wally?* A: *Through work.* □ *I saw you talking to Bill. How do you know him, if I might ask?*

How do you like it here? How do you like living here, going to school here, working here, etc.? □ *Welcome to Worth High School. How do you like it here?* □ *I see you have just joined the company. How do you like it here?*

How do you like school? a phrase used to start a conversation with a school-age person. □ BOB: *Well, Billy, how do you like school?* BILL: *I hate it.* BOB: *Too bad.* □ MARY: *How do you like school?* BOB: *It's okay. Almost everything else is better, though.*

How do you like that? 1. Do you like that?; Is that to your liking? □ TOM: *There's a bigger one over there. How do you like that?* BILL: *It's better, but not quite what I want.* □ CLERK: *Here's one without pleats. How do you like that?* FRED: *That's perfect!* **2.** an expression said when administering punishment. □ *"How do you like that?" growled Tom as he punched John in the stomach.* □ BILL (being spanked): *Ouch! Ow! No!* MOTHER (spanking): *How do you like that?* BILL: *Not much.* MOTHER: *It hurts me more than it hurts you.* **3.** an expression of surprise at someone's bad or strange behavior or at some surprising event. □ TOM (shouting at Sue): *Can it! Go away!* SUE (looking at Mary, aghast): *Well, how do you like that!* MARY: *Let's get out of here!* □ FRED: *How do you like that?* SUE: *What's the matter?* FRED: *My wallet's gone.*

How do you like this weather? a greeting inquiry. (A direct answer is expected.) □ HENRY: *Hi, Bill. How do you like this weather?* BILL: *Lovely weather for ducks. Not too good for me, though.* □ ALICE: *Gee, it's hot! How do you like this weather?* RACHEL: *You can have it!*

How dumb do you think I am? Your question is insulting. I am not stupid. (Shows agitation. An answer is not expected or desired.) □ MARY: *Are you really going to sell your new car?* SALLY: *Come on! How dumb do you think I am?* □ TOM: *Do you think you could sneak into that theater without paying?* BOB: *Good grief! How dumb do you think I am?*

How goes it (with you)? How are things going with you? □ TOM: *How goes it?* JANE: *Great! How goes it with you?* TOM: *Couldn't be better.* □ SALLY: *Greetings, Sue. How goes it?* SUE: *Okay, I guess. And you?* SALLY: *The same.*

How (have) you been? one of the standard greeting inquiries. □ BOB: *Hi, Fred! How have you been?* FRED: *Great! What about you?* BOB: *Fine.* □ BOB: *How you been?* SUE: *Okay, I guess. You okay?* BOB: *Yup.*

How many times do I have to tell you? a phrase admonishing someone who has forgotten instructions. □ MOTHER: *How many times do I have to tell you? Do your homework!* BILL: *Mom! I hate school!* □ MARY: *Clean this place up! How many times do I have to tell you?* BILL: *I'll do it! I'll do it!*

How may I help you? AND **How can I help you?; How can I serve you?; May I help you?; What can I do for you?** In what way can I serve you? (Usually said by shopkeepers and food service personnel. The first question is the most polite, and the last is the least polite.) □ WAITER: *How can I help you?* SUE: *I'm not ready to order yet.* □ CLERK: *May I help you?* JANE: *I'm looking for a gift for my aunt.*

How should I know? AND **Don't ask me.** I do not know. Why should I be expected to know? (Shows impatience or rudeness.) □ BILL: *Why is the orca called the killer whale?* MARY: *How should I know?* □ SALLY: *Where did I leave my glasses?* TOM: *Don't ask me.*

How something **is that!** Isn't that wonderful or awesome? (The *something* = cool, good, great, awesome, yummy, etc. More of an exclamation than a question, and either the question mark or the exclamation mark can be used.) □ A: *Here is my new jacket. Isn't the red bright?* B: *How cool is that?* □ *Now here is my latest creation. How great is that?*

How time flies. Go to (My,) how time flies.

How will I know you? Go to How will I recognize you?

How will I recognize you? AND **How will I know you?** a question asked by one of two people who have agreed to meet for the first time in a large busy place. □ *Tom: Okay, I'll meet you at the west door of the station. MARY: Fine. How will I recognize you? TOM: I'll be wearing dark glasses.* □ *BILL: I'll meet you at six. How will I recognize you? MARY: I'll be carrying a brown umbrella.*

How you been? Go to How (have) you been?

How you doing? Go to How (are) you doing?

How you feeling? Go to How (are) you feeling?

How-de-do. AND **Howdy(-do).** a greeting inquiry meaning How do you do.; a response to the greeting inquiry **How-de-do**. (These forms never have rising question intonation, but the first instance of either one calls for a response. Familiar and folksy.) □ *BILL: Well, here's my old pal, Tom. How-de-do, Tom. TOM: How-de-do. How you been?* □ *SALLY: How do you do, Mr. Johnson. TOM: Howdy, ma'am. SALLY: Charmed, I'm sure.*

Howdy(-do). Go to How-de-do.

How're things going? one of the standard greeting inquiries. □ *BOB: Hi, Fred! How're things going? FRED: Could be better. How's by you?* □ *BILL: How are things going? MARY: Fine, but I need to talk to you.*

How're things (with you)? a greeting inquiry. □ *SALLY: How are you? BILL: Fine. How are things?* □ *BILL: How are things going? MARY: Fine. How are things with you?*

How's business? a question asked in a conversation about the state of someone's business or job. □ *TOM: Hello, Sally. How's business? SALLY: Okay, I suppose.* □ *BOB: Good to see you, Fred. FRED: Hello, Bob. How's business? BOB: Just okay.*

How's by you? a greeting inquiry. (Informal.) □ *FRED: Hey, man! How's by you? JOHN: Groovy, Fred. Tsup?* □ *BOB: Hello. What's cooking? BILL: Nothing. How's by you?*

How's every little thing? How're things with you? (Informal and familiar.) □ *BILL: Hello, Tom. TOM: Hi, Bill. How's every little thing? BILL: Couldn't be better.* □ *BILL: Hi, Mary. How's every little thing? MARY: Things are fine. How are you? BILL: Fine, thanks.*

How's it going? one of the standard informal greeting inquiries. □ *SUE: How's it going? BILL: Just great! How are you? SUE: Fine,* *thanks.* □ MARY: *How are you, Sue?* SUE: *Things just couldn't be better! I'm gloriously in love!* MARY: *Anybody I know?*

How's (it) with you? a greeting inquiry. (Slang.) □ TOM: *Hey, man. How's with you?* BOB: *Great! And you?* TOM: *Okay.* □ BILL: *How's with you, old buddy?* JOHN: *Can't complain. And you?* BILL: *Couldn't be better.*

How's my boy? AND **How's the boy?** How are you? (Male to male, and familiar. The speaker may outrank the person addressed.) □ BOB: *How's my boy?* BILL: *Hi, Tom. How are you?* □ FRED: *Hello, old buddy. How's the boy?* BOB: *Hi, there! What's cooking?* FRED: *Nothing much.*

How's that again? Please say that again.; I did not hear what you said. □ SUE: *Would you like some coffee?* MARY: *How's that again?* SUE: *I said, would you like some coffee?* □ TOM: *The car door is frozen closed.* BOB: *How's that again?* TOM: *The car door is frozen closed.*

How's that working for you? Go to How's that working (out)?

How's that working (out)? AND **How's that working for you?; How's that working out (for you)?** And how did that so-called promising idea work out? (Sometimes sarcastic or ironic.) □ DON: *I tried to lose weight by giving up desserts.* HANNA: *How's that working out for you?* □ DALE: *I tried a new toothpaste that isn't as sweet-tasting as the last one.* IDA: *How's that working out for you?*

How's that working out (for you)? Go to How's that working (out)?

How's the boy? Go to How's my boy?

How's the family? AND **How's your family?** an expression that carries the greeting inquiries beyond the speakers present. □ BOB: *Hello, Fred. How are you?* FRED: *Fine, thanks.* BOB: *How's the family?* FRED: *Great! How's yours?* BOB: *Couldn't be better.* □ *"How's the family?" asked Bill, greeting his boss.*

How's the wife? How is your wife? (Usually male to male.) □ TOM: *Hi, Fred, how are you?* FRED: *Good. And you?* TOM: *Great! How's the wife?* FRED: *Okay, and yours?* TOM: *Couldn't be better.* □ BILL: *Hi, Bill. How's the wife?* BOB: *Doing fine. How's every little thing?* BILL: *Great!*

How's the world (been) treating you? How are things going for you? □ *SUE: Hello there, Bob. How's the world treating you? BOB: I can't complain. How are you? SUE: Doing just fine, thanks.* □ *MARY: Morning, Bill. BILL: Good morning, Mary. How's the world been treating you? MARY: Okay, I guess.*

How's tricks? a greeting inquiry. (Slang.) □ *BOB: Fred! How's tricks? FRED: How are you doing, Bob? BOB: Doing great!* □ *BILL: What's up? How's tricks? BOB: I can't complain. How are things going for you? BILL: Can't complain.*

How's with you? Go to How's (it) with you?

How's your family? Go to How's the family?

Hurry on! Keep going! Move faster! □ *TOM: Get going! Hurry on! SUE: I'm hurrying as fast as I can.* □ *MARY: Hurry on! CHILD: I can't go any faster!*

Hurry up! Come on, move faster. □ *SUE: Hurry up! We're late! BILL: I'm hurrying.* □ *BOB: We're about to miss the bus! SUE: Well, then, hurry up!*

Hush your mouth! Please be quiet! (Not very polite.) □ *I've heard enough of that talk. Hush your mouth!* □ *A: I hate her! I hate her! B: Now, hush your mouth! You shouldn't talk like that!*

(I) beg your pardon. 1. AND **Beg pardon.** a phrase said to excuse oneself for interrupting or committing some very minor social offence. □ *As Sue brushed by the old man, she turned and said, "Beg pardon."* □ *JANE: Ouch! That's my toe you stepped on! SUE: I beg your pardon. I'm so sorry.* **2.** a phrase that indicates the speaker's need to pass by another person. □ *The hallway was filled with people. Bob said, "I beg your pardon," and then he said it again and again.* □ *FRED: Beg pardon. Need to get by. SUE: I'm sorry.* **3.** an exclamation that shows, as politely as possible, one's indignation at something that someone has said. (In a way, this signals the offender of the magnitude of the offence and invites a revision of the original offending statement.) □ *BILL: I think you've really made a poor choice this time. MARY: I beg your pardon! BILL: I mean, you normally do better. MARY: Well, I never!* □ *SUE: Your spaghetti sauce is too sweet. SALLY: I beg your pardon! SUE: Maybe not.*

(I) beg your pardon, but AND **begging your pardon, but** please excuse me, but. (A very polite and formal way of interrupting, bringing something to someone's attention, or asking a question of a stranger.) □ *RACHEL: Beg your pardon, but I think your right front tire is a little low. HENRY: Well, I guess it is. Thank you.* □ *JOHN: Begging your pardon, ma'am, but weren't we on the same cruise ship in Alaska last July? RACHEL: Couldn't have been me.*

I believe so. Go to I guess (so).

I believe we've met. a phrase indicating that one has already met a person to whom one is being introduced. □ *JOHN: Alice, have you met Fred? ALICE: Oh, yes, I believe we've met. How are you, Fred? FRED: Hello, Alice. Good to see you again.* □ *ALICE: Tom, this is my cousin, Mary. TOM: I believe we've met. Nice to see you again, Mary. MARY: Hello, Tom. Good to see you again.*

I can accept that. I accept your evaluation as valid. □ *BOB: Now, you'll probably like doing the other job much better. It doesn't call for you to do the things you don't do well. TOM: I can accept that.* □ *SUE: On your evaluation this time, I noted that you need to work on telephone manners a little bit. BILL: I can accept that.*

I can live with that. That is something I can get used to.; That is all right as far as I'm concerned. □ *SUE: I want to do this room in green. BILL: I can live with that.* □ *CLERK: This one will cost twelve dollars more. BOB: I can live with that. I'll take it.*

(I) can too. You are wrong, I can.; Don't say I can't, because I can! (The response to **(You) can't!**) □ *SUE: I'm going to the party. MOTHER: You can't. SUE: I can too. MOTHER: Cannot! SUE: Can too!* □ *"Can too!" protested Fred. "I can, if you can!"*

I can't accept that. I do not believe what you said.; I reject what you said. □ *SUE: The mechanic says we need a whole new engine. JOHN: What? I can't accept that!* □ *TOM: You're now going to work on the night shift. You don't seem to be able to get along with some of the people on the day shift. BOB: I can't accept that. It's them, not me.*

(I) can't argue with that. I agree with what you said.; It sounds like a good idea. □ *TOM: This sure is good cake. BOB: Can't argue with that.* □ *SUE: What do you say we go for a swim? FRED: I can't argue with that.*

(I) can't beat that. AND **(I) can't top that.** I cannot do better than that.; I cannot exceed that. □ *HENRY: That was really great. I can't beat that. RACHEL: Yes, that was really good.* □ *"What a great joke! I can't top that," said Kate, still laughing.*

I can't believe (that)! That is unbelievable! □ *TOM: What a terrible earthquake! All the houses collapsed, one by one. JANE: I can't believe that!* □ *BILL: This lake is nearly two hundred feet deep. SUE: I can't believe! BILL: Take my word for it.*

(I) can't complain. AND **(I have) nothing to complain about.** a response to a greeting inquiry asking how one is or how things are going for one. □ *SUE: How are things going? MARY: I can't complain.* □ *MARY: Hi, Fred! How are you doing? FRED: Nothing to complain about.*

I can't get over something**!** I am just so amazed! (The *something* can be a fact or a pronoun, such as *that* or *it*. Also with *just*, as in the example.) □ *"I just can't get over the way everybody pitched in and* *helped," said Alice.* □ BOB: *The very idea, Sue and Tom doing something like that!* BILL: *I can't get over it!*

(I) can't help it. There is nothing I can do to help the situation.; That is the way it is.; There is nothing I can do. (Often in answer to a criticism.) □ MARY: *Your hair is a mess.* SUE: *It's windy. I can't help it.* □ FRED: *I wish you'd quit coughing all the time.* SALLY: *I can't help it. I wish I could too.*

(I) can't make heads or tails of something. I'm not able to figure out or understand something. (Also in other persons.) □ *He's read this book over and over, but he can't make heads or tails out of it.* □ *I got a new computer, but it just sits there. I can't make heads or tails of it.*

(I) can't rightly say. I do not know with any certainty. (Colloquial and a little folksy.) □ FRED: *When do you think we'll get there?* BILL: *Can't rightly say.* □ BOB: *Okay, how does this look to you?* BILL: *I can't rightly say. I've never seen anything like it before.*

(I) can't say (as) I do. Go to (I) can't say that I do.

(I) can't say for sure. I do not know with any certainty. □ TOM: *When will the next train come through?* JANE: *I can't say for sure.* □ BOB: *How can the driver hit so many potholes?* BILL: *Can't say for sure. I know he doesn't see too well, though.*

(I) can't say that I do. AND **(I) can't say's I do.; (I) can't say (as) I do.** a vague response to a question about whether one remembers, knows about, likes, etc., something or someone. (A polite way of saying no. Colloquial and folksy. The *say as* and *say's* are not standard English.) □ JANE: *You remember Fred, don't you?* JOHN: *Can't say as I do.* □ BOB: *This is a fine-looking car. Do you like it?* BILL: *I can't say I do.*

(I) can't say that I have. AND **(I) can't say's I have.; (I) can't say (as) I have.** a vague response to a question about whether one has ever done something or been somewhere. (A polite way of saying no. Colloquial and folksy. The *say as* and *say's* are not standard English.) □ BILL: *Have you ever been to a real opera?* BOB: *I can't say as I have.* □ MARY: *Well, have you thought about going with me to Fairbanks?* FRED: *I can't say I have, actually.*

(I) can't say's I do. Go to (I) can't say that I do.

(I) can't thank you enough. a polite expression of gratitude. □ BILL: *Here's the book I promised you.* SUE: *Oh, good. I can't thank you enough.* □ TOM: *Well, here we are.* BILL: *Well, Tom. I can't thank you enough. I really appreciate the ride.*

(I) can't top that. Go to (I) can't beat that.

I can't understand (it). Go to I don't understand (it).

(I) can't unring the bell. I cannot undo what's been done. (Also in other persons.) □ *I wish I wasn't pregnant, but you can't unring the bell.* □ Q: *Isn't there anything we can do about the bank failure?* A: *Sorry. We can't unring the bell.*

(I) changed my mind. I have reversed my previous decision or statement. □ TOM: *I thought you were going to Atlanta today.* BILL: *I changed my mind. I'm leaving tomorrow.* □ MARY: *I thought that this room was going to be done in red.* SUE: *I changed my mind.*

(I) could be better. Go to (Things) could be better.

(I) could be worse. Go to (Things) could be worse.

I could eat. I am hungry enough to eat a meal. □ HANNA: *There's a pizza place. Want to get one?* DON: *I could eat.* □ ANDREW: *It's past dinnertime. Are you hungry?* ISABEL: *I could eat.*

I could eat a cow! Go to (I'm so hungry) I could eat a horse!

I could eat a horse! Go to (I'm so hungry) I could eat a horse!

I could use a something. I would like to have something, usually food or drink. (Also in other persons.) □ *Man, I'm hot. I could use a cold beer.* □ A: *There's a man outside who looks very hungry and is offering to chop us some wood.* B: *I bet he could use a sandwich or two. Too bad we don't have any wood to chop.*

(I) couldn't ask for more. Everything is fine, and there is no more that I could want. □ BILL: *Are you happy?* SUE: *Oh, Bill. I couldn't ask for more.* □ WAITER: *Is everything all right?* BILL: *Oh, yes, indeed. Couldn't ask for more.*

I couldn't ask you to do that. That is a very kind offer, but I would not ask you to do it. (This is not a refusal of the offer.) □ SALLY: *Look, if you want, I'll drive you to the airport.* MARY: *Oh, Sally. I couldn't ask you to do that.* □ BILL: *I'll lend you enough money to get you through the week.* SALLY: *I couldn't ask you to do that.*

(I) couldn't be better. I am fine. □ JOHN: *How are you?* JANE: *Couldn't be better.* □ BILL: *I hope you're completely well now.* MARY: *I couldn't be better.*

(I) could(n't) care less. It doesn't matter to me. (The *less* bears the heaviest stress in both versions. Both versions are idiomatic. Despite the apparent contradiction, either reading of this—both the affirmative and negative—usually have the same meaning. The exception would be in a sentence where the *could* bears the heaviest stress: *I could care less, [but I don't].*) □ TOM: *It's raining in! The carpet will get wet!* MARY: *I couldn't care less.* □ BILL: *I'm going to go in there and tell him off!* JOHN: *I could care less.*

(I) couldn't help it. There was no way I could prevent it.; I was unable to prevent something from happening.; I was unable to control myself. □ SALLY: *You let the paint dry with brush marks in it.* MARY: *I couldn't help it. The telephone rang.* □ FRED: *You got fingerprints all over the window.* MARY: *Sorry. Couldn't help it.*

I didn't catch the name. AND **I didn't catch your name.** I don't remember your name from when I heard it.; I didn't hear your name when we were introduced. □ BILL: *How do you like this weather?* BOB: *It's not too good. By the way, I didn't catch your name. I'm Bob Wilson.* BILL: *I'm Bill Franklin.* BOB: *Nice to meet you, Bill.* □ BOB: *Sorry, I didn't catch the name.* BILL: *It's Bill, Bill Franklin. And you?* BOB: *I'm Bob Wilson.*

I didn't catch your name. Go to I didn't catch the name.

I didn't get that. Go to I didn't (quite) catch that (last) remark.

I didn't (quite) catch that (last) remark. AND **I didn't get that.; I didn't hear you.** I didn't hear what you said, so would you please repeat it. □ JOHN: *What did you say? I didn't quite catch that last remark.* JANE: *I said it's really a hot day.* □ BILL: *Have a nice time, if you can.* SALLY: *I didn't get that.* BILL: *Have a nice time! Enjoy!*

I (do) declare! I am surprised to hear that! (Old-fashioned.) □ MARY: *I'm the new president of my sorority!* GRANDMOTHER: *I declare! That's very nice.* □ *A plane had landed right in the middle of the cornfield. The old farmer shook his head in disbelief. "I do declare!" he said over and over as he walked toward the plane.*

I don't believe it! an expression of amazement and disbelief. □ BOB: *Tom was just elected president of the trade association!* MARY: *I* *don't believe it!* □ Bob: *They're going to build a Disney World in Moscow.* Sally: *I don't believe it!*

(I) don't believe I've had the pleasure. an expression meaning *I haven't met you yet.* □ Tom: *I'm Tom Thomas. I don't believe I've had the pleasure.* Bill: *Hello. I'm Bill Franklin.* Tom: *Nice to meet you, Bill.* Bill: *Likewise.* □ Bob: *Looks like rain.* Fred: *Sure does. Oh, I don't believe I've had the pleasure.* Bob: *I'm Bob, Bob Jones.* Fred: *My name is Fred Wilson. Glad to meet you.*

(I) don't believe so. Go to I guess not.

I don't believe this! This is very strange!; I do not believe that this is happening. □ *"I don't believe this!" muttered Sally as all the doors in the house slammed at the same time.* □ Sally: *You're expected to get here early and make my coffee every morning.* John: *I don't believe this.*

I don't care. It doesn't matter to me. □ Mary: *Can I take these papers away?* Tom: *I don't care. Do what you want.* □ Bill: *Should this room be white or yellow?* Sally: *I don't care.*

I don't have time to breathe. Go to I don't have time to catch my breath.

I don't have time to catch my breath. AND **I don't have time to breathe.** I am very busy.; I have been very busy. □ Henry: *I'm so busy these days. I don't have time to catch my breath.* Rachel: *Oh, I know what you mean.* □ Sue: *Would you mind finishing this for me?* Bill: *Sorry, Sue. I'm busy. I don't have time to breathe.*

I don't know. a common expression of ignorance. □ Father: *Why can't you do better in school?* Bill: *I don't know.* □ Bill: *Well, what are we going to do now?* Sue: *I don't know.*

I don't love something. I don't like something. (With an implication that someone's efforts have failed to please as much as had been expected.) □ *Well, it's a nice house, but I don't love the entrance.* □ *I don't love this sauce on the chicken.*

I don't mean maybe! I am very serious about my demand or order. □ Bob: *Do I have to do this?* Sue: *Do it now, and I don't mean maybe!* □ Father: *Get this place cleaned up! And I don't mean maybe!* John: *All right! I'll do it!*

(I) don't mind if I do. Yes, I would like to. □ Sally: *Have some more coffee?* Bob: *Don't mind if I do.* □ Jane: *Here are some lovely roses.*

Would you like to take a few blossoms with you? JOHN: I don't mind if I do.

(I) don't think so. Go to I guess not.

I don't think we've met. Hello, I don't know your name, but I want to greet you. □ *A: I'm Jane Smithers. I don't think we've met. B: I'm Wallace Wimple.* □ *A: I've seen you here often, but I don't think we've met. B: I'm Harry Bopp. I own this place.*

I don't understand (it). AND **I can't understand (it).** I am confused and bewildered (by what has happened). □ *BILL: Everyone is leaving the party. MARY: I don't understand. It's still so early.* □ *BOB: The very idea, Sue and Tom doing something like that! ALICE: It's very strange. I can't understand it.*

I don't want to alarm you, but AND **I don't want to upset you, but** an expression used to introduce bad or shocking news or gossip. □ *BILL: I don't want to alarm you, but I see someone prowling around your car. MARY: Oh, goodness! I'll call the police!* □ *BOB: I don't want to upset you, but I have some bad news. TOM: Let me have it.*

I don't want to sound like a busybody, but an expression used to introduce an opinion or suggestion. □ *BOB: I don't want to sound like a busybody, but didn't you intend to have your house painted? BILL: Well, I guess I did.* □ *BOB: I don't want to sound like a busybody, but some of your neighbors wonder if you could stop parking your car on your lawn. SALLY: I'll thank you to mind your own business!*

I don't want to upset you, but Go to I don't want to alarm you, but.

I don't want to wear out my welcome. a phrase said by a guest who doesn't want to be a burden to the host or hostess or to visit too often. □ *MARY: Good night, Tom. You must come back again soon. TOM: Thank you. I'd love to. I don't want to wear out my welcome, though.* □ *BOB: We had a fine time. Glad you could come to our little gathering. Hope you can come again next week. FRED: I don't want to wear out my welcome, but I'd like to come again. BOB: Good. See you next week. Bye. FRED: Bye.*

I don't wonder. Go to I'm not surprised.

I doubt it. I do not think so. □ *Tom: Think it will rain today? Sue: I doubt it.* □ *Sally: Think you'll go to New York? Mary: I doubt it.*

I doubt that. I do not believe that what you just said is so. □ *Bob: I'll be there exactly on time. Sue: I doubt that.* □ *John: Fred says he can't come to work because he's sick. Jane: I doubt that.*

I expect. Go to I guess.

I expect not. Go to I guess not.

I expect (so). Go to I guess (so).

I got it! I'll do this!; This is my task!; I'll do it! (Often literal in a ball game.) □ *Sam (moving ahead of Jane to open the door): I got it!* □ *The ball was hit way up over center field. John shouted, "I got it!" as he ran backwards with his eye on the ball.*

I guess AND **I expect; I suppose; I suspect 1.** a phrase that introduces a supposition. (Frequently, in speech, *suppose* is reduced to *'spose*, and *expect* and *suspect* are reduced to *'spect*. The apostrophe is not always used.) □ *Bob: I guess it's going to rain. Bill: Oh, I don't know. Maybe so, maybe not.* □ *Alice: I expect you'll be wanting to leave pretty soon. John: Why? It's early yet.* **2.** a vague way of answering yes. □ *John: You want some more coffee? Jane: I 'spose.* □ *Alice: Ready to go? John: I spect.*

I guess not. AND **(I) don't think so.; I expect not.; I suppose not.; I suspect not.; I think not.** a vague statement of negation. (More polite or gentle than no. Frequently, in speech, *suppose* is reduced to *'spose*, and *expect* and *suspect* are reduced to *'spect*. The apostrophe is not always used.) □ *Bill: It's almost too late to go to the movie. Shall we try anyway? Mary: I guess not.* □ *Tom: Will it rain? Mary: I 'spect not.*

I guess (so). AND **I believe so.; I expect (so).; I suppose (so).; I suspect (so).; I think so.** a vague expression of assent. (Frequently, in speech, *suppose* is reduced to *'spose*, and *expect* and *suspect* are reduced to *'spect*. The apostrophe is not always used.) □ *Tom: Will it rain today? Bob: I suppose so.* □ *Sue: Happy? Bill: I 'spect. Sue: You don't sound happy. Bill: I guess not.*

I had a lovely time. AND **We had a lovely time.** a polite expression of thanks to a host or hostess. □ *Fred: Good-bye. I had a lovely time. Bill: Nice to have you. Do come again.* □ *Jane: We had a lovely time. Mary: Thank you and thanks for coming.*

(I) had a nice time. the standard "good-bye and thank you" said to a host or hostess by a departing guest. □ JOHN: *Thank you. I had a nice time.* SALLY: *Don't stay away so long next time. Bye.* □ MARY: *Had a nice time. Bye. Got to run.* SUE: *Bye. Drive safely.*

(I) had it on the tip of my tongue. I just now remembered the information but forgot it just as I started to say it. □ *Sorry. I know your name. I had it on the tip of my tongue.* □ *This is called a, well, uh—had it on the tip of my tongue.*

(I) hate to eat and run. an apology made by someone who must leave a social event soon after eating. □ BILL: *Well, I hate to eat and run, but it's getting late.* SUE: *Oh, you don't have to leave, do you?* BILL: *I think I really must.* □ MARY: *Oh, my goodness! I hate to eat and run, but I have to catch an early plane tomorrow.* BOB: *Do you have to go?* MARY: *Afraid so.*

I have better things to do. Go to (I've) (got) better things to do.

(I have) no problem with that. That is okay with me. (See also (That causes) no problem.) □ BOB: *Is it okay if I sign us up for the party?* SALLY: *I have no problem with that.* □ BILL: *It looks as though we will have to come back later. They're not open yet. Is that all right?* JANE: *No problem with that. When do they open?*

(I have) nothing to complain about. Go to (I) can't complain.

(I) have to be moving along. AND **(I) have to move along.** It is time for me to leave. □ BILL: *Bye, now. Have to be moving along.* SALLY: *See you later.* □ RACHEL: *I have to be moving along. See you later.* ANDREW: *Bye, now.* □ SALLY: *It's late. I have to move along.* MARY: *If you must. Good-bye. See you tomorrow.*

(I) have to go now. an expression announcing the need to leave. □ FRED: *Bye, have to go now.* MARY: *See you later. Take it easy.* □ SUE: *Would you help me with this box?* JOHN: *Sorry. I have to go now.*

(I) have to move along. Go to (I) have to be moving along.

(I) have to push off. Go to (I) have to shove off.

(I) have to run along. an expression announcing the need to leave. □ JANE: *It's late. I have to run along.* TOM: *Okay, Jane. Bye. Take care.* □ JOHN: *Leaving so soon?* SALLY: *Yes, I have to run along.*

(I) have to shove off. AND **(I've) got to be shoving off.; (I've) got to shove off.; (I) have to push off.; (It's) time to shove off.** a phrase announcing one's need to depart. □ JOHN: *Look at* *the time! I have to shove off! JANE: Bye, John.* □ *JANE: Time to shove off. I have to feed the cats. JOHN: Bye, Jane.* □ *FRED: I have to push off. Bye. JANE: See you around. Bye.*

I have to wash a few things out. an excuse for not going out or for going home early. (Of course, it can be used literally.) □ *JANE: Time to shove off. I have to wash a few things out. JOHN: Bye, Jane.* □ *BILL: I have to wash out a few things. BOB: Why don't you use a machine? BILL: Oh, I'll see you later.*

(I) haven't got all day. Please hurry, because I don't have a lot of time. □ *RACHEL: Make it snappy! I haven't got all day. ALICE: Just take it easy. There's no rush.* □ *HENRY: I haven't got all day. When are you going to finish with my car? BOB: As soon as I can.*

(I) haven't seen you in a long time. an expression said as part of the greeting series. □ *MARY: Hi, Fred! Haven't seen you in a long time. FRED: Yeah. Long time no see.* □ *TOM: Well, John. Is that you? I haven't seen you in a long time. JOHN: Good to see you, Tom!*

(I) haven't seen you in a month of Sundays. I haven't seen you in a long time. (Colloquial and folksy.) □ *TOM: Hi, Bill. Haven't seen you in a month of Sundays! BILL: Hi, Tom. Long time no see.* □ *BOB: Well, Fred! Come right in! Haven't seen you in a month of Sundays! FRED: Good to see you, Uncle Bob.*

I hear what you're saying. AND **I hear you. 1.** I know exactly what you mean. □ *JOHN: The prices in this place are a bit steep. JANE: Man, I hear you!* □ *BILL: I think it's about time for a small revolution! ANDREW: I hear what you're saying.* **2.** an expression indicating that the speaker has been heard but implying that there is no agreement. □ *TOM: Time has come to do something about that ailing dog of yours. MARY: I hear what you're saying.* □ *JANE: It would be a good idea to have the house painted. JOHN: I hear what you're saying.*

I hear you. Go to I hear what you're saying.

(I) hope not. a phrase expressing the desire and wish that something is not so. □ *JOHN: It looks like it's going to rain. JANE: Hope not.* □ *JOHN: The Wilsons said they might come over this evening. JANE: I hope not. I've got things to do.*

(I) hope so. a phrase expressing the desire and wish that something is so. □ *BILL: Is this the right house? BOB: Hope so.* □ *JOHN: Will you be coming to dinner Friday? SUE: Yes, I hope so.*

(I) hope to see you again (sometime). an expression said when taking leave of a person one has just met. □ BILL: *Nice to meet you, Tom.* TOM: *Bye, Bill. Nice to meet you. Hope to see you again sometime.* □ BILL: *Good talking to you. See you around.* BOB: *Yes, I hope to see you again. Good-bye.*

I just have this feeling I have a premonition about this.; I have a strange feeling about this matter. □ *I really don't know that something is wrong. I just have this feeling.* □ *I just have this feeling that she is not telling us the truth.*

(I) just want(ed) to (do something**).** a polite but vague way of explaining what you are going to do. □ RACHEL: *I just wanted to say that we all loved your letter. Thank you so much.* ANDREW: *Thanks. Glad you liked it.* □ RACHEL: *I just wanted to tell you how sorry I am about your sister.* ALICE: *Thanks. I appreciate it.* □ ANDREW: *Just wanted to come by for a minute and say hello.* TOM: *Well, hello. Glad you dropped by.*

I kid you not. I am not kidding you.; I am not trying to fool you. □ BILL: *Whose car is this?* SALLY: *It's mine. It really is. I kid you not.* □ *"I kid you not," said Tom, glowing. "I outran the whole lot of them."*

I know (just) what you mean. I know exactly what you are talking about, and I feel the same way about it. □ JOHN: *These final exams are just terrible.* BOB: *I know just what you mean.* JOHN: *Why do we have to go through this?* □ MARY: *What a pain! I hate annual inventories.* JOHN: *I know what you mean. It's really boring.*

(I) love it! It is just wonderful! □ MARY: *What do you think of this car?* BILL: *Love it! It's really cool!* □ BOB: *What a joke, Tom!* JANE: *Yes, love it!* TOM: *Gee, thanks.*

I must be off. an expression announcing the speaker's intention of leaving. □ BILL: *It's late. I must be off.* BOB: *Me, too. I'm out of here.* □ SUE: *I must be off.* JOHN: *The game's not over yet.* SUE: *I've seen enough.*

(I) must be running along. It's time for me to go. □ *Oh, it's after midnight. Must be running along.* □ *Must be running along. Got a cake in the oven.*

I must say good night. an expression announcing the speaker's intention of leaving for the night. □ JANE: *It's late. I must say good night.* BOB: *Can I see you again?* JANE: *Call me. Good night, Bob.*

Bob: *Good night, Jane.* □ Sue: *I must say good night.* Mary: *Good night, then. See you tomorrow.*

I need it yesterday. an answer to the question "When do you need this?" (Indicates that the need is urgent.) □ Bob: *When do you need that urgent survey?* Bill: *I need it yesterday.* □ Mary: *Where's the Wilson contract?* Sue: *Do you need it now?* Mary: *I need it yesterday! Where is it?*

I never! Go to (Well,) I never!

(I) never heard of such a thing! an expression of amazement and disbelief. (Compare to (Well,) I never!) □ Bill: *The company sent out a representative to our very house to examine the new sofa and see what the problem was with the wobbly leg.* Jane: *I've never heard of such a thing! That's very unusual.* □ Bill: *The tax office is now open on Sunday!* Sue: *Never heard of such a thing!*

(I) never thought I'd see you here! I am surprised to see you here. □ Tom: *Hi, Sue! I never thought I'd see you here!* Sue: *Hi, Tom. I was thinking the same thing about you.* □ Bill: *Well, Tom Thomas. I never thought I'd see you here!* Tom: *Likewise. I didn't know you liked opera.*

(I) never would have guessed. 1. I never would have thought something to be so. (Not used in other tenses.) □ *He was the one who did it? I never would have guessed.* □ *He wanted the job. Never would have guessed. He kept it a very good secret.* **2.** I knew it all the time, because it was so obvious. (Sarcastic. Not used in other tenses.) □ *I never would have guessed that he wanted the job. He only begged and begged for it.* □ *Now she wants to go back home? I never would have guessed! She has been homesick for days.*

I owe you one. Thank you for doing something that benefits me, now I owe you a favor. □ Bob: *I put the extra copy of the book on your desk.* Sue: *Thanks. I owe you one.* □ Bill: *Let me pay for it.* Bob: *Thanks a lot. I owe you one.*

I promise you! I am telling you the truth! (Compare to **Trust me!**) □ John: *Things will work out, I promise you!* Jane: *Okay, but when?* □ Sue: *I'll be there exactly when I said.* Bob: *Are you sure?* Sue: *I promise you, I'm telling the truth!*

(I) read you loud and clear. 1. a response used by someone communicating by radio stating that the person listening understands the transmission clearly. (See also **Do you read me?**) □ Control-

LER: *This is Aurora Center. Do you read me?* PILOT: *Yes, I read you loud and clear.* □ CONTROLLER: *Left two degrees. Do you read me?* PILOT: *Roger. Read you loud and clear.* **2.** I understand what you are telling me. (Used in general conversation, not in radio communication.) □ BOB: *Okay. Now, do you understand exactly what I said?* MARY: *I read you loud and clear.* □ MOTHER: *I don't want to have to tell you again. Do you understand?* BILL: *I read you loud and clear.*

(I) really must go. an expression announcing or repeating one's intention to depart. □ BOB: *It's getting late. I really must go.* JANE: *Good night, then. See you tomorrow.* □ SALLY: *I really must go.* JOHN: *Do you really have to? It's early yet.*

I spoke out of turn. I said the wrong thing.; I should not have said what I did. (An apology.) □ BILL: *You said I was the one who did it.* MARY: *I'm sorry. I spoke out of turn. I was mistaken.* □ BILL: *I seem to have said the wrong thing.* BOB: *You certainly did.* BILL: *I spoke out of turn, and I'm sorry.*

I spoke too soon. 1. I am wrong.; I spoke before I knew the facts. □ BILL: *I know I said I would, but I spoke too soon.* SUE: *I thought so.* □ JOHN: *You said that everything would be all right.* JANE: *I spoke too soon. That was before I learned that you had been arrested.* **2.** What I had said was just now contradicted. □ BOB: *It's beginning to brighten up. I guess it won't rain after all.* JOHN: *I'm glad to hear that.* BOB: *Whoops! I spoke too soon. I just felt a raindrop on my cheek.* □ BILL: *Thank heavens! Here's John now.* BOB: *No, that's Fred.* BILL: *I spoke too soon. He sure looked like John.*

I 'spose. Go to I guess.

I 'spose not. Go to I guess not.

I 'spose (so). Go to I guess (so).

I suppose. Go to I guess.

I suppose not. Go to I guess not.

I suppose (so). Go to I guess (so).

I suspect. Go to I guess.

I suspect not. Go to I guess not.

I suspect (so). Go to I guess (so).

I think not. Go to I guess not.

I think so. Go to I guess (so).

(I was) just wondering. a comment made after hearing a response to a previous question. □ JOHN: *Do you always keep your film in the refrigerator?* MARY: *Yes. Why?* JOHN: *I was just wondering.* □ BOB: *Did this cost a lot?* SUE: *I really don't think you need to know that.* BOB: *Sorry. Just wondering.*

I was up all night with a sick friend. an unlikely but popular excuse for not being where one was supposed to be the night before. □ BILL: *Where in the world were you last night?* MARY: *Well, I was up all night with a sick friend.* □ *Mr. Franklin said rather sheepishly, "Would you believe I was up with a sick friend?"*

I wish I'd said that. a comment of praise or admiration for someone's clever remark. □ MARY: *The weed of crime bears bitter fruit.* SUE: *I wish I'd said that.* MARY: *I wish I'd said it first.* □ JOHN: *Tom is simply not able to see through the airy persiflage of Mary's prolix declamation.* JANE: *I wish I'd said that.* JOHN: *I'm sorry I did.*

(I) wonder if a phrase introducing a hypothesis. □ HENRY: *I wonder if I could have another piece of cake.* SUE: *Sure. Help yourself.* □ ANDREW: *Wonder if it's stopped raining yet.* RACHEL: *Why don't you look out the window?* □ ANDREW: *I wonder if I'll pass algebra.* FATHER: *That thought is on all our minds.*

(I) won't breathe a word (of it). AND **(I) won't tell a soul.** I will not tell anyone your secret. □ BILL: *Don't tell anybody, but Sally is getting married.* MARY: *I won't breathe a word of it.* □ ALICE: *The Jacksons are going to have to sell their house. Don't spread it around.* MARY: *I won't tell a soul.*

I won't give up without a fight. I will not give in easily. (Compare to Don't give up too eas(il)y.) □ SUE: *Stick by your principles, Fred.* FRED: *Don't worry, I won't give up without a fight.* □ BOB: *The boss wants me to turn the Wilson project over to Tom.* SUE: *How can he do that?* BOB: *I don't know. All I know is that I won't give up without a fight.*

(I) won't tell a soul. Go to (I) won't breathe a word (of it).

(I) would if I could(, but I can't). I simply can't do it. □ JANE: *Can't you fix this yourself?* JOHN: *I would if I could, but I can't.* □ BOB: *Can you go to the dance? Hardly anyone is going.* ALICE: *Would if I could.*

I would like (for) you to meet someone. AND **I would like to introduce you to** someone. an expression used to introduce one person to another. (The *someone* can be a person's name, the name of a relationship, or the word *someone*.) □ MARY: *I would like you to meet my Uncle Bill.* SALLY: *Hello, Uncle Bill. Nice to meet you.* □ TOM: *I would like to introduce you to Bill Franklin.* JOHN: *Hello, Bill. Glad to meet you.* BILL: *Glad to meet you, John.*

I would like to introduce you to someone. Go to I would like (for) you to meet someone.

(I) wouldn't bet on it. AND **(I) wouldn't count on it.** I do not believe that something will happen. (Also with *that* or some specific happening.) □ JOHN: *I'll be a vice president in a year or two.* MARY: *I wouldn't bet on that.* □ JOHN: *I'll pick up a turkey on the day before Thanksgiving.* MARY: *Did you order one ahead of time?* JOHN: *No.* MARY: *Then I wouldn't count on it.*

(I) wouldn't count on it. Go to (I) wouldn't bet on it.

(I) wouldn't if I were you. a polite way of advising someone not to do something. □ MARY: *Do you think I should trade this car in on a new one?* SALLY: *I wouldn't if I were you.* □ BOB: *I'm going to plant nothing but corn this year.* SUE: *I wouldn't if I were you.* BOB: *Why?* SUE: *It's better to diversify.*

(I) wouldn't know. There is no way that I would know the answer to that question. □ JOHN: *When will the flight from Miami get in?* JANE: *Sorry, I wouldn't know.* □ BOB: *Are there many fish in the Amazon River?* MARY: *Gee, I wouldn't know.*

I wouldn't touch something **with a ten-foot pole.** Something is totally unacceptable.; I wouldn't even get near it. (Also in other persons.) □ Q: *Did you guys hear that proposal that Roscoe is shopping around?* A: *Yeah. We wouldn't touch it with a ten-foot pole.* □ *I refuse to do business there. I won't even go in the door. I wouldn't touch that place with a ten-foot pole.*

(I'd be) happy to (do something). AND **Be happy to (do** something**).** I would do it with pleasure. (The *do something* is replaced with a description of an activity.) □ JOHN: *I tried to get the book you wanted, but they didn't have it. Shall I try another store?* MARY: *No, never mind.* JOHN: *I'd be happy to give it a try.* □ ALICE: *Would you fix this, please?* JOHN: *Be happy to.*

(I'd) better be going. AND **(I'd) better be off.** an expression announcing the need to depart. □ Bob: *Better be going. Got to get home.* Bill: *Well, if you must, you must. Bye.* □ Fred: *It's midnight. I'd better be off.* Henry: *Okay. Bye, Fred.* □ Henry: *Better be off. It's starting to snow.* John: *Yes, it looks bad out.*

(I'd) better be off. Go to (I'd) better be going.

(I'd) better get moving. an expression announcing the need to depart. □ Jane: *It's nearly dark. Better get moving.* Mary: *Okay. See you later.* □ Bob: *I'm off. Good night.* Bill: *Look at the time! I'd better get moving too.*

(I'd) better get on my horse. an expression indicating that it is time that one departed. (Casual and folksy.) □ John: *It's getting late. Better get on my horse.* Rachel: *Have a safe trip. See you tomorrow.* □ *"I'd better get on my horse. The sun'll be down in an hour," said Sue, sounding like a cowboy.*

(I'd) better hit the road. Go to (It's) time to hit the road.

I'd like some feedback on something. AND **I'd like some input about** something. I would like to get some advice or information about something. (A slight misunderstanding of the meanings of *feedback* and *input*.) □ *I've been thinking about going to Guatemala, and I'd like some feedback on that country.* □ *Can somebody give me some input about the current price of gold?*

I'd like some input about something. Go to I'd like some feedback on something.

I'd like (to have) a word with you. AND **Could I have a word with you?** I need to speak to you briefly in private. (The alternate entry is also used with *can* or *may* in place of *could*.) □ Bob: *Can I have a word with you?* Sally: *Sure. I'll be with you in a minute.* □ Sally: *Tom?* Tom: *Yes?* Sally: *I'd like to have a word with you.* Tom: *Okay. What's it about?*

I'd like to speak to someone**, please.** the standard way of requesting to speak with a specific person on the telephone or in an office. □ Sue *(answering the phone)*: *Hello?* Bill: *Hello, this is Bill Franklin. I'd like to speak to Mary Gray.* Sue: *I'll see if she's in.* □ *"I'd like to speak to Tom," said the voice at the other end of the line.*

if I ever saw one if I have identified it or someone correctly. (Used to give emphasis to an assertion. Usually used in reference to people.) □ *She's a natural-born leader if I ever saw one.* □ *Tom's gonna wreck this company. He's a selfish tyrant if I ever saw one.*

if I might ask if you will permit me to ask without taking offense. □ *How old are you, if I might ask?* □ *If I might ask, how long have you lived here?*

if I were you an expression introducing or following a piece of advice. □ JOHN: *If I were you, I'd get rid of that old car.* ALICE: *Gee, I was just getting to like it.* □ HENRY: *I'd keep my thoughts to myself, if I were you.* BOB: *I guess I should be careful about what I say.*

If it isn't someone! This is a person I didn't expect to see here! □ *Well, if it isn't Bob Jones! Where've you been keeping yourself, Bob?* □ *A: Say, don't I know you? B: If it isn't Fred Smith. How are you doing, Fred?*

If I've told you once, I've told you a thousand times. an expression that introduces a scolding, usually said to a child. □ MOTHER: *If I've told you once, I've told you a thousand times, don't leave your clothes in a pile on the floor!* BILL: *Sorry.* □ *"If I've told you once, I've told you a thousand times, keep out of my study!" yelled Bob.*

If that don't beat all! AND **That beats everything!** That surpasses everything!; That is amazing!; That takes the cake! (The grammar error, *that don't*, is part of this phrase.) □ TOM: *The mayor is kicking the baseball team out of the city.* BILL: *If that don't beat all!* □ JOHN: *Now, here's a funny thing. South America used to be attached to Africa.* FRED: *That beats everything!* JOHN: *Yeah.*

If there's anything you need, don't hesitate to ask. a polite phrase offering help in finding something or by providing something. (Often said by a host or by a person helping someone settle into something.) □ MARY: *This looks very nice. I'll be quite comfortable here.* JANE: *If there's anything you need, don't hesitate to ask.* □ *"If there is anything you need, don't hesitate to ask," said the room clerk.*

If you don't mind. 1. Please stop annoying me! (An expression that rebukes someone for some minor social violation. See also **Do you mind?**) □ *When Bill accidently sat on Mary's purse, which she had placed in the seat next to her, she said, somewhat angrily, "If you don't mind!"* □ BILL (*pushing his way in front of Mary in the checkout line*): *Excuse me. I'm in a hurry.* MARY: *If you don't mind! I was here first!* BILL: *I'm in a hurry.* MARY: *So am I!* **2.** Please, oblige me if it is not a bother. (A polite way of softening a request, equivalent to *please.*) □ *BILL: If you don't mind, could you move a little to the left? SALLY: No problem.* (Sally moves.) *Is this all right? BILL: Yeah. Great! Thanks!* □ *JANE: Could I have your broccoli, if you don't mind? JOHN: Help yourself.* **3.** Yes, please do so if it is not too much of a bother. (A vague "yes" answer to a question that asks whether one should do something.) □ *TOM: Do you want me to take these dirty dishes away? MARY: If you don't mind.* □ *BILL: Shall I close the door? SALLY: If you don't mind.*

If you don't see what you want, please ask (for it). AND **If you don't see what you want, just ask (for it).** a polite phrase intended to help people get what they want. □ *CLERK: May I help you? SUE: I'm just looking. CLERK: If you don't see what you want, please ask.* □ *CLERK: I hope you enjoy your stay at our resort. If you don't see what you want, just ask for it. SALLY: Great! Thanks.*

if you know what's good for you if you know what will work to your benefit; if you know what will keep you out of trouble. □ *MARY: I see that Jane has put a big dent in her car. SUE: You'll keep quiet about that if you know what's good for you.* □ *SALLY: My boss told me I had better improve my spelling. BILL: If you know what's good for you, you'd better do it too.*

If you must. All right, if you have to. □ *SALLY: It's late. I have to move along. MARY: If you must. Good-bye. See you tomorrow.* □ *ALICE: I'm taking these things with me. JANE: If you must. All right. They can stay here, though.*

if you please AND **if you would(, please) 1.** a polite phrase indicating assent to a suggestion. □ *BILL: Shall I unload the car? JANE: If you please.* □ *SUE: Do you want me to take you to the station? BOB: If you would, please.* **2.** a polite phrase introducing or following a request. □ *JOHN: If you please, the driveway needs sweeping. JANE: Here's the broom. Have at it.* □ *JANE: Take these down to the basement, if you would, please. JOHN: Can't think of anything I'd rather do, sweetie.*

if you would(, please) Go to if you please.

I'll be a monkey's uncle! I am surprised! □ *I'll be a monkey's uncle! Here's my old pocketknife from when I was a kid.* □ *A: Well, I'll be a monkey's uncle. If it isn't Bob Jones! B: Hey, Ted! What's cooking?*

I'll be damned! AND **I'll be hanged!** I am very surprised! □ *I'll be damned! Did you see that Rolls-Royce go by? I'd swear it was gold-plated!* □ *I'll be hanged! An Indian-head penny. You never see those any longer.*

I'll be hanged! Go to I'll be damned!

(I'll) be right there. I'm coming. □ BILL: *Tom! Come here.* TOM: *Be right there.* □ MOTHER: *Can you come down here a minute?* CHILD: *I'll be right there, Mom.*

(I'll) be right with you. Please be patient, and I will attend to you soon. (Often said by someone behind a sales counter or by an office receptionist.) □ MARY: *Oh, Miss?* CLERK: *I'll be right with you.* □ BOB: *Sally, can you come here for a minute?* SALLY: *Be right with you.*

I'll be saying good night. Good night. (Vague and polite. Not really future tense. Also with *we*.) □ *I'll be saying good night. I had a wonderful time.* □ *It's late. We'll be saying good night and thank you.*

(I'll) be seeing you. Good-bye, I will see you sometime in the (near) future. □ BOB: *Bye. Be seeing you.* SALLY: *Yeah. See you later.* □ JOHN: *Have a good time on your vacation. I'll be seeing you.* SALLY: *See you next week. Bye.*

I('ll) bet 1. I'm pretty sure that. □ BOB: *I bet you miss your plane.* RACHEL: *No, I won't.* □ SUE: *I'll bet it rains today.* ALICE: *No way! There's not a cloud in the sky.* **2.** (Usually *I('ll) bet.*) I agree. (Often sarcastic.) □ TOM: *They're probably going to raise taxes again next year.* HENRY: *I bet.* □ FRED: *If we do that again, we'll really be in trouble.* ANDREW: *I'll bet.*

I'll bite. Okay, I will answer your question.; Okay, I will listen to your joke or play your little guessing game. □ BOB: *Guess what is in this box.* BILL: *I'll bite.* BOB: *A new toaster!* □ JOHN: *Did you hear the joke about the used car salesman?* JANE: *No, I'll bite.*

I'll call back later. a standard phrase indicating that a telephone caller will call again at a later time. □ SALLY: *Is Bill there?* MARY: *Sorry, he's not here right now.* SALLY: *I'll call back later.* □ JOHN: *Hello. Is Fred there?* JANE: *No. Can I take a message?* JOHN: *No, thanks. I'll call back later.*

(I'll) catch you later. I will talk to you later. □ MARY: *Got to fly. See you around.* SALLY: *Bye. Catch you later.* □ JOHN: *I have to go to class now.* BILL: *Okay, catch you later.*

I'll drink to that! I agree with that totally, and I salute it with a drink. (The phrase is used even when no drinking is involved.) □ JOHN: *Hey, Tom! You did a great job!* MARY: *I'll drink to that!* TOM: *Thanks!* □ JANE: *I think I'll take everybody out to dinner.* SALLY: *I'll drink to that!*

I'll get back to you (on that). AND **Let me get back to you (on that).** I will report back later with my decision. (More likely said by a boss to an employee than vice versa.) □ BOB: *I have a question about the Wilson project.* MARY: *I have to go to a meeting now. I'll get back to you on that.* BOB: *It's sort of urgent.* MARY: *It can wait. It will wait.* □ SUE: *Shall I close the Wilson account?* JANE: *Let me get back to you on that.*

I'll get right on it. I will begin work on that immediately. □ BOB: *Please do this report immediately.* FRED: *I'll get right on it.* □ JANE: *Please call Tom and ask him to rethink this proposal.* JOHN: *I'll get right on it.*

I'll have the same. AND **The same for me.** I would like the same thing that the last person chose. □ WAITRESS: *What would you like?* TOM: *Hamburger, fries, and coffee.* JANE: *I'll have the same.* □ JOHN: *For dessert, I'll have strawberry ice cream.* BILL: *I'll have the same.*

I'll have to beg off. a polite expression used to turn down an informal invitation. □ ANDREW: *Thank you for inviting me, but I'll have to beg off. I have a conflict.* HENRY: *I'm sorry to hear that. Maybe some other time.* □ BILL: *Do you think you can come to the party?* BOB: *I'll have to beg off. I have another engagement.* BILL: *Maybe some other time.*

I'll look you up when I'm in town. I will try to visit you the next time I am in town. □ BILL: *I hope to see you again sometime.* MARY: *I'll look you up when I'm in town.* □ ANDREW: *Good-bye, Fred. It's been nice talking to you. I'll look you up when I'm in town.* FRED: *See you around, dude.*

I'll put a stop to that. I'll see that the undesirable activity is stopped. □ FRED: *There are two boys fighting in the hall.* BOB: *I'll put a stop* *to that.* □ SUE: *The sales force is ignoring almost every customer in the older neighborhoods.* MARY: *I'll put a stop to that!*

I'll say! I agree with you strongly! □ ANDY: *Man it's really hot today!* HANNA: *I'll say!* □ ZEKE: *That there is the ugliest baby I ever did see.* DARRELL: *I'll say!*

(I'll) see you in a little while. a phrase indicating that the speaker will see the person spoken to within a few hours at the most. □ JOHN: *I'll see you in a little while.* JANE: *Okay. Bye till later.* □ SALLY: *I have to get dressed for tonight.* FRED: *I'll pick you up about nine. See you in a little while.* SALLY: *See you.*

I'll see you later. AND **(See you) later.** Good-bye until I see you again. □ JOHN: *Good-bye, Sally. I'll see you later.* SALLY: *Until later, then.* □ BOB: *Time to go. Later.* MARY: *Later.*

(I'll) see you next year. an expression meaning good-bye said toward the end of one year. □ BOB: *Happy New Year!* SUE: *You, too! See you next year.* □ JOHN: *Bye. See you tomorrow.* MARY: *It's New Year's Eve. See you next year!* JOHN: *Right! I'll see you next year!*

(I'll) see you (real) soon. Good-bye. I will meet you again soon. □ BILL: *Bye, Sue. See you.* SUE: *See you real soon, Bill.* □ JOHN: *Bye, you two.* SALLY: *See you soon.* JANE: *See you, John.*

(I'll) see you then. I will see you at the time we've just agreed upon. □ JOHN: *Can we meet at noon?* BILL: *Sure. See you then. Bye.* JOHN: *Bye.* □ JOHN: *I'll pick you up just after midnight.* SALLY: *See you then.*

(I'll) see you tomorrow. I will see you when we meet again tomorrow. (Typically said to someone whose daily schedule is the same as one's own.) □ BOB: *Bye, Jane.* JANE: *Good night, Bob. See you tomorrow.* □ SUE: *See you tomorrow.* JANE: *Until tomorrow. Bye.*

(I'll) talk to you soon. I will talk to you on the telephone again soon. □ SALLY: *Bye now. Talk to you soon.* JOHN: *Bye now.* □ BILL: *Nice talking to you. Bye.* MARY: *Talk to you soon. Bye.*

I'll thank you to keep your opinions to yourself. I do not care about your opinion of this matter. □ JANE: *This place is sort of drab.* JOHN: *I'll thank you to keep your opinions to yourself.* □ BILL: *Your whole family is sort of long-legged.* JOHN: *I'll thank you to keep your opinions to yourself.*

I'll thank you to mind your own business. a polite version of Mind your own business. (Shows a little anger.) □ *Tom: How much did this cost? Jane: I'll thank you to mind your own business.* □ *Bob: Is your house in your name or your brother's? John: I'll thank you to mind your own business.*

(I'll) try to catch you later. Go to (I'll) try to catch you some other time.

(I'll) try to catch you some other time. AND **(I'll) try to catch you later.; I'll try to see you later.** We do not have time to talk now, so I'll try to see you later. □ *Bill: I need to get your signature on this contract. Sue: I really don't have a second to spare right now. Bill: Okay, I'll try to catch you some other time. Sue: Later this afternoon would be fine.* □ *Bill: I'm sorry for the interruptions, Tom. Things are very busy right now. Tom: I'll try to see you later.*

I'll try to see you later. Go to (I'll) try to catch you some other time.

(I'm) able to sit up and take (a little) nourishment. I am well.; I'm (feeling) good. (Also a jocular response to "How are you?" As if one had been recuperating from a disease and had been lying in bed.) □ *Q: How are you doing? Any better? A: Oh, able to sit up and take nourishment.* □ *Q: I see you are doing pretty well with your jogging. How are you feeling? A: Well, I guess I'm able to sit up and take nourishment okay.*

(I'm) afraid not. AND **'Fraid not.** I believe, regrettably, that the answer is no. (The apostrophe is not always used.) □ *Rachel: Can I expect any help with this problem? Henry: I'm afraid not.* □ *Andrew: Will you be there when I get there? Bill: Afraid not.*

(I'm) afraid so. AND **'Fraid so.** I believe, regrettably, that the answer is yes. (The apostrophe is not always used.) □ *Alice: Do you have to go? John: Afraid so.* □ *Rachel: Can I expect some difficulty with Mr. Franklin? Bob: I'm afraid so.*

I'm all ears. Go to I'm listening.

I'm as hungry as a bear. I am very hungry. □ *What's for dinner? I'm as hungry as a bear.* □ *I'm as hungry as a bear, and I'll eat almost anything—except okra.*

I'm busy. Do not bother me now.; I cannot attend to your needs now. □ *Bob: Can I talk to you? Bill: I'm busy. Bob: It's important. Bill: Sorry, I'm busy!* □ *Fred: Can you help me with this? Bill: I'm busy. Can it wait a minute? Fred: Sure. No rush.*

I'm cool. I'm fine. (Slang.) □ BOB: *How you been?* FRED: *I'm cool, man. Yourself?* BOB: *The same.* □ FATHER: *How are you, son?* BILL: *I'm cool, Dad.* FATHER *(misunderstanding): I'll turn up the heat.*

I'm damned if I do and damned if I don't. There are problems if I do something and problems if I don't do it. □ *I can't win. I'm damned if I do and damned if I don't.* □ *No matter whether I go or stay, I am in trouble. I'm damned if I do and damned if I don't.*

(I'm) delighted to have you (here). AND **(We're) delighted to have you (here).** You're welcome here any time.; Glad you could come. (See also **(It's) good to have you here.**) □ BILL: *Thank you for inviting me for dinner, Mr. Franklin.* BILL: *I'm delighted to have you.* □ *"We're delighted to see you," said Tom's grandparents. "It's so nice to have you here for a visit."*

(I'm) delighted to make your acquaintance. I am very glad to meet you. □ TOM: *My name is Tom. I work in the advertising department.* MARY: *I'm Mary. I work in accounting. Delighted to make your acquaintance.* TOM: *Yeah. Good to meet you.* □ FRED: *Sue, this is Bob. He'll be working with us on the Wilson project.* SUE: *I'm delighted to make your acquaintance, Bob.* BOB: *My pleasure.*

(I'm) doing okay. 1. I'm just fine. □ BOB: *How you doing?* BILL: *Doing okay. And you?* BOB: *Things could be worse.* □ MARY: *How are things going?* SUE: *I'm doing fine, thanks. And you?* MARY: *Doing okay.* **2.** I'm doing as well as can be expected.; I'm feeling better. □ MARY: *How are you feeling?* SUE: *I'm doing okay—as well as can be expected.* □ TOM: *I hope you're feeling better.* SALLY: *I'm doing okay, thanks.*

I'm easy (to please). I accept that. I am not particular. □ TOM: *Hey, man! Do you care if we get a sausage pizza rather than mushroom?* BOB: *Fine with me. I'm easy.* □ MARY: *How do you like this music?* BOB: *It's great, but I'm easy to please.*

(I'm) feeling okay. I am doing well.; I am feeling well. □ ALICE: *How are you feeling?* JANE: *I'm feeling okay.* □ JOHN: *How are things going?* FRED: *Feeling okay.*

(I'm) glad to hear it. a phrase expressing pleasure at what the speaker has just said. □ SALLY: *We have a new car, finally.* MARY: *I'm glad to hear it.* □ TOM: *Is your sister feeling better?* BILL: *Oh, yes, thanks.* TOM: *Glad to hear it.*

I'm glad to meet you. Go to **(I'm) (very) glad to meet you.**

(I'm) glad you could come. AND **(We're) glad you could come.** a phrase said by the host or hostess (or both) to a guest. □ Tom: *Thank you so much for having me.* Sally: *We're glad you could come.* John: *Yes, we are. Bye.* □ Bill: *Bye.* Sally: *Bye, Bill. Glad you could come.*

(I'm) glad you could drop by. AND **(We're) glad you could drop by.; (I'm) glad you could stop by.; (We're) glad you could stop by.** a phrase said by the host or hostess (or both) to a guest who has appeared suddenly or has come for only a short visit. □ Tom: *Good-bye. Had a nice time.* Mary: *Thank you for coming, Tom. Glad you could drop by.* □ Tom: *Thank you so much for having me.* Sally: *We're glad you could drop by.*

(I'm) glad you could stop by. Go to (I'm) glad you could drop by.

I'm gone. an expression said just before leaving. (Slang. See also I'm out of here.) □ Bob: *Well, that's all. I'm gone.* Bill: *See ya!* □ Jane: *I'm gone. See you guys.* John: *See you, Jane.* Fred: *Bye, Jane.*

I'm good. 1. I'm well. (In response to "How are you?" Now heard more often than "I'm well," or "Fine.") □ Hanna: *Hi, how you doing?* Ida: *I'm good.* □ Q: *I'd heard you were sick. You look fine now. How are you?* A: *I'm good.* **2.** I have enough; I don't require any more, thank you. □ Andy: *Everyone got enough to drink?* Don: *I'm good.* Hanna: *I'm good.* Ida: *I'm good.* □ Father: *There's still a few hot dogs left. Can I get you one, Ida?* Ida: *No, thanks. I'm good.*

(I'm) having a wonderful time; wish you were here. a catchphrase that is written on postcards by people who are away on vacation. □ *John wrote on all his cards, "Having a wonderful time; wish you were here." And he really meant it too.* □ *"I'm having a wonderful time; wish you were here," said Tom, speaking on the phone to Mary, suddenly feeling very insincere.*

I'm having quite a time. 1. I am having a very enjoyable time. □ John: *Having fun?* Jane: *Oh, yes. I'm having quite a time.* □ Bob: *Do you like the seashore?* Sally: *Yes, I'm having quite a time.* **2.** I am having a very difficult time. □ Doctor: *Well, what seems to be the problem?* Mary: *I'm having quite a time. It's my back.* Doctor: *Let's take a look at it.* □ Father: *How's school?* Bill: *Pretty tough. I'm having quite a time. Calculus is killing me.*

(I'm) having the time of my life. I am having the best time ever. □ Bill: *Are you having a good time, Mary?* Mary: *Don't worry* *about me. I'm having the time of my life.* □ MARY: *What do you think about this theme park?* BILL: *Having the time of my life. I don't want to leave.*

I'm in. I agree to be part of the team or project. □ A: *We're gonna rob the bank tonight. Are you in?* B: *Awesome! I'm in.* □ DON: *Are you part of this project?* ISABEL: *I'm in.*

I'm (just) dying to know. I am very eager to find something out. (Also in other persons.) □ JAN: *I'm not sure if I am supposed to tell you when Mary is leaving for New York.* ANN: *Oh, please! I'm just dying to know.* □ *I'm just dying to know what our new address will be. I'm hoping for Paris.*

(I'm) just getting by. an expression indicating that one is just surviving financially or otherwise. □ BOB: *How you doing, Tom?* TOM: *Just getting by, Bob.* □ *"I wish I could get a better job," remarked Tom. "I'm just getting by as it is."*

(I'm just) minding my own business. an answer to a greeting inquiry asking what one is doing. (This answer also can carry the implication "Since I am minding my own business, why aren't you minding your own business?") □ TOM: *Hey, man, what are you doing?* BILL: *Minding my own business. See you around.* □ SUE: *Hi, Mary. What have you been doing?* MARY: *I'm just minding my own business and trying to keep out of trouble.*

(I'm) (just) plugging along. I am doing satisfactorily.; I am just managing to function. □ BILL: *How are things going?* BOB: *I'm just plugging along.* □ SUE: *How are you doing, Fred?* FRED: *Just plugging along, thanks. And you?* SUE: *About the same.*

(I'm) (just) thinking out loud. I'm saying things that might better remain as private thoughts. (A way of characterizing or introducing one's opinions or thoughts. Also past tense.) □ SUE: *What are you saying, anyway? Sounds like you're scolding someone.* BOB: *Oh, sorry. I was just thinking out loud.* □ BOB: *Now, this goes over here.* BILL: *You want me to move that?* BOB: *Oh, no. Just thinking out loud.*

I'm like you. an expression introducing a statement of a similarity that the speaker shares with the person spoken to. □ MARY: *And what do you think about this pair?* JANE: *I'm like you, I like the ones with lower heels.* □ *"I'm like you," confided Fred. "I think everyone ought to pay the same amount."*

I'm listening. AND **I'm all ears.** You have my attention, so you should talk. □ *Bob: Look, old pal. I want to talk to you about something. Tom: I'm listening.* □ *Bill: I guess I owe you an apology. Jane: I'm all ears.*

I'm not finished with you. I still have more to say to you. □ *Bill started to turn away when he thought the scolding was finished. "I'm not finished with you," bellowed his father.* □ *When the angry teacher paused briefly to catch his breath, Bob turned as if to go. "I'm not finished with you," screamed the teacher, filled anew with breath and invective.*

(I'm) just looking. Go to I'm only looking.

I'm not kidding! I am telling the truth.; I am not trying to fool you. □ *Mary: Those guys are all suspects in the robbery. Sue: No! They can't be! Mary: I'm not kidding!* □ *John (gesturing): The fish I caught was this big! Jane: I don't believe it! John: I'm not kidding!*

I'm not having this conversation. I don't like discussing this with you.; I can't believe I'm discussing this with you. □ *Don: You are late again, and your workspace is a mess. We are all angry with you. Hanna: I'm not having this conversation.* □ *Isabel: This is so embarrassing! I'm not having this conversation! Dan: I'm so sorry.*

I'm not surprised. AND **I don't wonder.** It is not surprising.; It should not surprise anyone. □ *Mary: All this talk about war has my cousin very worried. Sue: No doubt. At his age, I don't wonder.* □ *John: All of the better-looking ones sold out right away. Jane: I'm not surprised.*

I'm off. an expression said by someone who is just leaving. (Slang.) □ *Bob: Time to go. I'm off. Mary: Bye.* □ *Sue: Well, it's been great. Good-bye. Got to go. Mary: I'm off too. Bye.*

I'm not picky. What you are offering me or suggesting is quite satisfactory, since I am easy to please. □ *Mother: These cookies are a little brown on the bottom, but they're quite tasty. Hanna: Thanks. I'm not picky. They look great to me.* □ *Dan (speaking to the room clerk): I'm not picky, but I really would prefer a room that doesn't look out on all the trash cans.*

I'm only looking. AND **(I'm) just looking.** I am not a buyer, I am only examining your merchandise. (A phrase said to a shopkeeper or clerk who asks, **May I help you?**) □ *Clerk: May I help you?*

MARY: No, thanks. I'm only looking. □ *CLERK: May I help you? JANE: I'm just looking, thank you.*

I'm out of here. I am going to leave immediately. (Slang. The *out of* is usually pronounced *outta*.) □ *JOHN: I'm out of here. JANE: Bye.* □ *SALLY: Getting late. I'm out of here. SUE: Me, too. Let's go.*

(I'm) pleased to meet you. an expression said when one is introduced to someone. □ *TOM: I'm Tom Thomas. BILL: Pleased to meet you. I'm Bill Franklin.* □ *JOHN: Have you met Sally Hill? BILL: I don't believe I've had the pleasure. I'm pleased to meet you, Sally. SALLY: My pleasure, Bill.*

I'm (really) fed up (with someone or something**).** I have had enough of someone or something, and something must be done. □ *TOM: This place is really dull. JOHN: Yeah. I'm fed up with it. I'm out of here!* □ *SALLY: Can't you do anything right? BILL: I'm really fed up with you! You're always picking on me!*

I'm on it. I am doing it now, or I will do it as soon as possible. □ *ANDY: You are supposed to be doing the accounts for this month. DON: I'm on it, I'm on it!* □ *I knew the boss was after me to get the report done on time. I was working on it when he called me the third time. "I'm on it, Chief," I said, sort of fibbing, but sincere this time.*

I'm set. 1. I have everything I need. (As in *ready, set, go.* Also in the third person.) □ *Q: Do you have what you need for the day, so you can work interrupted? A: I'm set.* □ *He's set and ready to go to work.* **2.** I have finished eating (in a restaurant) and would like to have the check. (Also in the other persons.) □ *I'm set. Check, please.* □ *He's set, but I want dessert.*

(I'm so hungry) I could eat a cow! Go to (I'm so hungry) I could eat a horse!

(I'm so hungry) I could eat a horse! AND **(I'm so hungry) I could eat a cow!** I am really hungry! □ *A: Man, I'm so hungry I could eat a cow! B: Great. We are having hamburgers.* □ *DON: What's for dinner? I could eat a horse! FATHER: We're clean out of horse. Would baked ham, sweet potatoes, creamed peas, macaroni and cheese, and cherry pie do? DON: Sure! FATHER: Sorry, we're out of that too.*

(I'm) sorry. the phrase used for a simple apology. □ *BILL: Oh! You stepped on my toe! BOB: I'm sorry.* □ *JOHN: You made me miss my bus! SUE: Sorry.*

(I'm) sorry to hear that. an expression of consolation. □ JOHN: *My cat died last week.* JANE: *I'm sorry to hear that.* □ BILL: *I'm afraid I won't be able to continue here as head teller.* MARY: *Sorry to hear that.*

(I'm) sorry you asked (that). I regret that you asked about something I wanted to forget. □ TOM: *What on earth is this hole in your suit jacket?* BILL: *I'm sorry you asked. I was feeding a squirrel and it bit through my pocket where the food was.* □ SALLY: *Why is there only canned soup in the cupboard?* JOHN: *Sorry you asked that. We're broke. We have no money for food.* SALLY: *Want some soup?*

I'm speechless. I am so surprised that I cannot think of anything to say. □ MARY: *Fred and I were married last week.* SALLY: *I'm speechless.* □ TOM: *The mayor just died!* JANE: *What? I'm speechless!*

(I'm) (very) glad to meet you. a polite expression said to a person to whom one has just been introduced. □ MARY: *I'd like you to meet my brother, Tom.* BILL: *I'm very glad to meet you, Tom.* □ JANE: *Hi! I'm Jane.* BOB: *Glad to meet you. I'm Bob.*

I'm with you. Go to I'm with you on that (one).

I'm with you on that (one). AND **I'm with you.** I agree with you (in this instance). (With a stress on both *I* and *you*.) □ HANNA: *I think that everyone ought to be told to clean up the kitchen after they eat.* IDA: *I'm with you on that.* □ A: *The government is spending too damn much money!* B: *I'm with you on that one.* □ SALLY: *I think this old bridge is sort of dangerous.* JANE: *I'm with you. Let's go back another way.*

Imagine that! Go to Fancy that!

in a manner of speaking Go to so to speak.

in any case a phrase that introduces or follows a conclusion. □ JANE: *In any case, I want you to do this.* JOHN: *All right. I'll do it.* □ MARY: *This one may or may not work out.* SUE: *In any case, I can do it if necessary.*

in black and white printed, as in a contract. □ *The terms of the agreement were printed in black and white.* □ *I have your very words right here in black and white.*

in denial in a state of refusing to believe something that is true. □ *Mary was in denial about her illness and refused treatment.* □ *Tom doesn't think he's an alcoholic. He's still in denial.*

in general referring to the entire class being discussed; speaking of the entire range of possibilities; in most situations or circumstances. □ *I like vegetables in general, but not beets.* □ *In general, I prefer a hotel room on a lower floor, but will take a higher room if it's special.*

in my humble opinion a phrase introducing the speaker's opinion. □ *"In my humble opinion," began Fred, arrogantly, "I have achieved what no one else ever could."* □ *Bob: What are we going to do about the poor condition of the house next door? Bill: In my humble opinion, we will mind our own business.*

in my opinion Go to as I see it.

in my view Go to as I see it.

in other words a phrase introducing a restatement of what has just been said. □ *Henry: Sure I want to do it, but how much do I get paid? Andrew: In other words, you're just doing it for the money.* □ *Bill: Well, I suppose I really should prepare my entourage for departure. Bob: In other words, you're leaving? Bill: One could say that, I suppose. Bob: Why didn't one?*

in plain English in very direct and clear language; in English that anyone can understand. □ *I told him what he was to do in plain English.* □ *That was too complicated. Please tell me again, this time in plain English.*

in someone's **face** annoying and bothering someone, urgently and possibly too closely. (Also literal.) □ *I really can't stand her manner. She's always in my face about something. With her, everything is urgent.* □ *Listen, I don't like you in my face all the time. Just step back and let's talk like equals.*

in the first place originally; basically; for openers. (This can run through **in the second place**, **in the third place**, but not much higher.) □ *Bill: What did I do? Bob: In the first place, you had no business being there at all. In the second place, you were acting rude.* □ *Bill: Why on earth did you do it in the first place? Sue: I don't know.*

in the interest of saving time in order to hurry things along. □ *Mary: In the interest of saving time, I'd like to save questions for the end of my talk. Bill: But I have an important question now!* □ *"In the interest of saving time," said Jane, "I'll give you the first three answers."*

in the main basically; generally. □ MARY: *Everything looks all right—in the main.* SALLY: *What details need attention?* MARY: *Just a few things here and there. Like on page 27.* □ JOHN: *Are you all ready?* SUE: *I think we're ready, in the main.* JOHN: *Then, we shall go.*

in the meantime the period of time between two events; the period of time between now and when something is supposed to happen. □ *The movie starts at 6:00. In the meantime, let's eat dinner.* □ *My flight was at 8:00. In the meantime, I played solitaire.*

in the nick of time just in time; at the last possible instant; just before it is too late. □ *The doctor arrived in the nick of time. The patient's life was saved.* □ *I reached the airport in the nick of time.*

in the wrong place at the wrong time in a location where something bad is going to happen, exactly when it happens. (Usually about something bad.) □ *I always get into trouble. I'm just in the wrong place at the wrong time.* □ *It isn't my fault. I was just in the wrong place at the wrong time.*

in this day and age now; in these modern times. □ BILL: *Ted flunked out of school.* MOTHER: *Imagine that! Especially in this day and age.* □ BILL: *Taxes keep going up and up.* BOB: *What do you expect in this day and age?*

in view of due to; because of. □ *"In view of the bad weather," began Tom, "the trip has been canceled."* □ ANDREW: *Can we hurry? We'll be late.* MARY: *In view of your attitude about going in the first place, I'm surprised you even care.*

incidentally Go to by the way.

(Is) anything going on? Is there anything exciting or interesting happening here? □ ANDREW: *Hey, man! Anything going on?* HENRY: *No. This place is dull as can be.* □ BOB: *Come in, Tom.* TOM: *Is anything going on?* BOB: *No. You've come on a very ordinary day.*

(Is) everything okay? How are you?; How are things? □ JOHN: *Hi, Mary. Is everything okay?* MARY: *Sure. What about you?* JOHN: *I'm okay.* □ WAITER: *Is everything okay?* BILL: *Yes, it's fine.*

(Is it) cold enough for you? a greeting inquiry made during very cold weather. □ BOB: *Hi, Bill! Is it cold enough for you?* BILL: *It's unbelievable!* □ JOHN: *Glad to see you. Is it cold enough for you?* BILL: *Oh, yes! This is awful!*

(Is it) hot enough for you? a greeting inquiry made during very hot weather. □ *Bob: Hi, Bill! Is it hot enough for you? Bill: Yup.* □ *John: Nice to see you here! Is it hot enough for you? Bill: Good grief, yes! This is awful!*

Is someone **there?** a way of requesting to talk to someone in particular over the telephone. (This is not just a request to find out where *someone* is. The *someone* is usually a person's name.) □ *Tom: Hello? Mary: Hello. Is Bill there? Tom: No. Can I take a message?* □ *Tom: Hello? Mary: Hello. Is Tom there? Tom: Speaking.*

Is that everything? Go to (Will there be) anything else?

Is that so? AND **Is that right? 1.** Is what you said correct? (With rising question intonation.) □ *Henry: These are the ones we need. Andrew: Is that right? They don't look so good to me.* □ *Fred: Tom is the one who came in late. Rachel: Is that so? It looked like Bill to me.* **2.** That is what you say, but I do not believe you. (No rising question intonation. Slightly rude.) □ *Mary: You are making a mess of this. Alice: Is that so? And I suppose that you're perfect?* □ *Bob: I found your performance to be weak in a number of places. Henry: Is that right? Why don't you tell me about those weaknesses.*

Is that x**, or is it** x**?** AND **Is that** x**, or what?** Isn't this a classical example of something (x)?; This thing is such a quintessential instance of itself that it could be nothing else. (The *x* can be anything, but a set of two *x*'s refer to the same thing.) □ *Hot scarlet! What a cool color! Is that red, or is that red?* □ *Man, try this pepper sauce. Is that hot, or is it hot?*

Is that x**, or what?** Go to Is that x, or is it x?

Is there anything else? Go to (Will there be) anything else?

Is there some place I can wash up? Go to Where can I wash up?

(Is) this (seat) taken? an inquiry made by a person in a theater, auditorium, etc., asking someone already seated whether an adjacent seat is available or already taken. □ *Finally, Bill came to a row where there was an empty seat. He leaned over to the person sitting beside the empty seat and whispered, "Is this seat taken?"* □ *Fred: 'Scuse me. This taken? Alice: No. Help yourself.*

issue a call for something to make an invitation or request for something. □ *The prime minister issued a call for peace.* □ *The person who organized the writing contest issued a call for entries.*

(It) beats me. AND **(It's) got me beat.; You got me beat.** I do not know the answer.; I cannot figure it out. The question has me stumped. (The stress is on *me*.) □ BILL: *When are we supposed to go over to Tom's?* BILL: *Beats me.* □ SALLY: *What's the largest river in the world?* BOB: *You got me beat.*

It blows my mind! It really amazes and shocks me. (Slang.) □ BILL: *Did you hear about Tom's winning the lottery?* SUE: *Yes, it blows my mind!* □ JOHN: *Look at all that paper! What a waste of trees!* JANE: *It blows my mind!*

(It) can't be helped. 1. Nothing can be done to help the situation.; It isn't anyone's fault. (Also in the past tense, **It couldn't be helped.**) □ JOHN: *The accident has blocked traffic in two directions.* JANE: *It can't be helped. They have to get the people out of the cars and send them to the hospital.* □ BILL: *My goodness, the lawn looks dead!* SUE: *It can't be helped. There's no rain, and water is rationed.* □ JOHN: *I'm sorry I broke your figurine.* SUE: *It couldn't be helped.* JOHN: *I'll replace it.* SUE: *That would be nice.* □ BILL: *I'm sorry I'm late. I hope it didn't mess things up.* BOB: *It couldn't be helped.*

(It) couldn't be better. AND **(Things) couldn't be better.** Everything is fine. □ JOHN: *How are things going?* JANE: *Couldn't be better.* □ BILL: *I hope everything is okay with your new job.* MARY: *Things couldn't be better.*

(It) couldn't be helped. Go to (It) can't be helped.

(It) doesn't bother me any. AND **(It) doesn't bother me at all.** It does not trouble me at all.; I have no objection. (Compare to (It) makes no difference to me. Not very polite or cordial. See also (It) won't bother me any.) □ JOHN: *Do you mind if I sit here?* JANE: *Doesn't bother me any.* □ SALLY (smoking a cigarette): *Do you mind if I smoke?* BILL: *It doesn't bother me any.*

(It) doesn't bother me at all. Go to (It) doesn't bother me any.

(It) doesn't hurt to ask. AND **(It) never hurts to ask.** a phrase said when one asks a question, even when knowing the answer is likely to be no. □ JOHN: *Can I take some of these papers home with me?* JANE: *No, you can't. You know that.* JOHN: *Well, it doesn't hurt* *to ask.* □ SUE: *Can I have two of these?* SALLY: *Certainly not!* SUE: *Well, it never hurts to ask.* SALLY: *Well, it just may!*

It doesn't quite suit me. Go to This doesn't quite suit me.

(It) don't bother me none. Go to (It) makes no difference to me.

(It) don't make me no nevermind. Go to (It) makes no difference to me.

(It) hasn't been easy. AND **Things haven't been easy.** Things have been difficult, but I have survived. □ BILL: *I'm so sorry about all your troubles. I hope things are all right now.* BOB: *It hasn't been easy, but things are okay now.* □ JOHN: *How are you getting on after your dog died?* BILL: *Things haven't been easy.*

It isn't worth it. 1. Its value does not justify the action proposed. □ MARY: *Should I write a letter in support of your request?* SUE: *No, don't bother. It isn't worth it.* □ JOHN: *Do you suppose we should report that man to the police?* JANE: *No, it isn't worth it.* **2.** Its importance does not justify the concern being shown. □ TOM: *I'm so sorry about your roses all dying.* MARY: *Not to worry. It isn't worth it. They were sort of sickly anyway.* □ JOHN: *Should I have this coat cleaned? The stain isn't coming out.* SUE: *It isn't worth it. I only wear it when I shovel snow anyway.*

It isn't worth the trouble. AND **It's not worth the trouble.** Don't bother. It isn't worth it. □ TOM: *Shall I wrap all this stuff back up?* MARY: *No. It's not worth the trouble. Just stuff it in a paper bag.* □ JANE: *Do you want me to try to save this little bit of cake?* JOHN: *Oh, no! It's not worth the trouble. I'll just eat it.*

(It) just goes to show (you) (something**).** That incident or story has an important moral or message. □ TOM: *The tax people finally caught up with Henry.* SALLY: *See! It just goes to show.* □ *Indignant over the treatment she received at the grocery store and angry at the youthful clerk, Sally muttered, "Young people. They expect too much. It just goes to show you how society has broken down."*

(It) makes me no difference. Go to (It) makes no difference to me.

(It) makes no difference to me. AND **(It) makes me no difference.; (It) makes me no nevermind.; (It) don't bother me none.; (It) don't make me no nevermind.** I really do not care, one way or the other. (The first one is standard, the others are colloquial.) □ BILL: *Mind if I sit here?* TOM: *Makes no difference to* me. □ BILL: *What would you say if I ate the last piece of cake?* BOB: *Don't make me no nevermind.*

(It) never hurts to ask. Go to (It) doesn't hurt to ask.

(It) (really) doesn't matter to me. I do not care. □ ANDREW: *What shall I do? What shall I do?* ALICE: *Do whatever you like. Jump off a bridge. Go live in the jungle. It really doesn't matter to me.* □ TOM: *I'm leaving you. Mary and I have decided that we're in love.* SUE: *So, go ahead. It doesn't matter to me. I don't care what you do.*

(It) sounds like a plan. What you say sounds promising and is a good plan. □ DON: *Let's meet tomorrow and settle the matter.* ANDREW: *Sounds like a plan.* □ A: *We'll sell the sofa and buy some comfortable chairs.* B: *Great! It sounds like a plan.*

It strikes me that it seems to me that. □ HENRY: *It strikes me that you are losing a little weight.* MARY: *Oh, I love you!* □ "*It strikes me that all this money we are spending is accomplishing very little,*" said Bill.

(It) suits me (fine). It is fine with me. □ JOHN: *Is this one okay?* MARY: *Suits me.* □ JOHN: *I'd like to sit up front where I can hear better.* MARY: *Suits me fine.*

It takes all kinds (of people) (to make a world). All kinds of people, even strange ones, make up the world's population. (A mild way of remarking about someone who has done something strange.) □ A: *I was shocked to hear that Fred had run away with his secretary and then wrote a series of bad checks. Who would have thought?* B: *It takes all kinds!* □ *Every time they tell me I am strange, I remind them that it takes all kinds to make a world.*

(It) won't bother me any. AND **(It) won't bother me at all.** It will not trouble me at all.; I have no objection if you wish to do that. (Not very polite or cordial.) □ JOHN: *Will you mind if I sit here?* JANE: *Won't bother me any.* □ SALLY (*lighting a cigarette*): *Do you mind if I smoke?* BILL: *It won't bother me at all.*

(It) won't bother me at all. Go to (It) won't bother me any.

(It) works for me. It is fine with me. (Slang. With stress on *works* and *me*. The answer to **Does it work for you?**) □ BOB: *Is it okay if I sign us up for the party?* SALLY: *It works for me.* □ TOM: *Is Friday all right for the party?* BILL: *Works for me.* BOB: *It works for me, too.*

It'll all come out in the wash. It will all be made clear at a future reckoning.; Bad things about someone will be revealed eventually.; It will all work out for the best. (This does not mean that bad actions will be neutralized in the way that stains are removed by washing. *Come out* = be revealed.) □ *A: Bob thinks he can keep getting away with padding his expense account. You'd think they'd figure out what's going on. B: Don't worry. It'll all come out in the wash.* □ *Everyone is pretty uncertain about the future now and wondering if we will have jobs next week. I say, just relax. It'll all come out in the wash.*

It'll never fly! AND **It'll never work!** It simply will not work as described. (A cliché.) □ *ANDY: I built this contraption to help me gather up lawn clippings. What do you think of it? FATHER: It'll never fly!* □ *It seems like a great idea when you first think about it, but in the long run, it'll never work.*

It'll never work! Go to It'll never fly!

It's a jungle out there! The world and the people in it can be quite cruel. □ *A: Man, I can't believe how rude people are. Whether they are driving or walking, they are just plain animals. B: Yeah. It's a jungle out there.* □ *Wow, about two dozen reporters have the mayor cornered on the sidewalk, and they're asking him all sorts of questions. It's a jungle out there!*

(It's) about that time. AND **It's that time.** It is the scheduled or customary time for something to happen or be done. □ *It's about that time. We'll be saying good night.* □ *It's that time. See you in the morning.* □ *About that time. Off to bed, kids.*

It's all someone **needs.** Go to That's all someone **needs.**

It's been. a phrase said on leaving a party or some other gathering. (Slang or familiar colloquial. A shortening of *It's been lovely* or some similar expression.) □ *MARY: Well, it's been. We really have to go, though. ANDREW: So glad you could come over. Bye.* □ *FRED: Bye, you guys. See you. SALLY: It's been. Really it has. Toodle-oo.*

(It's) been a long time. I haven't seen you for a long time. (Also literal.) □ *Well, Fred Jones, it's been a long time. How are you?* □ *HANNA: Hey, Ida. Good to see you again. You're looking well. IDA: Yes, it's been a long time.*

(It's) been a pleasure. AND **(It's been) my pleasure.** You are welcome, and I am happy to have come, been invited, or been able to serve you. □ DON: *Thanks so much for coming.* HANNA: *My pleasure.* □ *I'm glad you could help me with my problem.* ANDREW: *It's been my pleasure.*

(It's been) good talking to you. AND **(It's) been good to talk to you.; (It's been) nice talking to you.** a polite phrase said upon departure, at the end of a conversation. □ MARY *(as the elevator stops): Well, this is my floor. I've got to get off.* JOHN: *Bye, Mary. It's been good talking to you.* □ JOHN: *It's been good talking to you, Fred. See you around.* FRED: *Yeah. See you.*

(It's) been good to talk to you. Go to (It's been) good talking to you.

(It's been) nice talking to you. Go to (It's been) good talking to you.

(It's) better than nothing. Having something that is not satisfactory is better than having nothing at all. □ JOHN: *How do you like your dinner?* JANE: *It's better than nothing.* JOHN: *That bad, huh?* □ JOHN: *Did you see your room? How do you like it?* JANE: *Well, I guess it's better than nothing.*

(It's) close enough for government work. fairly close or accurate. (Jocular.) □ *I can do math pretty well. Close enough for government work, anyway.* □ *This isn't quite right, but it's close enough for government work.*

It's for you. This telephone call is for you. □ HENRY: *Hello?* FRED: *Hello. Is Bill there?* HENRY: *Hey, Bill! It's for you.* BILL: *Thanks. Hello?* □ *"It's for you," said Mary, handing the telephone receiver to Sally.*

(It's) good to be here. AND **(It's) nice to be here.** I feel welcome in this place. □ JOHN: *I'm so glad you could come.* JANE: *Thank you. It's good to be here.* □ ALICE: *Welcome to our house!* JOHN: *Thank you. It's nice to be here.*

(It's) good to have you here. AND **(It's) nice to have you here.** Welcome to this place.; It is good that you are here. □ JOHN: *It's good to have you here.* JANE: *Thank you for asking me.* □ ALICE: *Oh, I'm so glad I came!* FRED: *Nice to have you here.*

(It's) good to hear your voice. a polite phrase said upon beginning or ending a telephone conversation. □ BOB: *Hello?* BILL: *Hello, it's Bill.* BOB: *Hello, Bill. It's good to hear your voice.* □ BILL: *Hello,*

Tom. This is Bill. TOM: *It's good to hear your voice. What's cooking?*

(It's) good to see you (again). a polite phrase said when greeting someone whom one has met before. □ BILL: *Hi, Bob. Remember me? I met you last week at the Wilsons'.* BOB: *Oh, hello, Bill. Good to see you again.* □ FRED: *Hi. Good to see you again!* BOB: *Nice to see you, Fred.*

(It's) got me beat. Go to (It) beats me.

(It's) just what you need. Go to That's all someone needs.

(It's) my way or the highway. There is no choice other than the way I have described to you. □ *I hate that manager. Never any discussion. It's always my way or the highway.* □ *Just before I quit, the jerk said, "My way or the highway." I prefer the highway.* □ *Do it the way I tell you or else. It's my way or the highway.*

It's nice to be here. Go to (It's) good to be here.

It's nice to have you here. Go to (It's) good to have you here.

(It's) nice to meet you. an expression said just after being introduced to someone. □ TOM: *Sue, this is my sister, Mary.* SUE: *It's nice to meet you, Mary.* MARY: *How are you, Sue?* □ BOB: *I'm Bob. Nice to see you here.* JANE: *Nice to meet you, Bob.*

(It's) nice to see you. an expression said when greeting or saying good-bye to someone. □ MARY: *Hi, Bill. It's nice to see you.* BILL: *Nice to see you, Mary. How are things?* □ JOHN: *Come on in, Jane. Nice to see you.* JANE: *Thanks, and thank you for inviting me.*

(It's) no trouble. Do not worry, this is not a problem. □ MARY: *Do you mind carrying all this up to my apartment?* TOM: *It's no trouble.* □ BOB: *Would it be possible for you to get this back to me today?* BILL: *Sure. No trouble.*

(It's) none of your business! It is nothing that you need to know, and it is none of your concern. (Not very polite.) □ ALICE: *How much does a little diamond like that cost?* MARY: *None of your business!* □ JOHN: *Do you want to go out with me Friday night?* MARY: *Sorry, I don't think so.* JOHN: *Well, what are you doing then?* MARY: *None of your business?*

(It's) not half bad. It is not as bad as one might have thought. □ MARY: *How do you like this play?* JANE: *Not half bad.* □ JANE: *Well, how do you like college?* FRED: *It's not half bad.*

It's not over 'til it's over. There is still hope for things to go the way I want until the entire event is over. □ *Don't leave the stadium now! They haven't won the game yet. It's not over 'til it's over.* □ *It looks bad for our side, but it's not over 'til it's over.*

(It's) not supposed to. AND **(Someone's) not supposed to.** a phrase indicating that someone or something is not meant to do something. (Often with a person's name or a pronoun as a subject.) □ *FRED: This little piece keeps falling off. CLERK: It's not supposed to.* □ *BILL: Tom just called from Detroit and says he's coming back tomorrow. MARY: That's funny. He's not supposed to.*

It's not worth the trouble. Go to It isn't worth the trouble.

It's on me. I will pay this bill. (Usually a bill for a meal or drinks. Compare to This one's on me.) □ *As the waiter set down the glasses, Fred said, "It's on me" and grabbed the check.* □ *JOHN: Check, please. BILL: No, it's on me this time.*

(It's) out of the question. It cannot be done.; No! (A polite but very firm "No!") □ *JANE: I think we should buy a watchdog. JOHN: Out of the question.* □ *JOHN: Can we go to the mountains for a vacation this year? JANE: It's out of the question.*

It's six of one and half a dozen of another. AND **It's six of one and half a dozen of the other.** Either choice will have about the same result.; Neither choice is much better than the other. (Sometimes *a half dozen* rather than *half a dozen*.) □ *HANNA: I simply can't choose between going to Florida or Arizona for the winter. Lots of reasons on both sides. It's six of one and half a dozen of the other. IDA: Then just flip a coin, silly.* □ *What does it matter whether you choose pinkish red or reddish pink. It's six of one and half a dozen of another.*

It's six of one and half a dozen of the other. Go to It's six of one and half a dozen of another.

It's that time. Go to (It's) about that time.

(It's) time for a change. an expression announcing a decision to make a change. □ *BILL: Are you really going to take a new job? MARY: Yes, it's time for a change.* □ *JANE: Are you going to Florida for your vacation? FRED: No. It's time for a change. We're going skiing.*

(It's) time I left. The time has come for me to go. (Also in other persons. See also **(It's) time we were going.**) □ *It's almost dawn! Time I left.* □ *It's time we left. The party is totally over.*

(It's) time to go. It is now time to leave. □ JANE: *Look at the clock! Time to go!* JOHN: *Yup! I'm out of here too.* □ MOTHER: *It's four o'clock. The party's over. Time to go.* BILL: *I had a good time. Thank you.*

(It's) time to hit the road. AND **(I'd) better hit the road.; (I've) got to hit the road.** It's time to leave. □ HENRY: *Look at the clock. It's past midnight. It's time to hit the road.* ANDREW: *Yeah. We got to go.* SUE: *Okay, good night.* □ BILL: *I've got to hit the road. I have a long day tomorrow.* MARY: *Okay, good night.* BILL: *Bye, Mary.*

(It's) time to move along. Go to **(It's) time to run.**

(It's) time to move on. AND **(Let's) just move on.** Let's stop worrying, complaining, or feeling guilty (about something) and let things return to normal. □ DON: *Yes, it was a bad accident, but it's time to move on.* □ HANNA: *It's over. It can't be undone.* ANDREW: *Let's just move on.*

(It's) time to push along. Go to **(It's) time to run.**

(It's) time to run. AND **(It's) time to move along.; (It's) time to push along.; (It's) time to push off.; (It's) time to split.** It's time to leave. □ ANDREW: *Time to push off. I've got to get home.* HENRY: *See you, dude.* □ JOHN: *It's time to split. I've got to go.* SUE: *Okay. See you tomorrow.*

(It's) time to shove off. Go to **(I) have to shove off.**

(It's) time to split. Go to **(It's) time to run.**

It's time we should be going. a statement made by one member of a pair (or group) of guests to the other member(s). (Typically, a way for a husband or wife to signal the other spouse that it is time to leave.) □ *Mr. Franklin looked at his wife and said softly, "It's time we should be going."* □ TOM: *Well, I suppose it's time we should be going.* MARY: *Yes, we really should.* ALICE: *So early?*

(It's) time we were going. It's time for us to go. (Also in other persons. See also **(It's) time I left.**) □ *It's time we were going. It's really late.* □ *It's late, and it's time we were going.*

It's written all over one's **face.** One's face reveals everything about a particular matter. □ Q: *How did you know what naughty little* *thing I got away with at work today? A: It's written all over your face.* □ *You must have some good news for us. It's written all over your face.*

It's you! It suits you perfectly.; It is just your style. □ JOHN *(trying on jacket): How does this look?* SALLY: *It's you!* □ SUE: *I'm taking a job with the candy company. I'll be managing a store on Maple Street.* MARY: *It's you! It's you!*

It's your funeral. If that is what you are going to do, you will have to endure the consequences. □ TOM: *I'm going to call in sick and go to the ball game instead of to work today.* MARY: *Go ahead. It's your funeral.* □ BILL: *I'm going to take my car to the racetrack and see if I can race against someone.* SUE: *It's your funeral.*

It's yours! As you requested, it is now yours!; You are getting what you want! □ BOB: *I really think I would like to have the red one.* CLERK: *It's yours!* □ TOM: *I really want to read that book you've been reading. It looks very interesting.* BOB: *Here, it's yours! I'm finished with it.*

(I've) been getting by. a response to a greeting inquiry into one's well-being indicating that one is having a hard time surviving or that things are just all right but that they could be much better. (See also **(I'm) just getting by.**) □ JOHN: *How are things?* JANE: *Oh, I've been getting by.* □ SUE: *How are you doing?* MARY: *Been getting by. Things could be better.*

(I've) been keeping busy. AND **(I've been) keeping busy.** a typical response to a greeting inquiry asking what one has been doing. (Also reflexive: *keeping myself.*) □ BILL: *What have you been doing?* BOB: *I've been keeping myself busy. What about you?* BILL: *About the same.* □ JOHN: *Yo! What have you been up to?* BILL: *Been keeping myself busy.*

(I've) been keeping cool. AND **(I've been) keeping cool.** an answer to a question about what one has been doing during very hot weather. (Also reflexive: *keeping yourself.*) □ JANE: *How do you like this hot weather?* BILL: *I've been keeping cool.* □ MARY: *Been keeping cool?* BOB: *Yeah. Been keeping cool.*

(I've) been keeping myself busy. AND **(I've been) keeping myself busy.** a typical response to a greeting inquiry asking what one has been doing. □ BILL: *What have you been doing?* BOB: *I've been keeping myself busy. What about you?* BILL: *About the same.*

☐ JOHN: *Yo! What have you been up to?* BILL: *Been keeping myself busy.*

(I've) been keeping out of trouble. AND **(I've been) keeping out of trouble.** a response to any greeting inquiry that asks what one has been doing. (Also reflexive: *keeping yourself.*) ☐ JOHN: *What have you been doing, Fred?* FRED: *Been keeping out of trouble.* JOHN: *Yeah. Me, too.* ☐ MARY: *How are things, Tom?* TOM: *Oh, I've been keeping out of trouble.*

(I've) been okay. a response to any greeting inquiry that asks how one has been. ☐ BILL: *Well, how have you been, good buddy?* JOHN: *I've been okay.* ☐ SUE: *How you doing?* JANE: *Been okay. And you?* SUE: *The same.*

I've been there. I know exactly what you are talking about.; I know exactly what you are going through. ☐ JOHN: *Wow! Those sales meetings really wear me out!* JANE: *I know what you mean. I've been there.* ☐ SUE: *These employment interviews are very tiring.* BOB: *I know it! I've been there.*

(I've) been under the weather. a greeting response indicating that one has been ill. ☐ JOHN: *How have you been?* SALLY: *I've been under the weather, but I'm better.* ☐ DOCTOR: *How are you?* MARY: *I've been under the weather.* DOCTOR: *Maybe we can fix that. What seems to be the trouble?*

(I've) been up to no good. a vague greeting response indicating that one has been doing mischief. ☐ JOHN: *What have you been doing, Tom?* TOM: *Oh, I've been up to no good, as usual.* JOHN: *Yeah. Me, too.* ☐ MARY: *Been keeping busy as usual?* SUE: *Yeah. Been up to no good, as usual.* MARY: *I should have known.*

(I've) (got) better things to do. AND **I have better things to do.** There are better ways to spend my time.; I cannot waste any more time on this matter. ☐ ANDREW: *Good-bye. I've got better things to do than stand around here listening to you brag.* HENRY: *Well, good-bye and good riddance.* ☐ MARY: *How did things go at your meeting with the zoning board?* SALLY: *I gave up. Can't fight city hall. Better things to do.*

(I've) got to be shoving off. Go to (I) have to shove off.

(I've) got to fly. a phrase announcing one's need to depart. (Go to (I) have to shove off for other possible variations.) ☐ BILL: *Well,* *time's up. I've got to fly.* BOB: *Oh, it's early yet. Stay a while.* BILL: *Sorry. I got to go.* □ *"It's past lunchtime. I've got to fly,"* said Alice.

(I've) got to get moving. a phrase announcing one's need to depart. (Go to (I) **have to shove off** for other possible variations.) □ BILL: *Time to go. Got to get moving.* SALLY: *Bye, Tom.* □ MARY: *It's late and I've got to get moving.* SUE: *Well, if you must, okay. Come again sometime.* MARY: *Bye.*

(I've) got to go. a phrase announcing one's need to depart. (Go to (I) **have to shove off** for other possible variations.) □ ANDREW: *Bye, I've got to go.* RACHEL: *Bye, little brother. See you.* □ SALLY: *Ciao! Got to go.* SUE: *See ya! Take it easy.*

(I've) got to go home and get my beauty sleep. a phrase announcing one's need to depart. (Go to (I) **have to shove off** for other possible variations.) □ SUE: *Leaving so early?* JOHN: *I've got to go home and get my beauty sleep.* □ JANE: *I've got to go home and get my beauty sleep.* FRED: *Well, you look to me like you've had enough.* JANE: *Why, thank you.*

(I've) got to hit the road. Go to (It's) **time to hit the road.**

(I've) got to run. a phrase announcing one's need to depart. (Go to (I) **have to shove off** for other possible variations.) □ JOHN: *Got to run. It's late.* JANE: *Me, too. See ya, bye-bye.* □ MARY: *Want to watch another movie?* BILL: *No, thanks. I've got to run.*

(I've) got to shove off. Go to (I) **have to shove off.**

(I've) got to split. a phrase announcing one's need to depart. (Go to (I) **have to shove off** for other possible variations.) □ JANE: *Look at the time! Got to split.* MARY: *See you later, Jane.* □ BILL: *It's getting late. I've got to split.* SUE: *Okay, see you tomorrow.* BILL: *Good night.*

(I've) got to take off. a phrase announcing one's need to depart. (Go to (I) **have to shove off** for other possible variations.) □ MARY: *Got to take off. Bye.* BOB: *Leaving so soon?* MARY: *Yes. Time to go.* BOB: *Bye.* □ *"Look at the time. I've got to take off!"* shrieked Alice.

I've got work to do. 1. I'm too busy to stay here any longer. □ JANE: *Time to go. I've got work to do.* JOHN: *Me, too. See you.* □ BOB: *I have to leave now.* BILL: *So soon?* BOB: *Yes, I've got work to do.* **2.** Do not bother me. I'm busy. □ BILL: *Can I ask you a question?* JANE: *I've got work to do.* □ MARY: *There are some things we have to get* *straightened out on this Wilson contract. JOHN: I've got work to do. It will have to wait.*

I've had a lovely time. AND **We've had a lovely time.** a polite expression said to a host or hostess on departure. □ BOB: *I've had a lovely time. Thanks for asking me.* FRED: *We're just delighted you could come. Good night.* BOB: *Good night.* □ SUE: *We've had a lovely time. Good night.* BILL: *Next time don't stay away so long. Good night.*

I've had enough of this! I will not take any more of this situation! □ SALLY: *I've had enough of this! I'm leaving!* FRED: *Me, too!* □ JOHN (*glaring at Tom*): *I've had enough of this! Tom, you're fired!* TOM: *You can't fire me. I quit!*

I've had it up to here (with someone or something**).** I will not endure any more of someone or something. □ BILL: *I've had it up to here with your stupidity.* BOB: *Who's calling who stupid?* □ JOHN: *I've had it up to here with Tom.* MARY: *Are you going to fire him?* JOHN: *Yes.*

I've heard so much about you. a polite phrase said upon being introduced to a person one heard about from a friend or the person's relatives. □ BILL: *This is my cousin Kate.* BOB: *Hello, Kate. I've heard so much about you.* □ SUE: *Hello, Bill. I've heard so much about you.* BILL: *Hello. Glad to meet you.*

(I've) never been better. AND **(I've) never felt better.** a response to a greeting inquiry into one's health or state of being. □ MARY: *How are you, Sally?* SALLY: *Never been better, sweetie.* □ DOCTOR: *How are you, Jane?* JANE: *Never felt better.* DOCTOR: *Then, why are you here?*

(I've) never felt better. Go to (I've) never been better.

(I've) seen better. a noncommittal and not very positive judgment about something or someone. □ ALICE: *How did you like the movie?* JOHN: *I've seen better.* □ BILL: *What do you think about this weather?* BOB: *Seen better.*

(I've) seen worse. a noncommittal and not totally negative judgment about something or someone. □ ALICE: *How did you like the movie?* JOHN: *I've seen worse.* □ BILL: *What do you think about this weather?* BOB: *Seen worse. Can't remember when, though.*

jog someone's **memory** to stimulate someone's memory to recall something. □ *Hearing the first part of the song I'd forgotten really jogged my memory.* □ *I tried to jog Bill's memory about our childhood antics.*

Join the club! AND **Welcome to the club!** You are one of many in the same condition or with the same problem. □ *So, you just got your electric bill for last month, and you're astounded. Join the club!* □ DON: *I just found out that our company's pension plan is insolvent. I'm really screwed!* ANDY: *Welcome to the club!*

(Just) gotta love it! Go to (You) (just) gotta love it!

Just a minute. AND **Just a moment.; Just a sec(ond).; Wait a minute.; Wait a sec(ond). 1.** Please wait a short time. □ JOHN: *Just a minute.* BOB: *What's the matter?* JOHN: *I dropped my wallet.* □ SUE: *Just a sec.* JOHN: *Why?* SUE: *I think we're going in the wrong direction. Let's look at the map.* **2.** (Usually an exclamation.) Stop there.; Hold it! □ JOHN: *Just a minute!* MARY: *What's wrong?* JOHN: *That stick looked sort of like a snake. But it's all right.* MARY: *You scared me to death!* □ MARY: *Wait a minute!* BILL: *Why?* MARY: *We're leaving an hour earlier than we have to.*

Just a moment. Go to Just a minute.

Just a second. Go to Just a minute.

(Just) as I expected. I thought so.; I knew it would be this way. □ *Just as I expected. The window was left open and it rained in.* □ A: *He's not here.* B: *As I expected, he left work early again.*

Just getting by. Go to (I'm) just getting by.

Just goes to show (you). Go to (It) just goes to show (you) (something).

just let me say Go to let me (just) say.

just like that in just the way it was stated; without any (further) discussion or comment. □ *Sue: You can't walk out on me just like that. John: I can too. Just watch!* □ *Mary: And then she slapped him in the face, just like that! Sally: She can be so rude.*

Just looking. Go to (I'm) only looking.

Just plugging along. Go to (I'm) (just) plugging along.

(Just) taking care of business. an answer to the question "What have you been doing lately?" (Also abbreviated **T.C.B.**) □ *Bill: Hey, man. What you been doing? Tom: Just taking care of business.* □ *Andrew: Look, officer, I'm just standing here, taking care of business, and this Tom guy comes up and tries to hit me for a loan. Tom: That's not true!*

Just thinking out loud. Go to (I'm) (just) thinking out loud.

Just wait! Go to You (just) wait (and see)!

Just want(ed) to (do something**).** Go to (I) just want(ed) to (do something).

Just watch! Go to (You) (just) watch!

Just what you need. Go to That's all someone needs.

Just wondering. Go to (I was) just wondering.

Just (you) wait (and see)! Go to You (just) wait (and see)!

keep a secret to know a secret and not tell anyone. □ *Please keep our little secret private.* □ *Do you know how to keep a secret?*

keep harping on something to continue to talk or complain about something; to keep raising a topic of conversation. □ *Why do you keep harping on the same old complaint?* □ *You keep harping on my problems and ignore your own!*

keep in mind that Go to keep (it) in mind that.

Keep in there! Keep trying. □ ANDREW: *Don't give up, Sally. Keep in there!* SALLY: *I'm doing my best!* □ JOHN: *I'm not very good, but I keep trying.* FRED: *Just keep in there, John.*

Keep in touch. Please try to communicate occasionally. □ RACHEL: *Good-bye, Fred. Keep in touch.* FRED: *Bye, Rach.* □ SALLY (throwing kisses): *Good-bye, you two.* MARY (waving good-bye): *Be sure to write.* SUE: *Yes, keep in touch.*

keep (it) in mind that introduces something that the speaker wants remembered. □ BILL: *When we get there, I want to take a long hot shower.* FATHER: *Keep it in mind that we are guests, and we have to fit in with the routines of the household.* □ SALLY: *Keep it in mind that you don't work here anymore, and you just can't go in and out of offices like that.* FRED: *I guess you're right.*

Keep it up! Keep up the good work!; Keep on doing it.; Keep (on) trying. □ JANE: *I think I'm doing better in calculus.* JOHN: *Keep it up!* □ SALLY: *I can now jog for almost three miles.* FRED: *Great! Keep it up!* **2.** Just keep acting that way and see what happens to you. (Compare to **(Go ahead,) make my day!**) □ JOHN: *You're just not doing what is expected of you.* BILL: *Keep it up! Just keep it up, and I'll quit right when you need me most.* □ *"Your behavior is terrible, young man! You just keep it up and see what happens," warned Alice. "Just keep it up!"*

Keep (on) trying. AND **Don't quit trying.** a phrase encouraging continued efforts. □ JANE: *I think I'm doing better in calculus.* JOHN: *Keep trying! You can get an A.* □ SUE: *I really want that promotion, but I keep getting turned down.* BILL: *Don't quit trying! You'll get it.*

keep one's **opinions to** oneself to stop mentioning one's own opinions, especially when they disagree with someone else's. □ *You ought to keep your opinions to yourself if you are going to be offensive.* □ *Please keep your rude opinions to yourself!*

Keep out of my way. AND **Stay out of my way. 1.** Don't get in my pathway. □ JOHN: *Keep out of my way. I'm carrying a heavy load.* BILL: *Sorry.* □ *"Keep out of my way!" shouted the piano mover.* **2.** Do not try to stop me. □ HENRY: *I'm going to get even, no matter what. Keep out of my way.* ANDREW: *Keep it up! You'll really get in trouble.* □ JOHN: *I intend to work my way to the top in this business.* MARY: *So do I, so just keep out of my way.*

Keep out of this! AND **Stay out of this!** This is not your business, so do not try to get involved. □ JOHN: *Now, you listen to me, Fred!* MARY: *That's no way to talk to Fred!* JOHN: *Keep out of this, Mary! Mind your own business!* FRED: *Stay out of this, Mary!* MARY: *It's just as much my business as it is yours.*

Keep quiet. AND **Keep still.** Get quiet and stay that way. □ JOHN: *I'm going to go to the store.* BILL: *Keep quiet.* JOHN: *I just said . . .* BILL: *I said, keep quiet!* □ CHILD: *I want some candy!* MOTHER: *Keep still.*

Keep quiet about it. Go to Keep still about it.

Keep smiling. a parting phrase encouraging someone to have good spirits. □ JOHN: *Things are really getting tough.* SUE: *Well, just keep smiling. Things will get better.* □ BILL: *What a day! I'm exhausted and depressed.* BOB: *Not to worry. Keep smiling. Things will calm down.*

keep someone **in the loop** to make sure that someone is kept informed about all the news relating to a matter. □ *I need all the information about this deal as soon as possible. Please keep me in the loop.* □ *Keep Fred in the loop so he will have no excuse for not knowing what's going on.*

keep something **on the back burner** to temporarily remove a project, question, or piece of business from immediate consideration. □

This isn't the most important thing we have to deal with at the moment, so keep it on the back burner until we have some time. □ *Why has this been kept on the back burner so long? This is one of the most urgent issues that this company faces!*

Keep still. Go to Keep quiet.

Keep still about it. AND **Keep quiet about it.** Don't tell it to anyone. □ BILL: *Are you really going to sell your car?* MARY: *Yes, but keep quiet about it.* □ JOHN: *Someone said you're looking for a new job.* SUE: *That's right, but keep still about it.*

Keep talking. Continue to explain. See also Tell me more. □ DON: *I have a hot lead on a big deal with a Vegas land owner.* ANDY: *Keep talking. I'm interested.* □ A: *There's all sorts of good reasons to get this guy elected.* B: *Keep talking.*

Keep this to yourself. a phrase introducing something that is meant to be a secret. □ ANDREW: *Keep this to yourself, but I'm going to Bora Bora on my vacation.* HENRY: *Sounds great. Can I go too?* □ JOHN: *Keep this to yourself. Mary and I are breaking up.* SUE: *I won't tell a soul.*

Keep up the good work. Please keep doing the good things that you are doing now. □ FATHER: *Your grades are fine, Bill. Keep up the good work.* BILL: *Thanks, Dad.* □ *"Nice play," said the coach. "Keep up the good work!"*

Keep your chin up. an expression of encouragement to someone who has to bear some emotional burdens. □ FRED: *I really can't take much more of this.* JANE: *Keep your chin up. Things will get better.* □ JOHN: *Smile, Fred. Keep your chin up.* FRED: *I guess you're right. I just get so depressed when I think of this mess I'm in.*

Keep your mouth shut (about someone or something**).** Do not tell anyone about someone or something. □ BOB: *Are you going to see the doctor?* MARY: *Yes, but keep your mouth shut about it.* □ BOB: *Isn't Tom's uncle in tax trouble?* JANE: *Yes, but keep your mouth shut about him.*

Keep your nose out of my business. Go to Mind your own business.

Keep your opinions to yourself! I do not want to hear your opinions! □ JANE: *I think this room looks drab.* SUE: *Keep your opinions to yourself! I like it this way!* □ SALLY: *You really ought to do some-*

thing about your hair. It looks like it was hit by a truck. JOHN: Keep your opinions to yourself. This is the latest style where I come from. SALLY: I won't suggest where that might be.

Keep your shirt on! Be patient!; Just wait a minute! (Colloquial.) □ *JOHN: Hey, hurry up! Finish this! BILL: Keep your shirt on! I'll do it when I'm good and ready.* □ *JOHN: Waiter! We've been waiting fifteen minutes! What sort of place is this? WAITER: Keep your shirt on! JOHN (quietly): Now I know what sort of place this is.*

Keeping busy. Go to (I've) been keeping busy. See also (Have you) been keeping busy?

Keeping cool. Go to (I've) been keeping cool. See also (Have you) been keeping cool?

Keeping out of trouble. Go to (I've) been keeping out of trouble.

Kind of. Go to Sort of.

kiss and make up to make apologies and amends (to each other). (Probably not with actual kissing.) □ *That's enough screaming and shouting, you two. Now stop it and kiss and make up.* □ *I am really angry at Tom. There isn't any way on God's green earth that I'm going to kiss and make up.*

Knock it off! Be quiet!; Stop that noise! (Slang.) □ *JOHN: Hey, you guys! Knock it off! BOB: Sorry. BILL: Sorry. I guess we got a little carried away.* □ *SUE: All right. Knock it off! BILL: Yeah. Let's get down to business.*

Know something? Go to (Do you) want to know something?

Know what? Go to (Do you) know what?

Know what I mean? Go to (Do you) know what I'm saying?

Know what I'm saying? Go to (Do you) know what I'm saying?

know when one **is not wanted** to sense when one's presence is not welcome; to know when one is not among friends. (Usually said when someone feels hurt by being ignored by people.) □ *I'm leaving this place! I know when I'm not wanted!* □ *She doesn't know when she's not wanted. Can't she tell she's out of place?*

know where all the bodies are buried to know all the secrets and intrigue; to know all the important details. □ *He is a good choice for president because he knows where all the bodies are buried.* □ *Since he knows where all the bodies are buried, he is the only one who can advise us.*

Ladies first. an expression indicating that women should go first, as in going through a doorway. □ *Bob stepped back and made a motion with his hand indicating that Mary should go first. "Ladies first," smiled Bob.* □ Bob: *It's time to get in the food line. Who's going to go first?* BILL: *Ladies first, Mary.* MARY: *Why not gentlemen first?* BOB: *Looks like nobody's going first.*

late in the day almost too late in the sequence of things. (Also literal.) □ *Now that you've lost most of your money in bad investments, it's late in the day to think about looking for a stockbroker.* □ *At 85, it's a little late in the day to be thinking about marriage.*

Later. Go to I'll see you later.

Later, alligator. Go to See you later, alligator.

Later, bro. I will see you later, friend. (*Bro* = brother.) □ ANDY: *Bye, Don.* DON: *Later, bro.* □ *Gotta go. Later, bro.*

Leave it to me. I will attend to it by myself.; I will do it. □ JOHN: *This whole business needs to be straightened out.* SUE: *Leave it to me. I'll get it done.* □ JANE: *Will you do this as soon as possible?* MARY: *Leave it to me.*

Leave me alone! Stop harassing me!; **Don't bother me!** □ JOHN: *You did it. You're the one who always does it.* BILL: *Leave me alone! I never did it.* □ FRED: *Let's give Bill a dunk in the pool.* BILL: *Leave me alone!*

leave someone **high and dry** to leave someone helpless. □ *All my workers quit and left me high and dry.* □ *All the children ran away and left Billy high and dry to take the blame for the broken window.*

Leaving so soon? Go to (Are you) leaving so soon?

Less is more. Less of something is more manageable or economical than more of it.; There are positives in not having too much or too many. □ *A: This new gadget is much smaller than the old one,* *but it's supposed to be stronger. B: I guess that less is more in this case.* □ *Our working group is now smaller and more nimble—much more efficient. Less is more, definitely.*

the **lesser (of the two)** the smaller one (of two); the one having the least amount. □ *The last two pieces of pie were not quite the same size, and I chose the lesser of the two.* □ *Faced with a basket containing too much and one with too little, Tom chose the lesser.*

the **lesser of two evils** the less bad thing, of a pair of bad things. □ *I didn't like either politician, so I voted for the lesser of two evils.* □ *Given the options of going out with someone I don't like or staying home and watching a boring television program, I chose the lesser of the two evils and watched television.*

Let it be. Leave the situation as it is. □ ALICE: *I can't get over the way he just left me there on the street and drove off. What an arrogant pig!* MARY: *Oh, Alice, let it be. You'll figure out some way to get even.* □ JOHN: *You can't!* BILL: *Can too!* JOHN: *Can't!* BILL: *Can too!* JANE: *Stop! Let it be! That's enough!*

Let it go. Forget it.; Stop worrying about it. □ *Don't get so angry about it. Let it go.* □ *Let it go. Stop fretting.*

Let me get back to you (on that). Go to I'll get back to you (on that).

Let me have it! AND **Let's have it!** Tell me the news. □ BILL: *I'm afraid there's some bad news.* BOB: *Okay. Let me have it! Don't waste time!* BILL: *The plans we made did away with your job.* BOB: *What?* □ JOHN: *I didn't want to be the one to tell you this.* BOB: *What is it? Let's have it!* JOHN: *Your cat was just run over.* BOB: *Never mind that. What's the bad news?*

let me (just) say AND **just let me say** a phrase introducing a point that the speaker thinks is important. □ RACHEL: *Let me say how pleased we all are with your efforts.* HENRY: *Why, thank you very much.* □ BOB: *Since you ask, just let me say that we're extremely pleased with your efforts.* BILL: *Thanks loads. I did what I could.*

let out a sound to make [some kind of] a sound. □ *Be quiet. Don't let out a sound!* □ *Suddenly, Jane let out a shriek.*

let something **pass** to let an error or offense go unnoticed or unchallenged. □ *Bob let Bill's insult pass because he didn't want to argue.* □ *A: I'm really sorry. B: Don't worry, I'll let this little incident pass.*

Let the buyer beware. The person who buys something should investigate the goods or property thoroughly for damage or suitability. □ *Be careful when buying things from street vendors. Let the buyer beware.* □ *It's the purchaser's job to make sure the goods are okay. Let the buyer beware.*

Let's call it a day. Let us end what we are doing for the day. □ *MARY: Well, that's the end of the reports. Nothing else to do. SUE: Let's call it a day.* □ *BOB: Let's call it a day. I'm tired. TOM: Me, too. Let's get out of here.*

Let's change something **up (a little).** Let's do something a little differently. (The *up* is colloqial.) □ *Q: Aren't things okay the way they are? A: No, Let's change things up a little.* □ *ANDREW: This stuff is boring. HANNA: Okay, let's change it up.*

Let's do lunch (sometime). Go to We('ll) have to do lunch sometime.

Let's do it. AND **Let's do this.** We are ready, and it's time to begin doing something. □ *HANNA: Do you have everything you need to know? Is everybody ready? IDA: Yes. Let's do this.* □ *COACH (standing on the bridge): Okay, bungee jumpers! Let's do it!*

Let's do this. Go to Let's do it.

Let's do this again (sometime). AND **We must do this again (sometime).** an expression indicating that one member of a group or pair has enjoyed doing something and would like to do it again. □ *BILL: What a nice evening. MARY: Yes, let's do this again sometime. BILL: Bye. MARY: Bye, Bill.* □ *SUE (saying good night): So nice to see both of you. MARY: Oh, yes. We must do this again sometime.*

Let's eat. 1. an announcement that a meal is ready to be eaten. □ *FATHER: It's all ready now. Let's eat. BILL: Great! I'm starved.* □ *JOHN: Soup's on! Let's eat! BILL: Come on, everybody. Let's eat!* **2.** AND **Let's eat something.** a suggestion that it is time to eat. □ *MARY: Look at the clock. We only have a few minutes before the show. Let's eat.* □ *BILL: What should we do? We have some time to spare. SUE: Let's eat something. BILL: Good idea. SUE: Food is always a good idea with you.*

Let's eat something. Go to Let's eat.

Let's get down to business. a phrase marking a transition to a business discussion or serious talk. □ *JOHN: Okay, enough small* *talk. Let's get down to business. MARY: Good idea.* □ *"All right, ladies and gentlemen, let's get down to business," said the president of the board.*

Let's get out of here. Let us leave (and go somewhere else). □ *ALICE: It's really hot in this room. Let's get out of here. JOHN: I'm with you. Let's go.* □ *BILL: This crowd is getting sort of angry. BOB: I noticed that too. Let's get out of here.*

Let's get together (sometime). a vague invitation to meet again, usually said upon departing. (The *sometime* can be a particular time or the word *sometime*.) □ *BILL: Good-bye, Bob. BOB: See you, Bill. Let's get together sometime.* □ *JANE: We need to discuss this matter. JOHN: Yes, let's get together next week.*

Let's go somewhere where it's (more) quiet. Let us continue our conversation where there is less noise or where we will not be disturbed. □ *TOM: Hi, Mary. It's sure crowded here. MARY: Yes, let's go somewhere where it's quiet.* □ *BILL: We need to talk. SALLY: Yes, we do. Let's go somewhere where it's more quiet.*

Let's have it! Go to **Let me have it!**

(Let's) just move on. Go to **(It's) time to move on.**

Let's not go through all that again. We are not going to discuss that matter again. (Compare to **Do we have to go through all that again?**) □ *BILL: Now, I still want to explain again about last night. SALLY: Let's not go through all that again!* □ *SALLY: I can't get over the way you spoke to me at our own dinner table. FRED: I was only kidding! I said I was sorry. Let's not go through all that again!*

Let's shake on it. Let us mark this agreement by shaking hands on it. □ *BOB: Do you agree? MARY: I agree. Let's shake on it. BOB: Okay.* □ *BILL: Good idea. Sounds fine. BOB (extending his hand): Okay, let's shake on it. BILL (shaking hands with Bob): Great!*

Let's talk (about it). Let us talk about the problem and try to settle things. □ *TOM: Bill! Bill! I'm sorry about our argument. Let's talk. BILL: Get lost!* □ *SALLY: I've got a real problem. BOB: Let's talk about it.*

level the playing field to make things fair and balanced for all people concerned. □ *It really isn't fair that you should get the first choice of everything just because the boss is your uncle. We need to do something to level the playing field around here.* □ *A: Come on,* *you guys! Let's level the playing field. Throw Bob off the team and put me on! B: How does that level the playing field?*

Life's been good (to me). I am grateful that I am doing well in life. □ *I can't complain. Life's been good to me.* □ *I'm doing fine. Life's been good.*

Like I care! AND **As if (I cared)!** What makes you think I could possibly care?; I don't care at all! □ ANN: *He treated me soooo badly. He took me to the prom in a crummy car, failed to pay me any attention all evening, and then wanted to leave early. JAN: Like I care! I didn't even have a date to the prom.* □ JOHN: *I expect you to greet everyone at the door with a smile on your face and a friendly word for each of my guests. JAN: As if!*

like I said AND **as I said** as I said (before); to repeat myself; as I said previously. (The first entry is more prevalent but less acceptable in style.) □ *Like I said, we have more serious problems than the ones you know about.* □ *It's time we began to take him seriously. Like I said, he needs our support.*

like I was saying Go to as I was saying.

Like it or lump it! There is no other choice. Take that or none. (Slang.) □ JOHN: *I don't like this room. It's too small.* BILL: *Like it or lump it. That's all we've got.* □ JANE: *I don't want to be talked to like that.* SUE: *Well, like it or lump it! That's the way we talk around here.*

Like it's such a big deal! It really isn't all that important! (Informal. Sarcastic.) □ *So I dropped the glass. Like it's such a big deal.* □ *Like it's such a big deal. Who cares?*

like to hear oneself **talk** [for someone] to enjoy one's own talking more than other people enjoy listening to it. □ *I guess I don't really have anything to say. I just like to hear myself talk, I guess.* □ *There he goes again. He just likes to hear himself talk.*

like you say Go to as you say.

like(ly) as not Go to (as) like(ly) as not.

Likewise(, I'm sure). The same from my point of view. □ ALICE: *I'm delighted to make your acquaintance.* BOB: *Likewise, I'm sure.* □ JOHN: *How nice to see you!* SUE: *Likewise.* JOHN: *Where are you from, Sue?*

little by little AND **bit by bit** a small amount at a time; gradually. □ *ANDY: Why are you so slow, Don? When on earth will this job get done? DON: Don't worry. I'll get it done little by little.* □ *I can't pay you everything I owe you all at once. I'll have to pay it off bit by bit.*

live up to one's **end of the bargain** to carry through on a bargain; to do as was promised in an agreement. □ *You can't quit now. You have to live up to your end of the bargain.* □ *Bob isn't living up to his end of the bargain, so I am going to sue him.*

Long time no see. I have not seen you in a long time.; We have not seen each other in a long time. □ *TOM: Hi, Fred. Where have you been keeping yourself? FRED: Good to see you, Tom. Long time no see.* □ *JOHN: It's Bob! Hi, Bob! BOB: Hi, John! Long time no see.*

look a sentence opener seeking the attention of the person spoken to. (Words such as this often use intonation to convey the connotation of the sentence that is to follow. The brief intonation pattern accompanying the word may indicate sarcasm, disagreement, caution, consolation, sternness, etc. See also **look here**.) □ *SUE: How could you! FRED: Look, I didn't mean to.* □ *ANDREW: Look, can't we talk about it? SUE: There's no more to be said.* □ *JOHN: I'm so sorry! ANDREW: Look, we all make mistakes.* □ *"Look, let me try again," begged Fred.* □ *ANDREW: Look, I've just about had it with you! SALLY: And I've had it with you.* □ *ANDREW: Look, that can't be right. RACHEL: But it is.*

Look alive! Act alert and responsive! □ *"Come on, Fred! Get moving! Look alive!" shouted the coach, who was not happy with Fred's performance.* □ *BILL: Look alive, Bob! BOB: I'm doing the best I can.*

Look (at) what the cat dragged in! Look who's here! (A good-humored and familiar way of showing surprise at someone's presence in a place, especially if the person looks a little rumpled. Compare to (Someone) **looks like something the cat dragged in.**) □ *Bob and Mary were standing near the doorway talking when Tom came in. "Look what the cat dragged in!" announced Bob.* □ *MARY: Hello, everybody. I'm here! JANE: Look at what the cat dragged in!*

look here a phrase emphasizing the point that follows. (Can show some impatience. See also **look**.) □ *HENRY: Look here, I want to try to help you, but you're not making it easy for me. RACHEL: I'm just so upset.* □ *ANDREW: Look here, I just asked you a simple question! BOB: As I told you in the beginning, there are no simple answers.*

Look me up when you're in town. When you next come to my town, try to find me (and we can visit). (A vague and perhaps insincere invitation.) □ BOB: *Nice to see you, Tom. Bye now.* TOM: *Yes, indeed. Look me up when you're in town. Bye.* □ SALLY (on the phone): *Bye. Nice talking to you.* MARY: *Bye, Sally. Sorry we can't talk more. Look me up when you're in town.*

Look out! AND **Watch out!** Be careful.; Be aware of the danger near you! □ *Bob saw the scenery starting to fall on Tom. "Look out!" he cried.* □ *"Watch out! That sidewalk is really slick with ice!" warned Sally.*

look under the hood to examine the engine of a car; to check the oil and water associated with the engine of a car. □ *I finished putting gas in. I need to look under the hood.* □ *Do you want me to look under the hood, sir?*

Look who's here! an expression drawing attention to someone present at a place. □ BILL: *Look who's here! My old friend Fred. How goes it, Fred?* FRED: *Hi, there, Bill! What's new?* BILL: *Nothing much.* □ BILL: *Look who's here!* MARY: *Yeah. Isn't that Fred Morgan?*

Look who's talking! You are guilty of doing what you have criticized someone else for doing or accused someone else of doing. □ ANDREW: *You criticize me for being late! Look who's talking! You just missed your flight!* JANE: *Well, nobody's perfect.* □ MARY: *You just talk and talk, you go on much too long about practically nothing, and you never give a chance for anyone else to talk, and you just don't know when to stop!* SALLY: *Look who's talking!*

Looking good. AND **Lookin' good.** Someone is doing well.; Things are progressing nicely. □ A: *Our project is halfway completed and beginning to take shape.* B: *Sure is. Lookin' good, chum. Keep up the good work.* □ *Nice work, Sally. Looking good. Glad you'll finish on time.*

Looks like something the cat dragged in. Go to (Someone) looks like something the cat dragged in.

Loose lips sink ships. Idle talk can reveal secret or privileged information. (From a World War II slogan, which was more literal.) □ *Okay, people. We're going to be working on a top secret project that management wants to present to the board. This is not to be discussed with anyone else inside the company and, of course, no one on the outside. Remember: "Loose lips sink ships."* □ *Now keep this quiet. Not a word to anyone. Loose lips sink ships, as they used to say.*

Lord knows I've tried. I certainly have tried very hard. □ ALICE: *Why don't you get Bill to fix this fence? MARY: Lord knows I've tried. I must have asked him a dozen times—this year alone.* □ SUE: *I can't seem to get to class on time. RACHEL: That's just awful. SUE: Lord knows I've tried. I just can't do it.*

lose one's **train of thought** to forget what one was talking about. □ ANDREW: *I had something important on my mind, but that telephone call made me lose my train of thought. MARY: Did it have anything to do with money, such as the money you owe me? ANDREW: I can't remember.* □ TOM: *Now, let's take a look at, uh. Well, next I want to talk about something that is very important. MARY: I think you lost your train of thought. TOM: Don't interrupt. You'll make me forget what I'm saying.*

Lots of luck! I wish you luck, and you will need it, but it probably will not do any good. □ BILL: *I'm going to try to get my tax bill lowered. TOM: Lots of luck!* □ MARY: *I'll go in there and get him to change his mind, you just watch! SALLY: Lots of luck!*

Love it! Go to (I) love it!

Lovely weather for ducks. a greeting phrase meaning that this unpleasant rainy weather must be good for something. □ BILL: *Hi, Bob. How do you like this weather? BOB: Lovely weather for ducks.* □ SALLY: *What a lot of rain! TOM: Yeah. Lovely weather for ducks. Don't care for it much myself.*

lucky for you 1. a phrase usually introducing a description of an event that favors the person being spoken to. □ ANDREW: *Lucky for you the train was delayed. Otherwise you'd have to wait till tomorrow morning for the next one. FRED: That's luck, all right. I'd hate to have to sleep in the station.* □ JANE: *I hope I'm not too late. SUE: Everyone else is late too, lucky for you.* **2.** (Usually **Lucky for you!**) You are fortunate. (An independent sentence in this sense. Sometimes sarcastic.) □ A: *Wow, I just got a big check in the mail from my grandmother! B: Lucky for you!* □ TOM: *I am the only one who passed the test. BILL: Lucky for you!*

lull before the storm a quiet period just before a period of great activity or excitement. □ *It was very quiet in the cafeteria just before the students came in for lunch. It was the lull before the storm.* □ *In the brief lull before the storm, the clerks prepared themselves for the doors to open and bring in thousands of shoppers.*

Ma'am? 1. Did you call me, ma'am? (Said to a woman.) □ MOTHER: *Tom!* TOM: *Ma'am?* MOTHER: *Come take out the garbage.* TOM: *Yuck!* □ DOCTOR: *Now, Bill, I need you to do something for me.* BILL: *Ma'am?* DOCTOR: *Stick out your tongue.* **2.** Will you please repeat what you said, ma'am? □ SALLY: *Bring it to me, please.* BILL: *Ma'am?* SALLY: *Bring it to me.* □ *Uncle Fred turned his good ear to the clerk and said, "Ma'am?"*

Make a lap. Sit down. (Slang.) □ ANDREW: *Hey, you're in the way, Tom! Make a lap, why don't you?* TOM: *Sorry.* □ RACHEL: *Come over here and make a lap. You make me tired, standing there like that.* JOHN: *You just want me to sit by you.* RACHEL: *That's right.*

Make it fast. Hurry up and tell me what you have to say.; Do it quickly. □ A: *I have to stop at the rest room on the way.* B: *Make it fast.* □ Q: *Do you mind if I stop here for a smoke?* A: *Just make it fast.*

Make it snappy! Hurry up!; Move quickly and smartly. □ ANDREW: *Make it snappy! I haven't got all day.* BOB: *Don't rush me.* □ MARY: *Do you mind if I stop here and get some film?* BOB: *Not if you make it snappy!* MARY: *Don't worry. I'll hurry.*

make it (to something**)** to manage to attend something; to manage to attend some event. □ *"I'm sorry," said Mary, "I won't be able to make it to your party."* □ RACHEL: *Can you come to the rally on Saturday?* ANDREW: *Sorry. I can't make it.*

Make it two. I wish to order the same thing that someone else just ordered. (Said to food or drink service personnel.) □ BILL *(speaking to the waiter): I'll have the roast chicken.* MARY: *Make it two.* □ WAITER: *Would you like something to drink?* TOM: *Just a beer.* WAITER *(turning to Mary): And you?* MARY: *Make it two.*

Make mine something. I wish to have something. (The *something* can be a particular food or drink, a flavor of a food, a size of a garment, or a type of almost anything. Most typically used for food or drink.) □ BILL: *I want some pie. Yes, I'd like apple.* TOM: *Make mine cherry.* □ WAITER: *Would you care for some dessert? The ice cream is homemade.* TOM: *Yes, indeed. Make mine chocolate.*

Make my day! Go to (Go ahead,) make my day!

Make no mistake (about it)! Do not be mistaken! □ SALLY: *I'm very angry with you! Make no mistake about it!* FRED: *Whatever it's about, I'm sorry.* □ CLERK: *Make no mistake, this is the finest carpet available.* SALLY: *I'd like something a little less fine, I think.*

Make up your mind. AND **Make your mind up.** Please make a decision.; Please choose. □ HENRY: *I don't have all day. Make up your mind.* RACHEL: *Don't rush me.* □ MARY: *I'm not sure I want to go.* BOB: *Make your mind up. We have to catch the plane.*

Make your mind up. Go to Make up your mind.

Make yourself at home. Please make yourself comfortable in my home. (Also a signal that a guest can be less formal.) □ ANDREW: *Please come in and make yourself at home.* SUE: *Thank you. I'd like to.* □ BILL: *I hope I'm not too early.* BOB: *Not at all. Come in and make yourself at home. I've got a few little things to do.* BILL: *Nice place you've got here.*

Makes me no difference. Go to (It) makes no difference to me.

Makes me no nevermind. Go to (It) makes no difference to me.

Makes no difference to me. Go to (It) makes no difference to me.

Makes no nevermind to me. Go to (It) makes no difference to me.

man up to do the honorable and responsible thing; to exhibit manly courage to overcome fears of the negative consequences of doing the right thing. □ *Come on, you guys gotta man up! Who put the snake in Private Klinger's footlocker?* □ *Well, I guess I have to man up and take over responsibility for the entire incident.*

may as well (do something) Go to **might as well** (do something).

May I help you? Go to How may I help you?

May I speak to someone? Go to Could I speak to someone?

Maybe some other time. AND **We'll try again some other time.** a polite phrase said by a person whose invitation has just been turned down by another person. □ *BILL: Do you think you can come to the party? BOB: I'll have to beg off. I have another engagement. BILL: Maybe some other time.* □ *JOHN: Can you and Alice come over this Friday? BILL: Gee, sorry. We have something else on. JOHN: We'll try again some other time.*

Me neither. Also not me. □ *TOM: I definitely am not going. BOB: Me neither.* □ *A: There is no way I'm going to do this. B: Me neither.*

might as well (do something**)** AND **may as well (**do something**) 1.** a phrase indicating that it is probably better to do something than not to do it. □ *BILL: Should we try to get there for the first showing of the film? JANE: Might as well leave now. Nothing else to do.* □ *Might as well keep the gift. We can't return it.* **2.** (Usually **Might as well.; May as well.**) Yes, it will be done.; Yes, do it. (A reluctant yes, in answer to a question.) □ *Q: It's late. Time for bed. Should I put the cat out? A: Might as well.* □ *Q: Should I carry this crate out to the garage? I keep tripping over it. A: May as well.*

Might be better. Go to (Things) could be better.

Mind if I do something**?** Go to (Do you) mind if I do something?

Mind if I join you? Go to Could I join you?

Mind your manners. Go to Remember your manners.

Mind your own business. AND **Get your nose out of my business.; Keep your nose out of my business.** Stop prying into my affairs. (Not at all polite. The expressions with *get* and *keep* can have the literal meanings of removing and keeping removed.) □ *ANDREW: This is none of your affair. Mind your own business. SUE: I was only trying to help.* □ *BOB: How much did you pay in federal taxes last year? JANE: Good grief, Bob! Keep your nose out of my business!* □ *TOM: How much did it cost? SUE: Tom! Get your nose out of my business!* □ *"Hey!" shrieked Sally, jerking the checkbook out of Sue's grasp. "Get your nose out of my business!"*

Minding my own business. Go to (I'm just) minding my own business.

more and more an increasing amount; additional amounts. □ *As I learn more and more, I see how little I know.* □ *Dad seems to be smoking more and more lately.*

more or less somewhat. (Used to express vagueness or uncertainty.) □ *HENRY: I think this one is what I want, more or less. CLERK: A* *very wise choice, sir.* □ HENRY: *Is this one the biggest, more or less?* JOHN: *Oh, yes. It's the biggest there is.*

More power to you! Well done!; You really stood up for yourself!; You really did something for your own benefit! (The stress is on *to*, and the *you* is usually "ya.") □ BILL: *I finally told her off, but good.* BOB: *More power to you!* □ SUE: *I spent years getting ready for that job, and I finally got it.* MARY: *More power to you!*

more than you('ll ever) know a great deal, more than you suspect. □ BOB: *Why did you do it?* BILL: *I regret doing it. I regret it more than you know.* □ JOHN: *Oh, Mary, I love you.* MARY: *Oh, John, I love you more than you'll ever know.*

Morning. Go to (Good) morning.

(Most) folks (around here) call me name. My name is *my name.*; I go by the name of *my name.* (Rural or folksy. Also in other persons.) □ *Folks call me Travis.* □ *Most folks around here call me Darrell. What's your name?*

Much obliged. Thank you.; I am obligated to you for your assistance. □ A: *Thank you, and here's five dollars for your trouble.* B: *Much obliged.* □ *Thanks for helping me get my truck out of the mud. I'm much obliged.*

Mum's the word. No one will be told (this secret). □ BOB: *I hope you won't tell all this to anyone.* BILL: *Don't worry. Mum's the word.* □ *"Mum's the word," said Jane to ease Mary's mind about the secret.*

Must be running along. Go to (I) must be running along.

my a sentence opener expressing a little surprise or amazement. (See also My(, my). Words such as this often use intonation to convey the connotation of the sentence that is to follow. The brief intonation pattern accompanying the word may indicate sarcasm, disagreement, caution, consolation, sternness, etc.) □ *"My, what a nice place you have here," said Gloria.* □ RACHEL: *My, it's getting late!* JOHN: *Gee, the evening is just beginning.* □ *"My, it's hot!" said Fred, smoldering.*

My bad. Sorry, it's my fault. □ DON: *Who left the door unlocked?* HANNA: *I did. My bad.* □ ANDREW: *My bad. I won't do it again.*

(My) goodness (gracious)! a general expression of interest or mild amazement. □ BILL: *My goodness! The window is broken!* ANDREW: *I didn't do it!* BILL: *Who did, then?* □ *"Goodness! I'm late!" said*

Kate, glancing at her watch. □ *"Goodness gracious! Are you hurt?" asked Sue as she helped the fallen student to his feet.*

(My) hand to God! I pledge that what I am saying is the truth. (Refers to raising one hand as when taking an oath.) □ *Q: Is there something wrong with her? A: No. I saw her standing right there on the corner with no shoes on! Hand to God!* □ *Hand to God! I've never seen him before in my life!*

(My) heavens! a mild exclamation of surprise or amazement. □ BILL: *Heavens! The clock has stopped.* BOB: *Don't you have a watch?* □ SALLY: *The police are parked in our driveway, and one of them is getting out!* MARY: *My heavens!*

My house is your house. AND **Our house is your house.** a polite expression said to make a guest feel at home. (From the Spanish phrase *Mi casa, su casa*.) □ BILL: *Hello, Tom.* TOM *(entering): So nice you can put me up for the night.* BILL: *My house is your house. Make yourself at home.* □ MARY: *Come in, you two.* BILL: *Thanks.* SUE: *Yes, thank you.* MARY: *Well, what can I get you? My house is your house.*

(My,) how time flies. 1. Time has gone by quickly, and it is now time for me to go. □ BILL: *Look at the clock!* MARY: *How time flies! I guess you'll be going.* TOM: *Oh, no. I just noticed that it's time for the late show on television.* □ JOHN: *My watch says it's nearly midnight. How time flies!* JANE: *Yes, it's late. We really must go.* **2.** Time passes quickly. (Said especially when talking about how children grow and develop.) □ *"Look at how big Billy is getting," said Uncle Michael. "My, how time flies."* □ TOM: *It seems it was just yesterday that I graduated from high school. Now I'm a grandfather.* MARY: *My, how time flies.*

My lips are sealed. I will tell no one this secret or this gossip. □ MARY: *I hope you don't tell anyone about this.* ALICE: *Don't worry. My lips are sealed.* □ BOB: *Don't you dare tell her I told you.* BILL: *My lips are sealed.*

My(, my). an expression of mild surprise or interest. (See also **my.**) □ FRED: *My, my! How you've grown, Bill.* BILL: *Of course! I'm a growing boy. Did you think I would shrink?* □ DOCTOR: *My, my, this is interesting.* JANE: *What's wrong?* DOCTOR: *Nothing that a little exercise won't fix.*

my one and only my spouse, fiancé, girlfriend, boyfriend, or other romantically special person. (See also the **one and only,** someone.) □ *Fred, meet my one and only, Sally Orpington.* □ *I'll meet you at the stadium. I have to stop and pick up my one and only.*

My pleasure. 1. You're welcome.; It is my pleasure to do so. (From *It's my pleasure.* There is a stress on both words.) □ *MARY: Thank you for bringing this up here. BILL: My pleasure.* □ *JANE: Oh, doctor, you've really helped Tom. Thank you so much! DOCTOR: My pleasure.* **2.** Happy to meet you.; Happy to see you. □ *SALLY: Bill, meet Mary, my cousin. BILL: My pleasure.* □ *BILL: Good to see you again. MARY: My pleasure.*

My sentiments exactly. You have just said what I was thinking.; I agree completely. □ *DAN: We generally spend too much time talking and not enough time doing! ANDY: My sentiments exactly.* □ *IDA: I think Tom is too silly for words. HELEN: My sentiments exactly.*

My way or the highway. Go to (**It's**) **my way or the highway.**

My word! Goodness gracious! (A mild oath or exclamation.) □ *My word! He actually arrived on time for work!* □ *My word! A hole in one! This is only my second round of golf in my entire life.*

N

Name your poison. Go to What'll it be?

need I remind you that a phrase that introduces a reminder. (A little haughty or parental.) □ BILL: *Need I remind you that today is Friday?* BOB *(sarcastically): Gee, how else would I have known?* □ JOHN: *Need I remind you that you must return immediately?* JANE: *Sorry, I forgot.*

Need I say more? Is it necessary for me to say any more? □ MARY: *There's grass to be mowed, weeds to be pulled, dishes to be done, carpets to be vacuumed, and there you sit! Need I say more?* TOM: *I'll get right on it.* □ *"This project needs to be finished before anyone sleeps tonight," said Alice, hovering over the office staff. "Need I say more?"*

need something **like a hole in the head** not to need something at all. (Informal.) □ *I need a housecat like I need a hole in the head!* □ *She needs a car like she needs a hole in the head.*

need something **yesterday** to require something in a very big hurry. (Informal.) □ *Yes, I'm in a hurry! I need it yesterday!* □ *When do I need it? Now! Now! No, I need it yesterday!*

need to make a pit stop to have to go to the toilet. (From auto racing, where a car makes a stop at a crew *pit*—from *grease pit*—for servicing.) □ ANDY: *Hey, Dad. When do we stop next? I really gotta go.* FATHER: *I need to make a pit stop too. We'll try the next exit ramp.* □ *Anybody need to make a pit stop? This is your last chance. There are no more rest stops until we get to the other side of the city.*

Neither can I. I cannot do that either. □ BILL: *No matter what they do to them, I just can't stand sweet potatoes!* BOB: *Neither can I.* □ JOHN: *Let's go. I cannot tolerate the smoke in here.* JANE: *Neither can I.*

Neither do I. I do not do that either. □ *BILL: No matter what they do to them, I just don't like sweet potatoes! BOB: Neither do I.* □ *JANE: I really don't like what the city council is doing. FRED: Neither do I.*

Never been better. Go to (I've) never been better.

Never felt better. Go to (I've) never been better.

Never heard of such a thing. Go to (I) never heard of such a thing.

Never hurts to ask. Go to (It) doesn't hurt to ask.

Never in a thousand years! Go to Not in a thousand years!

Never mind! Forget it!; It's not important! □ *SALLY: What did you say? JANE: Never mind! It wasn't important.* □ *JOHN: I tried to get the book you wanted, but they didn't have it. Shall I try another store? MARY: No, never mind. JOHN: I'd be happy to give it a try.*

Never thought I'd see you here! Go to (I) never thought I'd see you here!

Never would have guessed. Go to (I) never would have guessed.

Next question. That is settled, so let's move on to something else. (Usually a way of evading further discussion.) □ *MARY: When can I expect this construction noise to stop? BOB: In about a month. Next question.* □ *BILL: When will the board of directors raise the dividend again? MARY: Oh, quite soon. Next question.*

Nice call! Go to Good call!

Nice going! AND **Good job!; Nice job! 1.** That was done well. □ *JOHN: Well, I'm glad that's over. SALLY: Nice going, John! You did a good job.* □ *TOM: Nice job, Bill! BILL: Thanks, Tom!* **2.** That was done poorly. (Sarcastic.) □ *FRED: I guess I really messed it up. BILL: Nice job, Fred! You've now messed us all up! FRED: Well, I'm sorry.* □ *"Nice going," frowned Jane, as Tom upset the bowl of potato chips.*

Nice job! Go to Nice going!

Nice place you have here. Your home is nice. (A compliment paid by a guest. The word *place* might be replaced with *home, house, room, apartment,* etc.) □ *Jane came in and looked around. "Nice place you have here," she said.* □ *BOB: Come in. Welcome. MARY: Nice place you have here. BOB: Thanks. We like it.*

Nice talking to you. Go to (It's been) good talking to you.

Nice to be here. Go to (It's) good to be here.

Nice to have you here. Go to (It's) good to have you here.

Nice to meet you. Go to (It's) nice to meet you.

Nice to see you. Go to (It's) nice to see you.

Nice weather we're having. 1. Isn't the weather nice? (Sometimes used to start a conversation with a stranger.) □ BILL: *Nice weather we're having.* BOB: *Yeah. It's great.* □ *Mary glanced out the window and said to the lady sitting next to her, "Nice weather we're having."* **2.** Isn't this weather bad? (A sarcastic version of sense 1.) □ BILL: *Hi, Tom. Nice weather we're having, huh?* TOM: *Yeah. Gee, it's hot!* □ MARY: *Nice weather we're having!* SALLY: *Sure. Lovely weather for ducks.*

Night. Go to Good night.

Nighty-night. Good night. (As said to a child.) □ FATHER: *Nighty-night, Bill.* BILL: *Catch you later, Pop.* □ *The mother smiled at the tiny sleeping form and whispered, "Nighty-night, little one."*

No big deal! Not a big problem! (Informal.) □ *It didn't hurt. No big deal!* □ *It isn't a problem. No big deal!*

No can do. I cannot do it. (The opposite of Can do.) □ BOB: *Can you do this now?* SALLY: *Sorry. No can do.* □ FRED: *Will you be able to fix this, or do I have to buy a new one?* ALICE: *No can do. You'll have to buy one.*

No chance. Go to (There is) no chance.

No comment. I have nothing to say on this matter. □ Q: *When did you stop beating your dog?* A: *No comment.* □ Q: *Georgie, did you chop down the cherry tree?* A: *No comment.*

no doubt a transitional or interpretative phrase strengthening the rest of a previous sentence. □ SUE: *Mary is giving this party for herself?* RACHEL: *Yes. She'll expect us to bring gifts, no doubt.* □ MARY: *All this talk about war has my cousin very worried.* SUE: *No doubt. At his age, I don't wonder.*

No doubt about it. Go to (There is) no doubt about it.

No fair! That isn't fair! □ BILL: *No fair! You cheated!* BOB: *I did not!* □ *"No fair," shouted Tom. "You stepped over the line!"*

No harm done. It is all right. No one or nothing has been harmed. (Informal.) □ *It's okay. No harm done.* □ A: *I am sorry I stepped on your toe.* B: *No harm done.*

No kidding! 1. You are not kidding me, are you? (An expression of mild surprise.) □ *Jane: I got elected vice president. Bill: No kidding! That's great!* **2.** Everyone already knows that! Did you just find that out? (Sarcastic.) □ *Sue: It looks like taxes will be increasing. Tom: No kidding! What do you expect?* □ *Alice: I'm afraid I'm putting on a little weight. Jane: No kidding!*

No lie? You are not lying, are you? □ *Bill: A plane just landed on the interstate highway outside of town! Tom: No lie? Come on! It didn't really, did it? Bill: It did too! Tom: Let's go see it!* □ *Bob: I'm going to take a trip up the Amazon. Sue: No lie?*

No more than I have to. an answer to the greeting question "What are you doing?" □ *Bob: Hey, Fred. What you been doing? Fred: No more than I have to.* □ *Sue: Hi, Bill. How are you? Bill: Okay. What have you been doing? Sue: No more than I have to.*

No need (to). Go to (There is) no need (to).

No news is good news. Hearing nothing (about a matter) indicates that all is well. □ *Don: Has anyone heard anything about the results of the storm? Was anyone injured? Hanna: Not yet. In this case, no news is good news.* □ *Somebody tell me! Have they accepted my proposal? Why are they taking so long? No news is good news, but is no news good for me or them?*

No, no, a thousand times no! Very definitely, no! (Jocular.) □ *Bob: Here, have some sweet potatoes. Bill: No, thanks. Bob: Oh, come on! Bill: No, no, a thousand times no!* □ *Sue: The water is a little cold, but it's great. Come on in. Bill: How cold? Sue: Well, just above freezing, I guess. Come on in! Bill: No, no, a thousand times no!*

No offense meant. I did not mean to offend by what I just said, did, or implied. (A formulaic way of asking for pardon or forgiveness. See No offense taken.) □ *Sorry. I know that sounded rude. No offense meant.* □ *Jan: That perfume's a little strong. Oops. No offense meant. Maria: No offense taken.*

No offense taken. I was not offended by what was just said, done, or implied. (A formulaic way of assuring someone that one was not offended by something. See No offense meant.) □ *Don't worry. No offense taken.* □ *Q: No offense meant. Are we still friends? A: No offense taken. Of course, we're friends!*

No pain, no gain. Efforts to achieve something will probably result in some kind of pain, usually physical. □ *Keep working those leg* *muscles if you want to build up your stamina. Yes, it hurts! No pain, no gain.* □ *I know you've been working almost every night on this campaign, and that's not going unnoticed. You are definitely proving yourself. Keep plugging along, even if it is a burden. No pain, no gain.*

No point in doing something. Go to (There's) no point in doing something.

No problem. Go to (That causes) no problem.

No problem with that. Go to (I have) no problem with that.

No rest for the wicked. Go to (There's) no rest for the wicked.

No siree(, Bob)! Absolutely no! (Not necessarily said to a male.) □ BILL: *Do you want to sell this old rocking chair?* JANE: *No siree, Bob!* □ BILL: *You don't want sweet potatoes, do you?* FRED: *No siree!*

No skin off my nose. Go to (That's) no skin off my nose.

No skin off my teeth. Go to (That's) no skin off my nose.

No such luck. No, and only luck could provide the positive outcome you envision. □ *A: Well, I guess that by now you should have completed your degree and are gainfully employed. B: No such luck.* □ *Q: Can you get a car to take us out Sunday night? A: No such luck.*

No such thing as a free lunch. Go to (There's) no such thing as a free lunch.

No sweat. (That causes) no problem.; There is no difficulty. (Slang or colloquial.) □ TOM: *I'm sorry I'm late.* MARY: *No sweat. We're on a very flexible schedule.* □ BILL: *Thanks for carrying this up here.* BOB: *No sweat. Glad to help.*

No, thank you. AND **No, thanks.** a phrase used to decline an offer of something. □ BOB: *Would you care for some more coffee?* MARY: *No, thank you.* □ JOHN: *Do you want to go downtown tonight?* JANE: *No, thanks.*

No, thanks. Go to No, thank you.

No thanks to you. I cannot thank you for what happened, because you did not cause it.; I cannot thank you for your help, because you did not give it. □ BOB: *Well, despite our previous disagreement, he seemed to agree to all our demands.* ALICE: *Yes, no thanks to you. I wish you'd learn to keep your big mouth shut!* □ JANE: *It looks like the picnic wasn't ruined despite the fact that I forgot the potato salad.* MARY: *Yes, it was okay. No thanks to you, of course.*

No trouble. Go to (It's) no trouble.

No way! No!; Absolutely not! □ *BILL: Will you take my calculus test for me? BOB: No way!* □ *BOB: You don't want any more sweet potatoes, do you? JANE: No way!*

No way, José! No! (Slang. An elaboration of *No. José* is pronounced with an initial *H*.) □ *BOB: Can I borrow a hundred bucks? BILL: No way, José!* □ *SALLY: Can I get you to take this nightgown back to the store for me and get me the same thing in a slightly smaller size? BOB: No way, José!*

No way to tell. Go to (There's) no way to tell.

None of your business! Go to (It's) none of your business!

None of your lip! Please don't complain or argue! □ *None of your lip! I've heard nothing but whining from you since we started out, and now you want to tell me how to drive!* □ *Shut up! None of your lip! Don't say another word!*

Nope. No. (Colloquial. The opposite of **Yup**.) □ *BOB: Tired? BILL: Nope.* □ *BILL: Are you sorry you asked about it? MARY: Nope.*

Not a chance! There is no chance at all that the event named will happen. (A variation of **(There is) no chance.**) □ *SALLY: Do you think our team will win today? MARY: Not a chance!* □ *JANE: Can I have this delivered by Saturday? CLERK: Not a chance!*

Not again! I cannot believe that it happened again! □ *MARY: The sink is leaking again. SALLY: Not again! MARY: Yes, again.* □ *FRED: Here comes Tom with a new girlfriend. SUE: Not again!*

Not always. a conditional negative response. □ *JOHN: Do you come here every day? JANE: No, not always.* □ *JOHN: Do you find that this condition usually clears up by itself? DOCTOR: Not always.*

Not anymore. The facts just mentioned are no longer true.; A previous situation no longer exists. □ *MARY: This cup of coffee you asked me to bring you looks cold. Do you still want it? SALLY: Not anymore.* □ *TOM: Do the Wilsons live on Maple Street? BOB: Not anymore.*

Not at all. a very polite response to **Thank you** or some other expression of gratitude. □ *JOHN: Thank you. JANE: Not at all.* □ *MARY: I want to thank you very much for all your help. SUE: Not at all. Happy to do it.*

Not bad. 1. It is quite satisfactory. □ BILL: *How do you like your new teacher? JANE: Not bad.* □ BOB: *Is this one okay? BILL: I guess. Yeah. Not bad.* **2.** It is really quite good. (The person or thing can be named, as in the examples.) □ JOHN: *How do you like that new car of yours? MARY: Not bad. Not bad at all.* □ TOM: *This one looks great to me. What do you think? SUE: It's not bad.*

Not by a long shot. Under no circumstances. (A negative characterization of one's appraisal of someone or something.) □ BILL: *Are you generally pleased with the new president? MARY: No, indeed, not by a long shot.* □ JOHN: *Do you find this acceptable? BILL: Good grief, no! Not by a long shot.*

Not for love nor money. Absolutely not!; No way! □ JOHN: *Would you be willing to drive through the night to get to Florida a day earlier? MARY: Not for love nor money!* □ JANE: *Someone needs to tell Sue that her favorite cat was just run over. Would you do it? BOB: Not for love nor money!*

Not for my money. Not as far as I'm concerned. (Has nothing to do with money or finance.) □ SUE: *Do you think it's a good idea to build all these office buildings in this part of the city? MARY: Not for my money. That's a real gamble.* □ JOHN: *We think that Fred is the best choice for the job. Do you think he is? MARY: Not for my money, he's not.*

not for publication not to be talked about openly; secret. □ *Please tell no one about this. It's not for publication.* □ *This report is not for publication, so keep the results to yourself.*

Not for the world! Absolutely not!; Not even if you gave me the world! □ *Q: Would you be able to work late on Friday evening? A: Not for the world!* □ TOM: *Can I ask you to loan my cousin's friend a hundred dollars until next month? ANN: Not for the world!*

Not half bad. Go to (It's) not half bad.

Not if I see you first. Go to Not if I see you sooner.

Not if I see you sooner. AND **Not if I see you first.** a jocular response to I'll see you later. (This means that you will not see me if I see you first, because I will avoid you.) □ TOM: *See you later. MARY: Not if I see you sooner.* □ JOHN: *Okay. If you want to argue, I'll just leave. See you later. MARY: Not if I see you first.*

Not in a thousand years! AND **Never in a thousand years!** No, never! □ *JOHN: Will you ever approve of her marriage to Tom? SUE: No, not in a thousand years!* □ *MARY: Will all this trouble ever subside? JOHN: Never in a thousand years!*

Not in my book. Not according to my views. (Compare to Not for my money.) □ *JOHN: Is Fred okay for the job, do you think? MARY: No, not in my book.* □ *SUE: My meal is great! Is yours a real winner? BOB: Not in my book.*

Not in this life! Never!; Not while I am still alive! □ *BOB: Now, we need someone to stay late and clean up after everyone and put all the tables and chairs away. Would you be willing to do that, Tom? TOM: Not in this life! I got a date afterward!* □ *I'm hoping to earn a million dollars by the time I'm thirty. I want to have two cars, a boat, a villa in Italy, and a fine collection of vintage wines. Can I do it? Not in this life!*

Not likely. That is probably not so. □ *MARY: Is it possible that you'll be able to fix this watch? SUE: Not likely, but we can always try.* □ *SALLY: Will John show up on time, do you think? BOB: Not likely.*

Not much. Go to Not (too) much.

Not on your life! No!; Absolutely not! □ *SALLY: Do you want to go downtown today? BILL: Not on your life! There's a parade this afternoon.* □ *SUE: I was cheated out of fifty dollars. Do you think I need to see a lawyer? JOHN: Not on your life! You'll pay more than that to walk through a lawyer's door.*

Not right now, thanks. No for the present. (It is hoped that one will be asked again later. Usually used for a temporary refusal of food or drink. There is an implication that more will be wanted later.) □ *WAITER: Do you want some more coffee? MARY: Not right now, thanks.* □ *JOHN: Can I take your coat? SUE: Not right now, thanks. I'm still a little chilly.*

not to mention someone or something even ignoring the mention of someone or something; additionally taking into account someone or something. □ *You have caused me a great deal of trouble. Not to mention the distress you have caused your aunt Octavia!* □ *Everyone was there. Fred, Mary, Jane, not to mention their children.*

Not supposed to. Go to (It's) not supposed to.

not to put too fine a point on it a phrase introducing a negative or controversial point. □ RACHEL: *Not to put too fine a point on it, Mary, but you're still acting a little rude to Tom.* MARY: *I'm sorry, but that's the way I feel.* □ JOHN: *I think, not to put too fine a point on it, you ought to do exactly as you are told.* ANDREW: *And I think you ought to mind your own business.*

Not to worry. Please do not worry. □ BILL: *The rain is going to soak all our clothes.* TOM: *Not to worry. I put them all in plastic bags.* □ SUE: *I think we're about to run out of money.* BILL: *Not to worry. I have some more traveler's checks.*

Not (too) much. a response to greeting inquiries into what one has been doing. □ JOHN: *What have you been doing?* MARY: *Not much.* □ SUE: *Been keeping busy? What are you up to?* BOB: *Not too much.* SUE: *Yeah. Me, too.*

Not under any circumstances. Go to Under no circumstances.

not worth mentioning 1. not important enough to require a comment. □ *There are others, but they are not worth mentioning.* □ *A small number of books hint at the phenomenon, but they aren't worth mentioning.* **2.** [of an error or wrong] not worth apologizing for. □ *This isn't a problem at all. It's not worth mentioning.* □ *No need to apologize to me. No harm done. It's not worth mentioning.*

not worth one's **while** not worth bothering with; not worth spending time on. □ *It's not worth my while to discuss it with you.* □ *Don't bother trying to collect money from them. It isn't worth your while.*

Nothing. 1. I did not say anything. □ MARY: *What did you say?* SUE: *Nothing.* □ TOM: *Did you have something to say? What do you want?* MARY: *Nothing.* **2.** a response to greeting inquiries into what one has been doing. □ BOB: *What you been doing?* MARY: *Nothing.* □ BILL: *What have you been up to?* MARY: *Nothing, really.*

Nothing doing! I will not permit it!; I will not participate in it! □ JOHN: *Can I put this box in your suitcase?* BILL: *Nothing doing! It's too heavy now.* □ SUE: *We decided that you should drive us to the airport. Do you mind?* JANE: *Nothing doing! I've got work to do.*

Nothing for me, thanks. I do not want any of what was offered. (Typically used to decline a serving of food or drink.) □ WAITER: *Would you care for dessert?* BOB: *Nothing for me, thanks.* □ BOB:

We have beer and wine. Which would you like? MARY: Nothing for me, thanks.

Nothing much. Not much.; Hardly anything.; Nothing of importance. □ *JOHN: Hey, man! How's by you? BOB: Hiya! Nothing much.* □ *BILL: What have you been doing? TOM: Nothing much.*

Nothing to complain about. Go to (I) can't complain.

Nothing to it! Go to (There's) nothing to it!

now a sentence opener having no specific meaning. (See also now, now. Words such as this often use intonation to convey the connotation of the sentence that is to follow. The brief intonation pattern accompanying the word may indicate sarcasm, disagreement, caution, consolation, sternness, etc.) □ *JOHN: I'm totally disgusted with you. BOB: Now, don't get angry!* □ *ANDREW: I'm fighting mad. Why did you do that? BILL: Now, let's talk this over.* □ *ANDREW: Now, try it again, slowly this time. SALLY: How many times do I have to rehearse this piece?* □ *FRED: Now, who do you think you are? TOM: Well, who do you think you are, asking me that question?*

now, now a calming and consoling phrase that introduces good advice. □ *"Now, now, don't cry," said the mother to the tiny baby.* □ *JANE: I'm so upset! ANDREW: Now, now, everything will work out all right.*

now then a sentence opener indicating that a new topic is being opened or that the speaker is getting down to business. (Expressions such as this often use intonation to convey the connotation of the sentence that is to follow. The brief intonation pattern accompanying the expression may indicate sarcasm, disagreement, caution, consolation, sternness, etc.) □ *"Now then, where's the pain?" asked the doctor.* □ *MARY: Now then, let's talk about you and your interests. BOB: Oh, good. My favorite subject.* □ *SUE: Now then, what are your plans for the future? ALICE: I want to become a pilot.* □ *"Now then, what did you have in mind when you took this money?" asked the police investigator.*

Now what? AND **What now?** What is going to happen now?; What kind of new problem has arisen? □ *The doorbell rang urgently, and Tom said, rising from the chair, "Now what?"* □ *BOB: There's a serious problem—sort of an emergency—in the mail room. SUE: What now? BOB: They're out of stamps or something silly like that.*

(Now,) where was I? I was interrupted, so please help me remember what I was taking about. (The emphasis is on *was*.) □ *Now, where was I? I think I lost my place.* □ *Q: Where was I? A: You had just described the War of 1812.*

Now you're cooking (with gas)! Now you are doing what you should be doing! □ *As Bob came to the end of the piece, the piano teacher said, "Now you're cooking with gas!"* □ *Tom (painting a fence): How am I doing with this painting? Any better? Jane: Now you're cooking. Tom: Want to try it?*

Now you're talking! Now you are saying the right things. □ *Tom: I won't put up with her behavior any longer. I'll tell her exactly what I think of it. Bill: Now you're talking!* □ *John: When I get back to school, I'm going to study harder than ever. Mother: Now you're talking!*

Of all the nerve! Go to What (a) nerve!

Of course. Yes.; Certainly!; For sure. □ SALLY: *Are you ready to go?* BOB: *Of course.* SALLY: *Then, let's go.* □ JANE: *Are you coming with us?* JOHN: *Of course. I wouldn't miss this for the world.* □ *"And you'll be there, of course?" asked Alice.* □ *"I would be happy to help, of course," confided Tom, a little insincerely.*

Of all things! How surprising! (With a sight sense of dismay.) □ JAN: *Did you hear that Fred and Mary sold their house and bought a small hotel in the Bahamas?* JOHN: *No. Of all things!* □ A: *Good grief! The stock market's crashed again!* B: *Of all things!*

off and running started and continuing. (Literal with racing.) □ A: *It's going to be a very busy day like all Saturdays. Everyone wants to shop on Saturday. So, I guess it's time to unlock the door and let them in.* B: *Okay, we're off and running.* □ *It's Monday morning, and we're off and running again.*

off the subject not concerned with the subject being discussed. □ *I got off the subject and forgot what I was supposed to be talking about.* □ *The speaker was off the subject, telling about his vacation in Hawaii.*

off the top of one's **head** Go to (right) off the top of one's head.

off to a flying start started and continuing to do well. □ A: *We started early this morning and are still going strong.* B: *Yes, we're off to a flying start. I hope we can continue at this pace.* □ *She's off to a flying start on her sales job. She has already sold her monthly quota in just one week.*

Oh, boy. 1. Wow! (Usually **Oh, boy!** An exclamation. It has nothing to do with boys.) □ BILL: *Oh, boy! An old-fashioned circus!* BOB: *So what?* □ *"Oh, boy!" shouted John. "When do we eat?"* **2.** I dread this.; This is going to be awful. □ *"Oh, boy," moaned Fred. "Here*

153

we go again." □ DOCTOR: *It looks like something fairly serious.* JANE: *Oh, boy.* DOCTOR: *But nothing modern medicine can't handle.*

Oh, sure (someone or something **will)!** a sarcastic expression implying that someone or something will not do something or that something will not happen as claimed. □ ANDREW: *Don't worry. I'll do it.* RACHEL: *Oh, sure you will! That's what you always say.* □ BOB: *I'll fix this fence the first chance I get.* MARY: *Oh, sure! When will that be? Next year?*

Oh, yeah? Is that what you think? (Rude and hostile.) □ TOM: *You're getting to be sort of a pest.* BILL: *Oh, yeah?* TOM: *Yeah.* □ BOB: *This sauce tastes bad. I think you ruined it.* BILL: *Oh, yeah? What makes you think so?* BOB: *My tongue tells me!*

OK. Go to Okay.

O.K. Go to Okay.

Okay. AND **OK.; O.K. 1.** Yes.; All right. □ JOHN: *Can we go now?* SUE: *Okay. Let's go.* □ MARY: *Can I have one of these?* FRED: *Okay.* MARY: *Thanks.* **2.** an expression indicating that the speaker accepts the current situation. (Not an answer to a question.) □ *"Okay, we're all here. Let's go now," said Tom.* □ BILL: *Okay, I can see the house now.* RACHEL: *This must be where we turn, then.* **3.** (usually **Okay?**) a question word asking if the person spoken to accepts the current situation. (Very close to sense 1.) □ BILL: *I'm going to turn here, okay?* RACHEL: *Sure. It looks like the right place.* □ ANDREW: *I'll take this one, okay?* MARY: *Yes, that's okay.*

Okay by me. Go to (That's) fine with me.

Okay with me. Go to (That's) fine with me.

on balance Go to all in all.

on the contrary a phrase disagreeing with a previous statement. □ TOM: *It's rather warm today.* BOB: *On the contrary, I find it too cool.* □ MARY: *I hear that you aren't too happy about my decision.* SUE: *On the contrary, I find it fair and reasonable.*

on the other hand a phrase introducing an alternate view. □ JOHN: *I'm ready to go; on the other hand, I'm perfectly comfortable here.* SALLY: *I'll let you know when I'm ready, then.* □ MARY: *I like this one. On the other hand, this is nice too.* SUE: *Why not get both?*

once and for all finally; permanently. □ SUE: *I'm going to get this place organized once and for all!* ALICE: *That'll be the day!* □ "We *need to get this straightened out once and for all," said Bob, for the fourth time today.*

once more AND **one more time** Please do it one more time. □ MARY: *You sang that line beautifully, Fred. Now, once more.* FRED: *I'm really tired of all this rehearsing.* □ JOHN *(finishing practicing his speech): How was that?* SUE: *Good! One more time, though.* JOHN: *I'm getting bored with it.*

the **one and only,** someone (announcing or presenting) someone famous or important. (Also used as sarcasm or exaggeration. See also **my one and only.**) □ *And now, without further ado, I give you the one and only, Mayor La Trivia!* □ *May I present to you the one and only, Joe Doaks, our favorite clerk.*

one final thing Go to **one final word.**

one final word AND **one final thing; one more thing** a phrase introducing a parting comment or the last item in a list. □ JOHN: *One final word: keep your chin up.* MARY: *Good advice!* □ SUE: *And one final thing: don't haul around a lot of expensive camera stuff. It just tells the thieves who to rob.* JOHN: *There are thieves here?* SUE: *Yeah. Everywhere.*

One moment, please. Please wait a minute.; Just a minute. □ JOHN: *Can you help me?* CLERK: *One moment, please. I will be with you shortly.* □ BILL *(answering the phone): Hello?* BOB: *Hello. Can I speak to Tom?* BILL: *One moment, please. (handing phone to Tom) It's for you.* TOM: *Hello, this is Tom.*

one more thing Go to **one final word.**

one more time Go to **once more.**

one way or another somehow. □ TOM: *Can we fix this radio, or do I have to buy a new one?* MARY: *Don't fret! We'll get it repaired one way or another.* □ JOHN: *I think we're lost.* ALICE: *Don't worry. We'll get there one way or another.*

open a conversation to start a conversation. □ *I tried to open a conversation with him, but he had nothing to say.* □ *She opened the conversation with an inquiry into my health, which got me talking about my favorite subject.*

or else or suffer the consequences. □ *Do what I tell you, or else.* □ *Don't be late for work, or else!*

or what? a way of adding emphasis to a yes-or-no question that the speaker has asked. (In effect, *if it wasn't what I said, what is it?*) □ *Bob: Now, is this a fine day or what? John: Looks okay to me.* □ *Tom: Look at Bill and Mary. Do they make a fine couple or what? Bob: Sure, they look great.*

or words to that effect or similar words meaning about the same thing. □ *John: It says right here in the contract, "You are expected to attend without fail," or words to that effect. Mary: That means I have to be there, huh? John: You got it!* □ *Sally: She said that I wasn't doing my job well, or words to that effect. Jane: Well, you ought to find out exactly what she means. Sally: I'm afraid I know.*

ought to be here any time Go to should be here any time.

Our house is your house. Go to My house is your house.

Out of the question. Go to (It's) out of the question.

Out, please. Please let me get out. (Said by someone trying to get out of an elevator. Compare to Coming through(, please.)) □ *The elevator stopped again, as it had at every floor, and someone said, "Out, please," as someone had said at every floor.* □ *Jane: Out, please. This is my floor. John: I'll get out of your way. Jane: Thanks.*

Over my dead body! a defiant phrase indicating the strength of one's opposition to something. (A joking response is "That can be arranged.") □ *Sally: Alice says she'll join the circus no matter what anybody says. Father: Over my dead body! Sally: Now, now. You know how she is.* □ *Bill: I think I'll rent out our spare bedroom. Sue: Over my dead body! Bill (smiling): That can be arranged.*

owing to something because of something; due to something. □ *Owing to the lateness of the evening, I must go home.* □ *We were late owing to the heavy traffic.*

P

Pardon (me). Go to Excuse me.

Pardon me for living! a very indignant response to a criticism or rebuke. □ *FRED: Oh, I thought you had already taken yourself out of here! SUE: Well, pardon me for living!* □ *TOM: Butt out, Mary! Bill and I are talking. MARY: Pardon me for living!*

Pardon my French. Excuse me for swearing or saying naughty words. □ *Pardon my French, but get that damn cat out of here!* □ *He slipped and fell on his butt, pardon my French.*

Perhaps a little later. Not now, but possibly later. □ *WAITER: Would you like your coffee now? BOB: Perhaps a little later. WAITER: All right.* □ *SALLY: Hey, Bill, how about a swim? BOB: Sounds good, but not now. Perhaps a little later. SALLY: Okay. See you later.*

Permit me. Go to Allow me.

pick and choose to choose very carefully from a number of possibilities; to be selective. □ *You must take what you are given. You cannot pick and choose.* □ *Jane is so beautiful. She can pick and choose from a whole range of suitors.*

pick the low-hanging fruit to do only the things that are easily done. □ *A: You're lazy, you know. There are lots of things to do around here, but you only pick the low-hanging fruit. B: Yes, I leave the challenges for others. It builds character, you know.* □ *Start out slowly. Look for customers who offer the least sales resistance. You know, pick the low-hanging fruit. Then get a little more aggressive.*

Please. 1. a response to a denial or refusal, essentially repeating the request. □ *BILL: Can I go to the picnic on the Fourth of July? MOTHER: No, you can't go to the picnic. BILL: Please!* □ *TOM: No, Bill. You can't have a raise. BILL: Please. I can hardly afford to live. TOM: You'll manage.* **2.** You go first.; Give yourself priority.; Attend to your interests first. □ *Bob stepped back and made a motion with* *his hand indicating that Mary should go first. "Please," smiled Bob.* □ MARY: *Do you mind if I take the last piece of cake?* BOB: *Please.* MARY: *Thanks.* **3.** (usually **Please!**) Please stop what you are doing!; Please do not do that!; Please do not say that! (Compare to **I beg your pardon.**) □ MARY: *You always make a mess wherever you go.* ALICE: *Please! I do not!* □ *Andrew kept bumping up against Mary in line. Finally Mary turned to him and said, "Please!"*

Please hold. Go to **Hold the wire(, please.)**

Pleased to meet you. Go to **(I'm) pleased to meet you.**

Plugging along. Go to **(I'm) (just) plugging along.**

point of view a way of thinking about something; [someone's] viewpoint; an attitude or expression of self-interest. □ *From my point of view, all this talk is a waste of time.* □ *I can understand her point of view. She has made some good observations about the problem.*

pose a question to ask a question; to imply the need for asking a question. □ *Genetic research poses many ethical questions.* □ *My interviewer posed a hypothetical question.*

Pretty good. I'm feeling good or well.; Things are going good or well. □ Q: *How are things going?* A: *Pretty good.* □ Q: *How are you doing?* A: *Pretty good.*

Pssst! Look here!; Give me your attention! (A soft sound made to attract someone's attention. See also **Ahem!**) □ *Pssst! Look over here. Pssst! Charlie!* □ LARRY (whispering): *Pssst! There's a telephone call for you. Take it in the hall, please.*

Pull up a chair. Please find a chair and sit down and join us. (Assumes that there is seating available. The speaker does not necessarily mean that the person spoken to actually has to move a chair.) □ TOM: *Well, hello, Bob!* BOB: *Hi, Tom. Pull up a chair.* □ *The three men were sitting at a table for four. Bob came up and said hello. Bill said, "Pull up a chair." Bob sat in the fourth chair at the table.*

Punch it! AND **Floor it! 1.** Press the accelerator to the floor! □ *Floor it! Let's get out of here. The cops are coming!* □ *Punch it, Fred. This thing ought to go faster than this.* **2.** Make something stronger and more aggressive! □ *You have to make this paragraph read more forcefully. Punch it! Really stress the three major points.* □ *I suggest* *that you put a lot more energy into your presentation. The substance is good, but you've really got to floor it to drive your points home.*

push back (against someone or something**)** to counter someone or something; to argue or fight back against someone or something. □ *Q: Do you think the president will push back against his critics? A: Probably not. It's just not his style.* □ *The author was fed up with reading reviews of his work that showed the reviewer had clearly not read the book. He decided to push back by writing an exposé of inept critics in general.*

put a cap on something to put a limit on something. □ *We need to put a cap on spending in every department.* □ *The city put a cap on the amount each landlord could charge.*

put a spin on something to twist a report or story to one's own advantage; to interpret an event to make it seem favorable or beneficial to one side of an issue. □ *The mayor tried to put a positive spin on the damaging polls.* □ *The pundit's spin on the new legislation was highly critical.*

put another way Go to to put it another way.

Put 'er there. Go to Put it there.

put in one's **two cents(' worth)** to add one's comments (to something). □ *Can I put in my two cents' worth?* □ *Sure, go ahead—put your two cents in.*

Put it anywhere. 1. Set down your burden anyplace that is convenient. (Literal.) □ *MARY: What shall I do with this? JANE: Oh, put it anywhere.* □ *TOM: Where does this lamp go, lady? SUE: Please put it anywhere. I'll move it later.* **2.** AND **Put it there.** Sit down anywhere. (Literally, place your buttocks anywhere. Colloquial and very familiar.) □ *TOM: Hi, Fred. Is there room for me here? FRED: Sure, man! Put it anywhere.* □ *BOB: Come in and set a spell. We'll have a little talk. JOHN: Nice place you've got here. BOB: Put it there, old buddy. How you been?*

Put it there. 1. Go to Put it anywhere. **2.** AND **Put 'er there.** Shake hands with me. (Literally, put your hand there, in mine. Colloquial. The apostrophe on 'er is not always used.) □ *BOB (extending his hand): Sounds great to me, old buddy. Put it there. FRED: Thanks, Bob. I'm glad we could close the deal.* □ *BOB: Good to see you, Fred. FRED: Put 'er there, Bob.*

put some teeth into something to increase the power of something. □ *The mayor tried to put some teeth into the new law.* □ *The statement is too weak. Put some teeth into it.*

put someone or something **to the test** to test someone or something to see how much can be achieved. □ *I think I can jump that far, but no one has ever put me to the test.* □ *I'm going to put my car to the test right now, and see how fast it will go.*

put someone's **nose out of joint** to offend someone; to cause someone to feel slighted or insulted. □ *I'm afraid I put his nose out of joint by not inviting him to the picnic.* □ *A: I'm really insulted! B: I didn't mean to put your nose out of joint. I meant no harm.*

put two and two together to figure something out from the information available. □ *Well, I put two and two together and came up with an idea of who did it.* □ *Don't worry. John won't figure it out. He can't put two and two together.*

quite a bit much; a lot. (Normally, a bit is a tiny amount.) □ *Hanna: How much of the cake flour will we use? Ida: I don't know exactly. Quite a bit, I think.* □ *I sprained my ankle, and it hurts quite a bit.*

Quite frankly Go to (Speaking) (quite) frankly.

rain on someone's **parade** to ruin someone's planned event; to spoil someone's plans or scheme. (Informal.) □ *I hate to rain on your parade, but the guest of honor cannot come to the reception.* □ *The boss rained on our parade by making us all work overtime.*

raised in a barn brought up to behave like a barnyard animal; behaving crudely. (Folksy.) □ *Close the door behind you! Were you raised in a barn?* □ *Don't wipe your nose on your sleeve. Were you raised in a barn?*

Reach out to someone. to approach someone in a friendly and non-threatening manner. □ *Don: I reached out to Fred, since he is so shy. Hanna: I hope he felt comfortable with your proposition.* □ *I reached out to my cousin, hoping to restore our former friendship.*

Read you loud and clear. Go to (I) read you loud and clear.

Ready for this? Go to (Are you) ready for this?

Ready to order? Go to (Are you) ready to order?

Really. 1. I agree with what you just said. □ *Rachel: This cake is just too dry. Mary: Really. I guess it's getting stale.* □ *Henry: Taxes are just too high. Mary: Really. It's out of hand.* **2.** (as a question, **Really?**) Do you really mean what you just said? □ *Henry: I'm going to join the army. Mary: Really? Henry: Yes, I'm really going to do it.* □ *Sally: This will cost over two hundred dollars. Rachel: Really? I paid half that the last time.* **3.** (usually **Really!**) I can't believe what has just been said or done.; I'm shocked. □ *Fred: Then I punched him in the nose. Henry: Really! Fred: Well, I had too. Henry: Really!* □ *"Really!" cried Sally, seeing the jogger bump the elderly lady.*

Really doesn't matter to me. Go to (It) (really) doesn't matter to me.

Really must go. Go to (I) really must go.

religious about doing something strict about doing something; conscientious about doing something. □ *Bob is religious about paying his bills on time.* □ *Max tries to be religious about being polite to everyone.*

Remember me to someone. Please carry my good wishes to someone. (The *someone* can be a person's name or a pronoun.) □ *Tom: My brother says hello. Bill: Oh, good. Please remember me to him. Tom: I will.* □ *Fred: Bye. John: Good-bye, Fred. Remember me to your Uncle Tom.*

Remember to write. AND **Don't forget to write. 1.** a final parting comment made to remind someone going on a journey to write to those remaining at home. □ *Alice: Bye. Mary: Good-bye, Alice. Remember to write. Alice: I will. Bye.* □ *Sally: Remember to write! Fred: I will! Sally: I miss you already!* **2.** a parting comment made to someone in place of a regular good-bye. (Jocular.) □ *John: See you tomorrow. Bye. Jane: See you. Remember to write.* □ *John: Okay. See you after lunch. Jane: Yeah. Bye. Remember to write.*

Remember your manners. 1. a parting instruction, usually to a child, encouraging proper behavior. □ *As Jimmy was going out the door, his mother said, "Have a good time and remember your manners."* □ *John: It's time for me to go to the party, Mom. Mother: Yes, it is. Remember your manners. Good-bye.* **2.** AND **Mind your manners.** a comment intended to remind someone of proper behavior, such as saying **Thank you** or **Excuse me.** □ *After Mary gave a cookie to little Bobby, Bobby's mother said to him, "Remember your manners."* □ *Bob: Here, Jane. Have one of these. Jane (taking one): Wow! Bob: Okay. Have another. Mother: What do you say? Remember your manners. Jane: Thanks a lot!*

The **rest is history.** Everyone knows the rest of the story that I am telling. □ *Bill: Then they arrested all the officers of the corporation, and the rest is history. Sue: Can't trust anybody these days.* □ *Bob: Hey, what happened between you and Sue? Bill: Finally we realized that we could never get along, and the rest is history.*

Right. Correct.; What you said is right. □ *Jane: It's really hot today. John: Right. Jane: Keeping cool? John: No way.* □ *Sally: Let's go over to Fred's room and cheer him up. Sue: Right.*

right away AND **right now** immediately. □ JOHN: *Take this over to Sue.* BILL: *Right away.* □ JOHN: *How soon can you do this?* SUE: *Right now.*

Right back at you. Go to (The) same to you.

right now. Go to right away.

(right) off the top of one's **head** without giving it too much thought or without the necessary knowledge. □ MARY: *How much do you think this car would be worth on a trade?* FRED: *Well, right off the top of my head, I'd say about a thousand.* □ TOM: *What time does the morning train come in?* BILL: *Off the top of my head, I don't know.*

Righto. Yes.; I will comply. □ FRED: *Can you handle this project for me today?* SUE: *Righto.* □ JOHN: *Is that you, Tom?* TOM: *Righto. What do you want?*

ring a bell (with someone**)** to cause someone to remember something; to awaken a memory in someone. □ HANNA: *I don't seem to recall the name of the gentleman standing near the punch bowl. Is he one of your guests?* DON: *Well, his face rings a bell, but I really don't have any idea who he is.* □ *Let's see. Cosmology. It rings a bell but I'm not sure what it is. Does it have anything to do with makeup?*

Rise and shine! Get out of bed and get going! (Like the sun.) □ FATHER: *Come on and get up, Andy. Rise and Shine! You've got to be at school by 7:30!* ANDY: *Dad, today is Saturday!* □ *Hey, Blanche. The alarm just went off. Rise and shine! Go make some coffee and call me when it's ready.*

Roger (wilco). Yes. (From aircraft radio communication. *Wilco* means "will comply.") □ JOHN: *Can you do this right now?* BOB: *Roger.* □ MARY: *I want you to take this over to the mayor's office.* BILL: *Roger wilco.*

the **royal treatment** very good treatment; very good and thoughtful care of a person. □ *I was well cared for. They gave me the royal treatment.* □ *A: Is that hotel worth the high rate?* B: *Yes, I had the royal treatment when I stayed there.*

Run it by (me) again. Go to Run that by (me) again.

run rampant to run, develop, or grow out of control. □ *The children ran rampant through the house.* □ *Weeds have run rampant around the abandoned house.*

Run that by (me) again. AND **Run it by (me) again.** Please repeat what you just said.; Please go over that one more time. (Slang.) □ *ALICE: Do you understand? SUE: No. I really didn't understand what you said. Run that by me again, if you don't mind.* □ *JOHN: Put this piece into the longer slot and the remaining piece into the slot on the bottom. SUE: Run that by again. I got lost just after* put. □ *MARY: Keep to the right, past the fork in the road, then turn right at the crossroads. Do you follow? JANE: No. Run it by me again.*

S

safe and sound Go to alive and well.

Sakes alive! Go to (Goodness) sakes alive!

The **same for me.** Go to I'll have the same.

Same here. Me, too.; I hold the same opinion.; I choose the same thing. □ *A: I'll have a slice of pie and coffee. B: Same here.* □ *BOB: I must express myself in no uncertain terms. I absolutely refuse to be involved in such a perplexing and annoying campaign. TOM: Same here.*

Same to ya. Go to (The) same to you.

(The) same to you. AND **Right back at you.; You too.** (Both are slangy, and the second is more cheeky than the first.) **1.** a polite way of returning good wishes to someone. □ *CLERK: Have a nice day. SALLY: The same to you.* □ *BOB: I hope things work out for you. Happy New Year! BILL: You too. Bye-bye.* □ *A: Merry Christmas, Fred. B: Right back at you, Bob.* **2.** (Usually **Same to ya.**) I return your criticism or epithet. (Slang. With the accent on *to*.) □ *TOM: You're such a pest! BILL: Same to ya!* □ *TOM: I hope you go out and fall in a hole! BILL: Same to you.* □ *A: Hey, Matt! You really stunk in your last gig! B: Right back at you, amateur!*

Save it! Stop talking!; Shut up! (Informal.) □ *I've heard enough. Save it!* □ *Save it! You talk too much!*

say a word used to catch someone's attention and announce that a sentence—probably a question—follows. (Words such as this often use intonation to convey the connotation of the sentence that is to follow. The brief intonation pattern accompanying the word may indicate sarcasm, disagreement, caution, consolation, sternness, etc.) □ *BOB: Say, don't I know you from somewhere? RACHEL: I hope not.* □ *"Say, why don't you stay on your side?" screamed Tom at the other boys.* □ *ANDREW: Say, where did I see* *that can opener?* RACHEL: *You saw it where you left it after you last used it.*

Say cheese! an expression used by photographers to get people to smile, which they must do while saying the word *cheese*. □ *"All of you please stand still and say cheese!" said the photographer.* □ *"Is everybody ready? Say cheese!" asked Mary, holding the camera to her face.*

say grace to say a prayer of gratitude before a meal. □ *Grandfather always says grace at Thanksgiving.* □ *A local preacher said grace at the banquet.*

Say hello to someone **(for me).** Please convey my good wishes to someone. (The *someone* can be a person's name or a pronoun. See also **Give my best to** someone.; **Remember me to** someone.) □ ANDREW: *Good-bye, Tom. Say hello to your brother for me.* TOM: *Sure. Bye, Andy.* □ SALLY: *Well, good-bye.* MARY: *Bye.* SALLY: *And say hello to Jane.* MARY: *Sure. Bye-bye.*

Say no more. I agree.; I will do it.; I concede, no need to continue talking. □ JOHN: *Someone ought to take this stuff outside.* BILL: *Say no more. Consider it done.* □ MARY: *Shouldn't we turn here if we plan to visit Jane?* ALICE: *Say no more. Here we go.*

Say what? What did you say?; Please repeat what you said. □ SALLY: *Would you like some more salad?* FRED: *Say what?* SALLY: *Salad? Would you like some more salad?* □ JOHN: *Put this one over there.* SUE: *Say what?* JOHN: *Never mind, I'll do it.*

Say when. Tell me when I have given you enough of something. (Usually a liquid. Sometimes answered with *When.*) □ TOM (*pouring milk into Fred's glass*): *Say when, Fred.* FRED: *When.* □ JOHN: *Do you want some more juice?* MARY: *Yes.* JOHN: *Okay. Say when.*

Says me! the contentious response to **Says who?** □ BILL: *I think you're making a mess of this project.* BOB: *Says who?* BILL: *Says me!* □ JOHN: *What do you mean I shouldn't have done it? Says who?* MARY: *Says me!*

Says who? Who do you think you are to say that? □ TOM: *Fred, you sure can be dumb sometimes.* FRED: *Says who?* TOM: *Says me!* □ BILL: *You take this dog out of here right now!* BOB: *Says who?* BILL: *Says me!*

Says you! It is just you who are saying that, so it does not matter. □ *BILL: I think you're headed for some real trouble. BOB: Says you!* □ *FRED: Says who? TOM: Says me! FRED: Aw, says you!*

scared silly frightened very much. □ *I was scared silly by the big explosion.* □ *We were scared silly to go into the park after dark.*

'Scuse (me). Go to Excuse me.

'Scuse me? Go to Excuse me?

'Scuse, please. Go to Excuse me.

Search me. I do not know.; You can search my clothing and my person, but you won't find the answer to your question anywhere near me. (Colloquial and not too polite. The two words have equal stress.) □ *JANE: What time does Mary's flight get in? SALLY: Search me.* □ *JOHN: What kind of paint should I use on this fence? BILL: Search me.*

See? Go to Don't you know?

See if I care! I do not care if you do it. □ *MARY: That does it! I'm going home to Mother! JOHN: See if I care!* □ *SUE: I'm putting the sofa here, whether you like it or not. BILL: Go ahead! See if I care!*

see someone **as** something to consider someone to be something; to picture someone as something. □ *The manager saw the skilled employee as a godsend.* □ *John saw the new salesman as a threat to his territory.*

See ya! Good-bye! (Colloquial.) □ *ANDREW: Good-bye, Tom, see ya! TOM: Bye. Take it easy.* □ *MARY: Bye, Jane! See you later. JANE: See ya!*

See ya, bye-bye. Bye. (Colloquial and slang.) □ *BILL: I have to be off. BOB: See ya, bye-bye.* □ *MARY: See ya, bye-bye. SUE: Toodle-oo.*

See you. Go to I'll see you later.

See you around. I will see you again somewhere. □ *BOB: Bye for now. JANE: See you around.* □ *TOM: See you around, Fred. FRED: Sure, Tom. See you.*

See you in a little while. Go to (I'll) see you in a little while.

(See you) later. Go to I'll see you later.

See you later, alligator. AND **Later, alligator.** Good-bye. (A natural mate to After while(, crocodile).) □ *BOB: See you later, alligator.*

JANE: *After while, crocodile.* □ Bob: *Bye, Tom.* Tom: *See you later, alligator.* Bob: *Later.*

See you next year. Go to (I'll) see you next year.

See you (real) soon. Go to (I'll) see you (real) soon.

See you soon. Go to (I'll) see you (real) soon.

See you then. Go to (I'll) see you then.

See you tomorrow. Go to (I'll) see you tomorrow.

Seen better. Go to (I've) seen better.

Seen worse. Go to (I've) seen worse.

selling like hotcakes selling very well. □ CLERK: *I'm glad we ordered those red shoes. They're selling like hotcakes.* □ CHEF: *The boysenberry pancakes are selling like hotcakes! We can hardly make them fast enough.*

send out the wrong signals AND **send** someone **the wrong signals** to signify something that is not true; to imply something that is not true. □ *I hope I haven't been sending out the wrong signals, but I do not really care to continue this relationship.* □ *Q: Are you really angry with me? A: Not really. Sorry, I guess I sent you the wrong signals. I'm just a little grouchy today.*

send someone **the wrong signals** Go to send out the wrong signals.

Seriously? AND **Honestly?** Do you really mean that? □ FATHER: *I got a raise today, but higher taxes will eat up almost all of it.* MOTHER: *Seriously? How can we ever expect to get ahead?* □ *Honestly? You really think you've finished this report? No way!*

set someone **straight** to make certain that someone understands something exactly. (Often said in anger or domination.) □ *Please set me straight on this matter. Do you or do you not accept the responsibility for the accident?* □ *I set her straight about who she had to ask for permission to leave early.*

sever ties with someone to end a relationship or an agreement suddenly. □ *The company severed ties with the embezzling employee.* □ *John has severed all ties with his parents.*

Shake it (up)! Hurry up!; Move faster!; Run faster! □ FRED: *Move it, Tom! Shake it up!* Tom: *I can't go any faster!* □ JANE: *Move, you guys. Shake it!* BILL: *Hey, I'm doing the best I can!*

Shake the lead out! Go to Get the lead out!

The **shame of it (all)!** That is so shameful!; I am so embarrassed. (Considerable use as a parody. Compare to **For shame!**) □ JOHN: *Good grief! I have a pimple! Always, just before a date.* ANDREW: *The shame of it all!* □ TOM: *John claims that he cheated on his taxes.* BILL: *Golly! The shame of it!*

Shame on you! a phrase scolding someone for being naughty. (Typically said to a child or to an adult for a childish infraction.) □ JOHN: *I think I broke one of your figurines.* MARY: *Shame on you!* JOHN: *I'll replace it, of course.* MARY: *Thanks, I sort of liked it.* □ *"Shame on you!" said Mary. "You should have known better!"*

Shape up or ship out! Do what is expected of you or get out!; Do better work or you'll be fired! (Naval or nautical.) □ HANNA: *I've spent about as much time as I want trying to train you to do the simplest tasks around here. I have had it! You're gonna have to shape up or ship out!* IDA: *You mean you're gonna fire me?* HANNA: *You got it!* □ *You guys are going to have to do better than what you are doing now. Shape up or ship out!*

share someone's **pain** to understand and sympathize with someone's pain or emotional discomfort. (Said in order to sound sympathetic.) □ *I am sorry about the loss of your home. I share your pain.* □ *We sympathize about the loss of your mother. We share your pain.*

share someone's **sorrow** to grieve as someone else grieves. □ *We all share your sorrow on this sad, sad day.* □ *I am sorry to hear about the death in your family. I share your sorrow.*

Shoot! Say what you have to say!; Ask your question! □ BOB: *Can I ask you a question?* BILL: *Sure. Shoot!* □ MARY: *There are a few things I want to say before we go on.* TOM: *Shoot!*

should be here any time AND **will be here any** time; **ought to be here any** time (The *time* = minute, moment, second.) □ Q: *Where's John?* A: *He should be here any minute.* □ *The plane should be here any moment.* □ *She's not late yet. She will be here any second.*

Shut up! Be quiet! (Impolite.) □ BOB: *And another thing.* BILL: *Oh, shut up, Bob!* □ ANDREW: *Shut up! I've heard enough!* BOB: *But I have more to say!* □ *"Shut up! I can't hear anything because of all your noise!" shouted the director.*

Shut up about it. Do not tell anyone about it. □ *BILL: I heard that you had a little trouble with the police. TOM: Just shut up about it! Do you hear?* □ *ANDREW: Didn't you once appear in a movie? ALICE: Shut up about it. No one has to know.*

Shut your face! Be quiet!; Shut up! (Rude.) □ *HENRY: Shut your face! I'm tired of your constant chatter. BOB: I didn't say a single word!* □ *MARY: You make me sick! SALLY: Shut your face!*

since time immemorial since a very long time ago. □ *A: We had our first local parade on Independence Day this year. B: My hometown has had a big parade on the Fourth of July since time immemorial.* □ *Since time immemorial, the trees have blossomed each spring.*

Since when? When was that decided?; That's news to me.; When was that done? □ *TOM: You've been assigned to the night shift. JOHN: Since when?* □ *JANE: Fred is now the assistant manager. BOB: Since when? JANE: Since I appointed him, that's when.*

Sir? 1. Did you call me, sir? (Said to a man.) □ *JOHN: Tom! TOM: Sir? JOHN: Get over here!* □ *FRED: Bill! BILL: Sir? Did you call me? FRED: Yes. Have a seat. I want to talk to you.* **2.** I did not hear what you said, sir. □ *JOHN: I want you to take this to Mr. Franklin. CHILD: Sir? JOHN: Please take this to Mr. Franklin.* □ *BOB: Can you wait on me? CLERK: Sir? BOB: Can you wait on me? CLERK: Oh, yes, sir.*

Skin me! Go to Give me five!

Skip it! Never mind!; Forget it! (Shows impatience or disappointment.) □ *JOHN: I need some help on this project. MARY: You've got to be kidding! JOHN: Oh, skip it!* □ *JANE: Will you be able to do this, or should I get someone with more experience? BOB: What did you say? JANE: Oh, skip it!*

Skoal! Go to Bottoms up.

Slip me five! Go to Give me five!

Slip me some skin! Go to Give me five!

slow going the rate of speed when one is making little progress. □ *It was slow going at first, but I was able to finish the project by the weekend.* □ *Getting the heavy rocks out of the field is slow going.*

slower and slower at a decreasing rate of speed; slow and then even slower. □ *The car is going slower and slower and will stop soon.* □ *The dog's breathing got slower and slower as it went to sleep.*

Smile when you say that. I will interpret that remark as a joke or as kidding. □ *JOHN: You're a real pain in the neck. BOB: Smile when you say that.* □ *SUE: I'm going to bop you on the head! JOHN: Smile when you say that!*

Snap it up! Hurry up! (Colloquial.) □ *JOHN: Come on, Fred. Snap it up! FRED: I'm hurrying! I'm hurrying!* □ *SALLY: Snap it up! You're going to make us late. JOHN: That's exactly what I had in mind.*

Snap to it! Move faster!; Look alert! □ *BILL: Snap to it! MARY: Don't rush me!* □ *JOHN: Get in line there. Snap to it! SALLY: What is this, the army? You just wait till I'm ready!*

So? Go to So (what)?

so 1. a sentence opener used to break a silence in a conversation or aggressively start a new topic. (Words such as this often use intonation to convey the connotation of the sentence that is to follow. The brief intonation pattern accompanying the word may indicate sarcasm, disagreement, caution, consolation, sternness, etc.) □ *ANDREW: So, I'm new around here. Where's the fun? BOB: You must be new. There's never been any fun around here.* □ *"So, how are you?" asked Kate.* □ *ANDREW: So, when do we eat? RACHEL: Don't you have any manners?* □ *BOB: So, what you been doing? BILL: Not much.* □ *ANDREW: So, been keeping busy? BOB: No. I been taking it easy.* **2.** a defensive sentence opener that takes an offensive tone. □ *FRED: So I made a mistake. So what? JOHN: It caused us all a lot of trouble. That's what.* □ *ALICE: So I'm not perfect! What does that prove? ANDREW: Nothing, I guess.*

So be it. That is the way it shall be.; It shall be as just described. □ *A: I really want you to complete this list of things even if you have to work through the night. B: So be it. But you had better pay me well.* □ *If that is the way you want us to remember you, so be it. But you shouldn't burn your bridges behind you.*

So do I. I do too. □ *MARY: I want some more cake. SALLY: So do I.* □ *BOB: I have to go home now. TOM: So do I. BOB: Bye.*

so mad I could scream very mad. □ *I am just so mad I could scream! Why is he such a jerk?* □ *She makes me so mad I could scream.*

So much for that. That is the end of that.; We will not be dealing with that anymore. □ *John tossed the stub of a pencil into the trash. "So much for that," he muttered, fishing through his drawer for* *another.* □ MOTHER: *Here, try some carrots.* CHILD *(brushing the spoon aside): No! No!* MOTHER: *Well, so much for that.*

So much the better. That is even better (than expected or desired). □ *Tom, if you decide to leave now and pick up Jean at the airport, so much the better. It will save a lot of time in the long run.* □ *A: She finally agreed to use the old ones rather than replace them. B: So much the better. The new ones are really cheaply made.*

so soon early; before the regular time; ahead of schedule. □ *I got there early because my bus arrived so soon.* □ *Because the meeting ended so soon, I had some extra time.*

so to speak AND **in a manner of speaking** a way of saying something and softening the impact of the words one used—at the same time. □ *I was so mad that I just kicked him in the butt, so to speak.* □ *Well, she was, his, ah, girlfriend, in a manner of speaking.*

So (what)? Why does that matter? (Colloquial or familiar. Can be considered rude.) □ BOB: *Your attitude always seems to lack sincerity.* MARY: *So what?* □ JOHN: *Your car sure is dusty.* SUE: *So?*

(So) what else is new? This isn't new. It has happened before.; Not this again. □ MARY: *Taxes are going up again.* BOB: *So what else is new?* □ JOHN: *Gee, my pants are getting tight. Maybe I'm putting on a little weight.* SALLY: *What else is new?*

Some people (just) don't know when to give up. Go to Some people (just) don't know when to quit.

Some people (just) don't know when to quit. AND **Some people (just) don't know when to give up. 1.** You, or someone being talked about, should stop doing something, such as talking, arguing, scolding, etc. (Often directed at the person being addressed rather than some people in general.) □ BILL: *I hate to say it again, but that lipstick is all wrong for you. It brings out the wrong color in your eyes, and it makes your mouth look larger than it really is.* JANE: *Oh, stop, stop! That's enough! Some people just don't know when to quit.* □ JOHN: *Those bushes out in the backyard need trimming.* SALLY: *You keep criticizing! Is there no end to it? Some people don't know when to quit!* **2.** Some people do not know when to slow down and stop working so hard. □ BOB: *We were afraid that John might have had a heart attack.* BILL: *I'm not surprised. He works so hard. Some people don't know when to quit.* □

173

JANE: *He just kept on gambling. Finally, he had no money left.*
SALLY: *Some people don't know when to quit.*

(Someone had) better keep quiet about it. Go to (Someone had) better keep still about it.

(Someone had) better keep still about it. AND **(Someone had) better keep quiet about it.** an admonition that someone ought not to tell about or discuss something. (The *someone* can stand for any person's name, any pronoun, or even the word *someone* meaning "you-know-who." If there is no *Someone had,* the phrase is a mild admonition to keep quiet about something.) □ MARY: *I saw you with Bill last night.* JANE: *You'd better keep quiet about it.* □ JANE: *Tom found out what you're giving Sally for her birthday.* BILL: *He had better keep quiet about it!*

(Someone) looks like something the cat dragged in. Someone looks rumpled or worn out. (Jocular. Compare to **Look (at) what the cat dragged in!**) □ ALICE: *Tom just came in. He looks like something the cat dragged in. What do you suppose happened to him?* □ RACHEL: *Wow! Did you see Sue?* JANE: *Yes. Looks like something the cat dragged in.*

(Someone or something is) supposed to (do something). Someone or something was meant to do something. (Frequently, in speech, *supposed* is reduced to *'sposed.* The words *someone* or *something* can be replaced with nouns or pronouns, or used themselves.) □ MARY: *They didn't deliver the flowers we ordered.* SUE: *Supposed to. Give them a call.* □ SALLY: *This screw doesn't fit into hole number seven in the way the instructions say it should.* BILL: *It's supposed to. Something's wrong.*

(Someone will) be with you in a minute. AND **With you in a minute.** Please be patient, someone will help you very soon. (The *someone* can be any person's name or a pronoun, typically *I.* If there is no one mentioned, *I* is implied. The *minute* can be replaced by *moment* or *second.*) □ SUE: *Oh, Miss?* CLERK: *Someone will be with you in a minute.* □ BILL: *Please wait here. I'll be with you in a minute.* BOB: *Please hurry.*

(Someone's) not supposed to. Go to (It's) not supposed to.

Something's got to give. Emotions or tempers are strained, and there is going to be an outburst. □ ALICE: *There are serious problems with Mary and Tom. They fight and fight.* SUE: *Yes, something's* *got to give. It can't go on like this.* □ BILL: *Things are getting difficult at the office. Something's got to give.* MARY: *Just stay clear of all the bickering.*

(somewhere) in the neighborhood of something approximately a particular measurement. □ *I take somewhere in the neighborhood of ten pills a day for my various ailments.* □ *My rent is in the neighborhood of $700 per month.*

Sooner than you think. Sooner rather than later. □ SALLY: *I'm going to have to stop pretty soon for a rest.* MARY: *Sooner than you think, I'd say. I think one of our tires is low.* □ TOM: *The stock market is bound to run out of steam pretty soon.* BOB: *Sooner than you think from the look of today's news.*

The **sooner the better.** The sooner something gets done, the better things will be. (A cliché.) □ BOB: *When do you need this?* MARY: *The sooner the better.* □ BOB: *Please get the oil changed in the station wagon. The sooner the better.* ALICE: *I'll do it today.*

Sorry. Go to (I'm) sorry.

Sorry (that) I asked. Now that I have heard the answer, I regret asking the question. □ ALICE: *Can we get a new car soon? The old one is a wreck.* JOHN: *Are you kidding? There's no way that we could ever afford a new car!* ALICE: *Sorry I asked.* □ *After he heard the long list of all the reasons he wouldn't be allowed to go to the concert, Fred just shrugged and said, "Sorry that I asked."*

Sorry to hear that. Go to (I'm) sorry to hear that.

Sorry you asked. Go to (I'm) sorry you asked (that). See also (Are you) sorry you asked?

Sorry you asked? Go to (Are you) sorry you asked?

Sort of. AND **Kind of.** Yes, but only to a small degree. □ BOB: *Do you like what you're doing in school?* ALICE: *Kind of.* □ HENRY: *What do you think about all these new laws? Do they worry you?* JOHN: *Sort of.*

sound like a broken record to say the same thing over and over. (From an earlier age when a crack in a 78 rpm record would cause the needle, or stylus, to stay in the same groove and play it over and over.) □ *He's always complaining about the way she treats him. He sounds like a broken record!* □ *I hate to sound like a broken* *record, but we just don't have enough people on the payroll to work efficiently.*

Sounds like a plan. Go to (It) sounds like a plan.

Soup's on! The meal is ready to eat. (Said for any food, not just soup.) □ *Tom: Soup's on! Bill: The camp chef has dished up another disaster. Come on, we might as well face the music.* □ *John: Soup's on! Come and get it! Mary: Well, I guess it's time to eat again. Sue: Yeah, no way to avoid it, I guess.*

spare someone something to exempt someone from having to listen to or experience something unwelcome. □ *I'll spare you the details and get to the point.* □ *Please, spare me the story and tell me what you want.*

speak ill of someone to say something bad about someone. □ *I refuse to speak ill of any of my friends.* □ *Max speaks ill of no one and refuses to repeat gossip.*

Speak of the devil. a phrase said when someone whose name has just been mentioned suddenly appears on the scene. (Compare to **We were just talking about you.**) □ *Tom: Speak of the devil, here comes Bill. Mary: We were just talking about you, Bill.* □ *John: I wonder how Fred is doing in his new job. Fred: Hi, you two. What's up? John: Speak of the devil. Look who's here!*

Speak up. Please speak more loudly.; Do not be shy—speak more loudly. □ *"Speak up. I can hardly hear you," said Uncle Henry, cupping his hand to his ear.* □ *Mary: I'm sorry. Teacher: Speak up. Mary: I'm sorry, ma'am. I won't do it again.*

Speaking. AND **This is** someone. I am the person you have just asked for (on the telephone). (The *someone* can be a person's name or *he* or *she*.) □ *Tom: Hello? Mary: Is Tom there? Tom: Speaking.* □ *Tom: Hello? Mary: Is Tom there? Tom: This is he.*

speaking (quite) candidly an expression introducing a frank or forthright statement. □ *Speaking quite candidly, I find your behavior a bit offensive, stated Frank, obviously offended.* □ *Mary: Tell me what you really think about this skirt. Sally: Speaking candidly, I think you should get your money back.*

(speaking) (quite) frankly AND **frankly speaking** a transitional phrase announcing that the speaker is going to talk in a more familiar and totally forthright manner. □ *Tom: Speaking quite* *frankly, I'm not certain she's the one for the job.* Mary: *I agree.* □ Bob: *We ought to be looking at housing in a lower price bracket.* Bill: *Quite frankly, I agree.* □ *"Frankly speaking," said John, "I think you're out of your mind!"*

spend (some) quality time with someone to spend time, giving lots of attention and being solicitous to someone, especially with one's family. (See also **have some face time with** someone.) □ *I spent some quality time with my wife this weekend.* □ *I need to stop working at home on the weekends and spend some quality time with my kids.*

spin a yarn to tell a tale. □ *Grandpa spun an unbelievable yarn for us.* □ *My uncle is always spinning yarns about his childhood.*

'Spose not. Go to I guess not.

'Spose so. Go to I guess (so).

stand up and be counted to state one's support (for someone or something). □ *If you believe in more government help for farmers, write your representative—stand up and be counted.* □ *I'm generally in favor of what you propose, but not enough to stand up and be counted.*

Stay out of my way. Go to Keep out of my way.

Stay out of this! Go to Keep out of this!

Stay with me. Follow along with what I am explaining.; Pay attention. (The accent is on *with*. Also literal with the accent on *stay*.) □ *This explanation is going to be quite complicated, so stay with me, and ask lots of questions.* □ *I know it's late, and you're all tired, but stay with me until I cover this last graph.*

Step aside. Please move out of the way so there is a pathway. □ *"Step aside. Let the mayor through, please," called out the mayor's bodyguard.* □ Tom *(blocking the boss's door): Just a moment, sir.* Boss *(trying to exit): Step aside, please.* Tom: *But, sir!* Boss: *Step aside, please.* Tom: *But, sir, the tax people are here with an arrest warrant.*

Stick with it. Do not give up.; Stay with your task. □ Bill: *I'm really tired of calculus.* Father: *Stick with it. You'll be a better person for it.* □ Bill: *This job is getting to be such a pain.* Sue: *True, but it pays well, doesn't it? Stick with it.*

Stop the music! and **Stop the presses!** Stop everything!; Hold it! (*Presses* refers to the printing presses used to print newspapers.

This means that there is recent important news, and that the presses must be stopped so changes can be made.) □ *JOHN (entering the room): Stop the music! There's a fire in the kitchen! MARY: Good grief! Let's get out of here!* □ *"Stop the presses!" shouted Jane. "I have an announcement."*

Stop the presses! Go to Stop the music!

(stuck) in a rut staying in an established way of living that never changes. □ *David felt like he was stuck in a rut, so he went back to school.* □ *Anne was tired of being in a rut, so she moved to Los Angeles.*

stuck in traffic caught in a traffic jam. □ *I am sorry I am late. I was stuck in traffic.* □ *My taxi was stuck in traffic, and I thought I would never get to the airport on time.*

Stuff a sock in it! Shut up!; Stop talking! (Literally, stuff a sock in your mouth to stop the noise.) □ *TOM: Hey, Henry! Can you hear me? HENRY: Be quiet, Tom. Stuff a sock in it!* □ *FRED: Hey, you still here? I want to tell you a few things! JOHN: Oh, stuff a sock in it! You're a pain.*

Suit yourself. You decide the way you want it.; **Have it your way.** □ *MARY: I think I want the red one. TOM: Suit yourself.* □ *JOHN (reading the menu): The steak sounds good, but I'm helpless in the face of fried chicken. SALLY: Suit yourself. I'll have the steak.*

Suits me (fine). Go to (It) suits me (fine).

Suppose Go to Supposing.

Suppose I do? AND **Supposing I do?** And what does it matter if I do, and what are you going to do about it? (Not usually with question intonation.) □ *ALICE: Do you really think it's right to do something like that? SUE: Suppose I do?* □ *FRED: Are you going to drive up into the mountains as you said you would? SALLY: Supposing I do? FRED: I'm just asking.*

Suppose I don't? AND **Supposing I don't?** And what will happen if I don't? (Not usually with question intonation.) □ *BILL: You'd better get yourself over to the main office. TOM: Suppose I don't?* □ *FATHER: You simply must do better in school. TOM: Supposing I don't? FATHER: Your clothing and personal belongings will be placed on the curb for the garbage pickup, and we will have the locks changed. Next question.*

Supposed to. Go to (Someone or something **is**) **supposed to** (do something).

Supposing I do? Go to Suppose I do?

Supposing I don't? Go to Suppose I don't?

Sure. Yes, certainly. (See also **Oh, sure** (someone or something **will**)!) □ *MARY: This okay? JANE: Sure.* □ *BILL: Want to go to a movie with me Saturday? SUE: Sure, why not?*

Sure as shooting! Absolutely! (An elaboration of **Sure.**) □ *BILL: Are you going to be there Monday night? BOB: Sure as shooting!* □ *BOB: Will you take this over to the main office? BILL: Sure as shooting!*

Sure thing. Yes.; Of course. □ *SUE: Will you be at the reception? BOB: Sure thing.* □ *BILL: You remember my cousin, Tom, don't you? BOB: Sure thing. Hi, Tom.*

swap something **out** Go to change something out.

Tah-dah! a phrase introducing or pointing to something that is supposed to be exciting. □ *"Tah-dah," said Alice. "This is my new car!"* □ BILL: *Tah-dah! Everyone, meet Mrs. Wilson!* MARY: *Hello, Mrs. Wilson.*

take a potshot at someone or something to criticize someone or something; to include a criticism of someone or something in a broader or more general criticism. □ *Daily, the media took potshots at the foolish politician.* □ *John is taking potshots at me in his condemnation of office workers.*

Take a shotgun approach to the problem. Attempt to solve a problem with methods that are far broader and more general than what is required. (The blast of a shotgun is very wide and can hit many things in addition to the actual target.) □ *We need to concentrate on cause and effect here. Let's figure out exactly what is wrong and propose the best solution to fix just that. We are not just going to take a shotgun approach to the problem.* □ *The doctor prescribed a broad-spectrum antibiotic. He wanted to start out by taking a shotgun approach to the infection while the lab worked to identify the pathogen.*

take a toll (on someone or something**)** to cause harm to someone or something through abuse. □ *Years of sunbathing took a toll on Mary's skin.* □ *Drug abuse takes a heavy toll on the lives of people and their families.*

Take care (of yourself). 1. Good-bye and keep yourself healthy. □ JOHN: *I'll see you next month. Good-bye.* BOB: *Good-bye, John. Take care of yourself.* □ MARY: *Take care.* SUE: *Okay. See you later.* **2.** Take care of your health and get well. □ MARY: *Don't worry. I'll get better soon.* SUE: *Well, take care of yourself. Bye.* □ JANE: *I'm sorry you're ill.* BOB: *Oh, it's nothing.* JANE: *Well, take care of yourself.*

Take heart. Be brave.; Be consoled.; Be cheered. □ *Take heart. Things are not as bad as they seem.* □ *I'm sorry for your troubles, but take heart. Things are bound to improve.*

Take it easy. 1. Good-bye and be careful. □ MARY: *Bye-bye.* BILL: *See you, Mary. Take it easy.* □ SUE: *Take it easy, Tom. Don't do anything I wouldn't do.* TOM: *Could you give me a short list of things you wouldn't do?* **2.** Be gentle.; Treat someone carefully. □ SUE: *Then I want you to move the piano and turn all the mattresses.* ANDREW: *Come on. Take it easy! I'm not made of steel, you know.* □ HENRY: *Oh, I'm pooped.* ALICE: *You just need a little rest and you'll feel as good as new. Just take it easy.* **3.** Calm down.; Relax.; Do not get excited. □ ANDREW: *I am so mad, I could blow my top!* RACHEL: *Now, now. Take it easy. What's wrong?* □ *Mary could see that Sally was very upset at the news. "Now, just take it easy," said Mary. "It can't be all that bad."*

take it on the chin to experience and endure a direct blow or assault. □ *The bad news was a real shock, and John took it on the chin.* □ *The worst luck comes my way, and I always end up taking it on the chin.*

Take it or leave it. That is all there is.; There is no choice.; Take this one or none. □ BILL: *That's my final offer. Take it or leave it.* BOB: *Aw, come on! Take off a few bucks.* □ BILL: *Aw, I want eggs for breakfast, Mom.* MOTHER: *There's only Sweet Wheets left. Take it or leave it.*

take it to one's **grave** to carry a secret with one until one dies. □ *I will never tell anyone. I'll take your secret to my grave.* □ *She took the answer to the mystery to her grave.*

Take my word for it. Believe me.; Trust me, I am telling you the truth. □ BILL: *Take my word for it. These are the best encyclopedias you can buy.* BOB: *But I don't need any encyclopedias.* □ RACHEL: *No one can cook better than Fred. Take my word for it.* BILL: *Really?* FRED: *Oh, yes. It's true.*

take someone **by surprise** to startle someone; to surprise someone with something unexpected. □ *Oh! You took me by surprise. I didn't hear you come in.* □ *Bill took his mother by surprise by coming to the door and pretending to be a solicitor.*

take someone or something **at face value** to accept someone or something based on outward appearance. □ *Don't just take her offer at* *face value. Think of the implications.* □ *Jane tends to take people at face value, and so she is always getting hurt.*

take someone's **part** to take a side in an argument; to support someone in an argument. □ *My sister took my mother's part in the family argument.* □ *You are always taking the part of underdog!*

take something **personally** to interpret a remark as if it were mean or critical about oneself. □ *Don't take it personally, but you really need a haircut.* □ *A: I'm not sure I like what you just said. B: Please don't take it personally.*

take umbrage at something to feel that one has been insulted by something. □ *The employee took umbrage at not getting a raise.* □ *Mary took umbrage at the suggestion that she was being unreasonable.*

Taking care of business. Go to (Just) taking care of business.

the **talk of** somewhere the frequent subject of conversation in a particular place. □ *The handsome new teacher was the talk of the town.* □ *John's new car is the talk of the office.*

talk through one's **hat** to brag or boast; to tell small lies casually. □ *MARY: I've got the fastest feet in the dorm, and they're going to carry me all the way to the Olympics. SALLY: Oh, Mary, you're just talking through your hat.* □ *"Bill is always talking through his hat," said Fred. "Don't pay any attention to his bragging."*

Talk to you soon. Go to (I'll) talk to you soon.

Ta-ta. Go to Toodle-oo.

T.C.B. Go to (Just) taking care of business.

Tell me another (one)! Not true!; What you just told me was a lie, so tell me another lie while you're at it. □ *BILL: Did you know that the football coach was once a dancer in a movie? TOM: Go on! Tell me another one!* □ *"Tell me another one!" laughed Bill at Tom's latest exaggeration.*

Tell me more. Continue talking and give me more information. (See also Keep talking.) □ *JAN: Well, I hear that Mary is leaving Fred. ANN: Really? Tell me more.* □ *Q: Would you be interested in learning who is seeing whom on a regular basis, whose initials are F.G.? A: Sure. Tell me more.*

(Tell me) this isn't happening. I can't believe that this is happening.; Assure me that what seems to be happening isn't really happening. □ *Ye gods! That man just stole my purse! This isn't* *happening!* □ *My arm is bleeding, and I think my wrist is broken. I think I'm going to pass out. Tell me this isn't happening!*

Thank God for small favors. We are grateful that not everything went wrong. □ *Thank God for small favors. We got here on time through no fault of our own.* □ *What a mess! It's like trying to herd frogs into the desert around here. At least it didn't rain today. Thank God for small favors.*

Thank goodness! AND **Thank heavens!** Oh, I am so thankful! □ JOHN: *Well, we finally got here. Sorry we're so late.* MOTHER: *Thank goodness! We were all so worried.* □ JANE: *There was a fire on Maple Street, but no one was hurt.* BILL: *Thank heavens!*

Thank heavens! Go to Thank goodness!

Thank you. I am grateful to you and offer you my thanks. □ BILL: *Here, have some more cake.* BOB: *Thank you.* □ JOHN: *Your hair looks nice.* MARY: *Thank you.*

Thank you a lot. Go to Thanks (a lot).

Thank you for a lovely evening. an expression said by a departing guest to the host or hostess at the end of an evening. (Other adjectives, such as *nice*, can be used in place of *lovely*.) □ MARY: *Thank you for a lovely evening.* JOHN: *Will I see you again?* □ BILL: *Thank you for a nice evening.* MARY: *Thank you so much for coming. Good night.*

Thank you for a lovely time. an expression said by a departing guest to the host or hostess. (Other adjectives, such as *nice*, can be used in place of *lovely*.) □ BILL: *Thank you for a nice time.* MARY: *Thank you so much for coming. Bye now.* □ JOHN: *Thank you so much for coming.* JANE: *Well, thank you for a lovely time.* JOHN: *Don't stay away so long next time.*

Thank you for calling. Thank you for calling on the telephone. (Said when the call is helpful or a bother to the caller.) □ MARY: *Good-bye.* SUE: *Good-bye, thanks for calling.* □ JOHN: *Okay. Well, I have to get off the phone. I just wanted you to know what was happening with your order.* JANE: *Okay. Bye. Thanks for calling.*

Thank you for inviting me. AND **Thank you for inviting us.; Thank you for having me.; Thank you for having us.** a polite expression said to a host or hostess on departure. □ MARY: *Good-bye, glad you could come.* BILL: *I had a great time. Thank you for* *inviting me.* □ JOHN: *I had a good time. Thank you for inviting me.* SALLY: *Come back again, John. It was good talking to you.*

Thank you for inviting us. Go to Thank you for inviting me.

Thank you for sharing. a sarcastic remark made when someone tells something that is unpleasant, overly personal, disgusting, or otherwise annoying. □ *Thank you for sharing. I really need to hear about your operation.* □ *Thank you for sharing, Bob. I hope your parents' divorce goes well.*

Thank you so much. Go to Thank you very much.

Thank you very much. AND **Thank you so much.** a more polite and emphatic way of saying Thank you. □ TOM: *Welcome. Come in.* BOB: *Thank you very much.* □ BILL: *Here's the book I promised you.* SUE: *Thank you so much.*

Thanks (a lot). AND **Thank you a lot. 1.** Thank you, I am grateful. □ BILL: *Here, take mine.* BOB: *Thanks a lot.* □ MARY: *Well, here's your pizza.* BILL: *Thanks.* **2.** That is not worth much.; That is nothing to be grateful for. (Sarcasm is indicated by the tone of voice used with this expression.) □ JOHN: *I'm afraid that you're going to have to work the night shift.* BOB: *Thanks a lot.* □ FRED: *Here's your share of the money. We had to take out nearly half to make up for the damage you did to the car.* BILL: *Thanks a lot.*

Thanks a million. Thank you a lot. □ BILL: *Oh, thanks a million. You were very helpful.* BOB: *Just glad I could help.* □ JOHN: *Here's your book.* JANE: *Thanks a million. Sorry I needed it back in such a rush.*

Thanks awfully. Thank you very much. □ JOHN: *Here's one for you.* JANE: *Thanks awfully.* □ MARY: *Here, let me help you with all that stuff.* SUE: *Thanks awfully.*

Thanks, but no thanks. Thank you, but I am not interested. (A way of turning down something that is not very desirable.) □ ALICE: *How would you like to buy my old car?* JANE: *Thanks, but no thanks.* □ JOHN: *What do you think about a trip over to see the Wilsons?* SALLY: *Thanks, but no thanks. We don't get along.*

Thanks for coming. I am pleased that you accepted my invitation. (Said by the host on arrival or departure of the guests.) □ *So good to see you. Thanks for coming.* □ *Thanks for coming. We were delighted that you could join us this evening.*

Thanks for having me. Go to Thank you for inviting me.

Thanks for the lift. Go to Thanks for the ride.

Thanks for the ride. AND **Thanks for the lift.** Thank you for giving me a ride in your car. □ *JOHN (stopping the car): Here we are. BOB: Thanks for the ride. Bye. JOHN: Later.* □ *As Fred got out of the car, he said, "Thanks for the lift."*

Thanks loads. Thanks a lot. (Colloquial.) □ *MARY: Here, you can have these. And take these too. SALLY: Thanks loads.* □ *JOHN: Wow! You look great! SALLY: Thanks loads. I try.*

That ain't the way I heard it. That is not the way I heard the story told. (A catchphrase. The *ain't* is built into the expression.) □ *JOHN: It seemed like a real riot. Then Sally called the police, and things calmed down. SUE: That ain't the way I heard it. JOHN: What? SUE: Somebody said the neighbors called the police.* □ *FRED: Four of us went fishing and were staying in this cabin. These women stopped and said they were having car trouble. What could we do? SALLY: That ain't the way I heard it.*

That (all) depends. My answer depends on factors that have yet to be discussed. □ *TOM: Will you be able to come to the meeting on Thursday night? MARY: That all depends.* □ *BOB: Can I see you again? SALLY: That depends.*

That beats everything! Go to If that don't beat all!

That brings me to the (main) point. a transitional expression that introduces the main point of a conversation. (See also **which brings me to the (main) point.**) □ *FATHER: It's true. All of us had to go through something like this when we were young, and that brings me to the point. Aren't you old enough to be living on your own and making your own decisions and supporting yourself? TOM: Well, yes, I guess so.* □ *FRED: Yes, things are very expensive these days, and that brings me to the main point. You simply have to cut back on spending. BILL: You're right. I'll do it!*

(That causes) no problem. That will not cause a problem for me or anyone else. □ *MARY: Do you mind waiting for just a little while? BOB: No problem.* □ *SUE: Does this block your light? Can you still read? JANE: That causes no problem.*

That does it! 1. That completes it!; It is now done just right! □ *When Jane got the last piece put into the puzzle, she said, "That does it!"* □ *JOHN (signing a paper): Well, that's the last one! That does it! BILL: I thought we'd never finish.* **2.** That's the last straw!; Enough is enough! □ BILL: *We're still not totally pleased with your work.* BOB: *That does it! I quit!* □ SALLY: *That does it! I never want to see you again!* FRED: *I only put my arm around you!*

That makes two of us. I agree with you or some other person. □ DON: *I would actually prefer to have the taxi pick us up three hours ahead of the flight.* ANDY: *That makes two of us. The security checks take longer and longer each time we fly.* □ A: *I think she is being overly harsh with us.* B: *That makes two of us.*

That (really) burns me (up)! That makes me very angry! □ BOB: *Did you hear that interest rates are going back up?* MARY: *That really burns me up!* □ SUE: *Fred is telling everyone that you are the one who lost the party money.* MARY: *That burns me! It was John who had the money in the first place.*

That takes the cake! 1. That is good, and it wins the prize! (Referring to cake as a prize.) □ *"What a performance!" cheered John. "That takes the cake!"* □ SUE: *Wow! That takes the cake! What a dive!* RACHEL: *She sure can dive!* **2.** That is the end!; **That does it!** □ BOB: *What a dumb thing to do, Fred!* FRED: *Yeah. That takes the cake!* □ BOB: *Wow! That takes the cake!* BILL: *What is it? Why are you slowing down?* BOB: *That stupid driver in front of me just hit the car on the left and then swung over and hit the car on the right.*

That tears it! That's the absolute end! (*Tears* rhymes with *stairs*.) □ RACHEL: *Okay, that tears it! I'm going to complain to the landlord. Those people make noise day and night!* SUE: *Yes, this is too much.* □ TOM: *The boss thinks maybe you should work on the night shift.* MARY: *That tears it! I quit!*

That'll be the day! It will be an unusually amazing day when that happens! □ BILL: *I think I'll fix that lamp now.* ANDREW: *When you finally get around to fixing that lamp, that'll be the day!* □ SUE: *I'm going to get this place organized once and for all!* ALICE: *That'll be the day!*

That'll teach someone**!** What happened to someone is a suitable punishment! (The *someone* is usually a pronoun.) □ BILL: *Tom, who has cheated on his taxes for years, finally got caught.* SUE: *That'll teach him.* □ BILL: *Gee, I got a ticket for speeding.* FRED: *That'll teach you!*

That's a new one on me! I had not heard that before. □ BOB: *Did you hear? They're building a new highway that will bypass the town.*

FRED: *That's a new one on me! That's terrible!* □ SUE: *All of us will have to pay our taxes monthly from now on.* MARY: *That's a new one on me!*

That's about the size of it. That is the way it is. □ BOB: *We only have grocery money left in the bank.* SALLY: *That means that there isn't enough money for us to go to Jamaica?* BOB: *That's about the size of it.* □ BOB: *I'm supposed to take this bill to the county clerk's office and pay them four hundred dollars?* SALLY: *That's about the size of it.*

That's all, folks. That is everything.; It's over.; There is no more. (The formulaic announcement of the end of a Warner Brothers color cartoon in movie theaters, usually stuttered by Porky Pig.) □ *We've finished playing for the evening. That's all, folks!* □ *Q: Can I have some more popcorn? A: All gone. Sorry. That's all, folks.*

That's all someone **needs.** AND **It's all** someone **needs.; (It's) just what you need.; That's just what you need.** Someone does not need that at all.; That's the last straw! (Always sarcastic. The someone can be a person's name or a pronoun.) □ JANE: *The dog died, and the basement is just starting to flood.* FRED: *That's all we need.* □ SALLY: *Bill, the check you wrote to the Internal Revenue Service was returned. There's no more money in the bank.* BILL: *That's all we need.* □ BOB: *On top of all that, now I have car trouble!* MARY: *That's just what you need!*

That's easy for you to say. You can say that easily because it really does not affect you the way it affects others. □ WAITER: *Here's your check.* MARY: *Thanks. (turning to others) I'm willing to just split the check evenly.* BOB: *That's easy for you to say. You had lobster!* □ SALLY: *Let's each chip in ten bucks and buy him a sweater.* SUE: *That's easy for you to say. You've got ten bucks to spare.*

That's enough! No more!; Stop that! □ SUE: *Here, I'll stack another one on top.* MARY: *That's enough! It will fall.* □ JOHN: *I could go on with complaint after complaint. I could talk all week, in fact.* BOB: *That's enough!*

That's enough for now. No more of that for now.; Please stop for a while. □ MARY: *Here, have some more cake. Do you want a larger piece?* BILL: *Oh, no. That's enough for now.* □ BILL: *Shall I cut a little more off this tree, lady, or save the rest till spring?* JANE: *No, that's enough for now.*

(That's) enough (of this) foolishness! 1. Stop this foolishness. □ BILL: *Enough of this foolishness. Stop it!* SALLY: *Sorry.* □ FATHER: *That's enough of this foolishness. You two stop fighting over nothing.* BOB: *Okay.* BILL: *Sorry.* **2.** I have had enough of this. (Does not refer to something that is actual foolishness.) □ ANDREW: *Enough of this foolishness. I hate ballet. I'm leaving.* SUE: *Well, sneak out quietly.* ANDREW: *No, I'll lead an exodus.* □ SALLY: *That's enough foolishness. I'm leaving and I never want to see you again!* BOB: *Come on! I was only teasing.*

(That's) fine by me. Go to (That's) fine with me.

(That's) fine with me. AND **(That's) fine by me.; (That's) okay by me.; (That's) okay with me.** That is agreeable as far as I am concerned. (The expressions with *by* are colloquial.) □ SUE: *I'm giving away your old coat.* BOB: *That's fine with me.* □ SALLY: *Can I take twenty dollars out of your wallet?* FRED: *That's okay by me—if you can find it, of course.*

That's funny. That is strange or peculiar. □ BILL: *Tom just called from Detroit and says he's coming back tomorrow.* MARY: *That's funny. He's not supposed to.* □ SUE: *The sky is turning very gray.* MARY: *That's funny. There's no bad weather forecast.*

That's it! 1. That does it!; That's the last straw! □ *That's it! I'm leaving! I've had enough!* □ *Okay. That's it! I'm going to report you to human resources!* **2.** That is the answer! □ *That's it! You are right.* □ *That's it! You got the right answer.*

That's (just) too much! 1. That is unpleasant and unacceptable!; That is more than I can bear! □ *"That's just too much!" exclaimed Sue, and she walked out.* □ BILL: *I'm afraid this movie isn't what we thought it was going to be.* SUE: *Did you see that? That's too much! Let's go!* **2.** That is just too funny. (Compare to You're too much!) □ *After Fred finished the joke, and Bill had stopped howling with laughter, Bill said, "That's too much! Tell a sad one for a change."* □ *When Tom stopped laughing, his sides ached and he had tears in his eyes. "Oh, that's too much!" he moaned.*

That's just what you need. Go to That's all someone needs.

That's more like it. That is better.; That is a better response than the previous one. □ WAITER: *Here is your order, sir. Roast chicken as you requested. Sorry about the mix-up.* JOHN: *That's more like it.*

□ CLERK: *Now, here's one that you might like.* SALLY: *Now, that's more like it!*

That's neither here nor there. That is irrelevant. □ *I don't care if you prefer beef over lamb. That's neither here nor there. The preferences of our guests are what matter.* □ WAITER: *But it's raining, and everyone will come in with umbrellas and wet coats.* CHEF: *That's neither here nor there. If we don't have the food prepared on time, we'll be fired whether the customers are wet or dry.* □ A: *Fred can bring games for the children, and Mary can bring party hats.* B: *That's neither here nor there—since the party has been cancelled.*

That's news to me. I did not know that.; I had not been informed of that. □ BILL: *They've blocked off Maple Street for some repairs.* TOM: *That's news to me.* □ SALLY: *The telephones are out. None of them work.* BILL: *That's news to me. I made a call just five minutes ago.*

(That's) no skin off my nose. AND **(That's) no skin off my teeth.** That does not embarrass me.; That causes me no difficulty or harm. (Colloquial. The second form is borrowed from the metaphor **by the skin of** someone's **teeth**, meaning just barely. The first form has additional variations—most of them vulgar.) □ BILL: *Everybody around here seems to think you're the one to blame.* BOB: *So what? I'm not to blame. It's no skin off my teeth, whatever they think.* □ BILL: *Sally is going to quit her job and go to Tampa.* BOB: *No skin off my nose! I don't care what she does.*

(That's) okay by me. Go to (That's) fine with me.

(That's) okay with me. Go to (That's) fine with me.

That's old school. That is old-fashioned or out of date. (See also from the old school.) □ *Don't bother holding the door open for me just because I am a woman. That's so old school.* □ *Well, it's not in the same category as buggy whips and spats, but that's totally old school in some circles.*

That's that! That is the end of that! Nothing more can be done. □ TOM: *Well, that's that! I can do no more.* SALLY: *That's the way it goes.* □ DOCTOR *(finishing an operation): That's that! Would you close for me, Sue?* SUE: *Nice job, doctor. Yes, I'll close.*

That's the last straw! That is going too far! Something will have to be done. □ BOB: *Now they say I have to have a tutor to pass calculus.* MARY: *That's the last straw! I'm going straight up to that school and* *find out what they aren't doing right.* □ *"That's the last straw!" cried Fred when he got another special tax bill from the city.*

That's the story of my life. That kind of thing is very typical in my life history. □ HANNA: *What a day this has been. Nothing seems to go right.* IDA: *One day's not as bad as weeks on end. That's the story of my life.* □ *A day late and a dollar short. That's the story of my life.*

That's the stuff! That is the right attitude or action. □ BOB: *I'm sure I can do it!* FRED: *That's the stuff!* □ *"That's the stuff!" cried the coach as Mary crossed the finish line.*

That's the ticket! That is what is required! □ MARY: *I'll just get ready and drive the letter directly to the airport!* SUE: *That's the ticket. Take it right to the airport post office.* □ BOB: *I've got it! I'll buy a new computer!* BILL: *That's the ticket!*

That's the way it goes. That is fate. □ MARY: *All my roses died in the cold weather.* SUE: *That's the way it goes.* □ SALLY: *Someone stole all the candy we left out in the front office.* JANE: *That's the way it goes.*

That's the way the ball bounces. Go to That's the way the cookie crumbles.

That's the way the cookie crumbles. AND **That's the way the ball bounces.; That's the way the mop flops.** That is life.; That's the way it goes. □ SUE: *I lost out on the chance for a promotion.* ALICE: *That's the way the cookie crumbles.* □ JOHN: *All this entire week was spent on this project. Then they canceled it.* SALLY: *That's the way the ball bounces.*

That's the way the mop flops. Go to That's the way the cookie crumbles.

(That's the) way to go! a phrase encouraging someone to continue the good work. □ *As John ran over the finish line, everyone cried, "That's the way to go!"* □ *"Way to go!" said Mary when Bob finally got the car started.*

(That's) too bad. It is unfortunate.; I'm sorry to hear that. □ TOM: *I hurt my foot on our little hike.* FRED: *That's too bad. Can I get you something for it?* TOM: *No, I'll live.* □ BOB: *My uncle just passed away.* TOM: *That's too bad. I'm sorry to hear that.* BOB: *Thanks.*

That's what I say. I agree with what was just said. □ *Tom: We've got to get in there and stand up for our rights! Mary: That's what I say.* □ *Bob: They shouldn't do that! Mary: That's what I say! Bob: They should be put in jail! Mary: That's what I say!*

That's what I'm talking about. This (or that) is definitely what I want or mean. (Often the speaker has not actually talked about the subject before.) □ *Andy: Well, Don, it's eight o'clock, and here I am. Right on time. Don: That's what I'm talking about. Promptness!* □ *Hey, I think I like the red one best. Yeah! That's what I'm talking about.*

that's why! a tag on the end of a statement that is an answer to a question beginning with *why*. (Shows a little impatience.) □ *Sue: Why do you always put your right shoe on first? Bob: Because, when I get ready to put on my shoes, I always pick up the right one first, that's why!* □ *Mary: Why do you eat that awful peppermint candy? Tom: Because I like it, that's why!*

Them's fighting words! That is a very provocative statement!; Those words could lead to a fight! (Humorous and only slightly threatening. The bad grammar is an attempt at rural humor.) □ *What do you mean by saying I took your parking place? Them's fighting words.* □ *A: You know, I don't like the way you drive. You scare me to death. B: Where I come from, them's fighting words.*

There aren't enough hours in the day. There are too many things to do and not enough time. □ *I am behind in all my work. There aren't enough hours in the day!* □ *We can't handle all the problems that come our way. There aren't enough hours in the day.*

(There is) no chance. There is no chance that something will happen. □ *Tom: Do you think that some little country like that will actually attack England? John: There's no chance.* □ *Bill: No chance you can lend me a few bucks, is there? Bill: Nope. No chance.*

(There is) no doubt about it. It cannot be doubted.; It is obvious. □ *Jane: It's really cold today. Fred: No doubt about it!* □ *Sue: Things seems to be getting more and more expensive. Tom: There's no doubt about that. Look at the price of oranges!*

(There is) no need (to). You do not have to.; It is not necessary. □ *Mary: Shall I try to save all this wrapping paper? Sue: No need. It's all torn.* □ *Bob: Would you like me to have it repaired? I'm so sorry I broke it. Bill: There is no need to. I can just glue it, thanks.*

There will be hell to pay. There will be a lot of trouble as a result of some action. □ *FRED: If you break another window, there will be hell to pay. ANDREW: I didn't do it! I didn't.* □ *BILL: I'm afraid there's no time to do this one. I'm going to skip it. BOB: There will be hell to pay if you do.*

There you are. That's the way things are.; This is the way things have worked out. □ *"There's nothing more that can be done. We've done what we could. So, there you are," said Fred, dejected.* □ *ANDREW: Then what happened? BOB: Then they put me in a cell until they found I was innocent. Somebody stole my watch in there, and I cut myself on a broken wine bottle left on a bench. And now I've got lice. All because of mistaken identity. So, there you are.*

There you go! Now you are doing it right!; Now you have the right attitude! □ *ALICE: I know I can do it. I just need to try harder. JANE: There you go!* □ *BOB: I'll devote my full time to studying and stop messing around. FATHER: There you go! That's great!*

There's more than one way to skin a cat. There is more than one way to do something. (Some suggest that this refers to skinning a catfish, but there are not really many ways to skin a catfish.) □ *Q: Isn't there a better way to do this? A: Sure! There's more than one way to skin a cat.* □ *A: I've done everything I can to convince cousin Sally to join us for the trip to Rome. I've appealed to her sense of family, her need for a vacation, and her love of Italian food. Nothing seems to work. B: Let me take a stab at it. There's more than one way to skin a cat.*

(There's) no point in doing something. There is (no longer) any purpose in doing something. □ *There is no point in locking the barn door now that the horse has been stolen.* □ *No point in crying over spilled milk.*

(There's) no rest for the wicked. Someone is extremely busy. (A catchphrase said to or about someone, including oneself.) □ *Gee, I've been working my butt off all day. Not a moment's rest. Oh, well. No rest for the wicked, I guess.* □ *Come on. Get up and go back to work. There's no rest for the wicked.*

(There's) no such thing as a free lunch. Nothing is really free because there is always some obligation. (Perhaps from a time when you could get a meal's worth of free food at a bar with the purchase of a beer or two.) □ *I ended up paying even more when* *they added on tax and carrying charges. There's no such thing as a free lunch.* □ Q: *Why won't my insurance pay for my cousin's operation also? A: No such thing as a free lunch.*

There's no time like the present. Do it now.; Don't put it off. □ A: *I think I will try to find a lawyer in a few weeks to help me with my will. B: Do it now. There's no time like the present.* □ *Don't wait another moment. You need a new bicycle while you're still young. There's no time like the present.*

(There's) no way to tell. No one can find out the answer. □ Tom: *How long are we likely to have to wait before the plane takes off?* Clerk: *Sorry, sir. There's no way to tell.* □ Bill: *Will the banks be open when we arrive?* Bob: *No way to tell. They don't keep regular hours.*

(There's) nothing to it! It's easy! □ John: *Is it hard to learn to fly a small plane?* Sue: *There's nothing to it!* □ Bill: *Me? I can't dive off a board that high! I can hardly dive off the side of the pool!* Bob: *Aw, come on! Nothing to it!*

They (just) don't make them like they used to. Goods are not as well made now as they were in the past. (Often used as a catchphrase. *Them* is often *'em.*) □ A: *Look at this flimsy door! B: They don't make 'em like they used to.* □ A: *Why don't cars last longer? B: They just don't make 'em like they used to.*

They must have seen you coming. You were really cheated.; When they saw you, they decided they could cheat you easily. □ Andrew: *It cost two hundred dollars.* Rachel: *You paid two hundred dollars for that thing? Boy, they must have seen you coming.* □ Bob: *Do you think I paid too much for this car? It's not as good as I thought it was.* Tom: *It's almost a wreck. They must have seen you coming.*

a **thing of the past** something that is old-fashioned or obsolete. (See also What's the world coming to?) □ *Taking off hats in elevators is a thing of the past.* □ Q: *What happened to good old decency and respect for others? A: Sure seems like it's a thing of the past.*

(Things) could be better. AND **(I) could be better.; (Things) might be better.** an answer to a greeting inquiry meaning "Life is not as good as it might be." (Not necessarily a direct answer.) □ John: *How are things going, Fred?* Fred: *Things could be better. And you?* John: *About the same.* □ Bob: *Hi, Bill! How are you?* Bill: *I could be better. What's new with you?* Bob: *Nothing much.*

(Things) could be worse. AND **(I) could be worse.** an answer to a greeting inquiry meaning "My state is not as bad as it might be." (Not necessarily a direct answer.) □ *JOHN: How are you, Fred? FRED: Things could be worse. And you? JOHN: Okay, I guess.* □ *BOB: Hi, Bob! What's happening? BOB: I could be worse. What's new with you?*

Things getting you down? Go to (Are) things getting you down?

Things haven't been easy. Go to (It) hasn't been easy.

(Things) might be better. Go to (Things) could be better.

Things will work out (all right). AND **Everything will work out (all right).; Everything will work out for the best.; Things will work out for the best.** The situation will reach a satisfactory conclusion.; The problem(s) will be resolved. □ *"Cheer up!" Mary said to a gloomy Fred. "Things will work out all right."* □ *MARY: Oh, I'm so miserable! BILL: Don't worry. Everything will work out for the best.* □ *"Now, now, don't cry. Things will work out," consoled Sally, hoping that what she was saying was really true.*

Things will work out for the best. Go to Things will work out (all right).

Think nothing of it. AND **Don't give it another thought.; Don't give it a (second) thought. 1.** You're welcome.; It was nothing.; I was glad to do it. □ *MARY: Thank you so much for driving me home. JOHN: Think nothing of it.* □ *SUE: It was very kind of you to bring these all the way out here. ALICE: Think nothing of it. I was delighted to do it.* **2.** You did no harm at all. (A very polite way of reassuring someone that an action has not caused any great harm or hurt the speaker.) □ *SUE: Oh, sorry. I didn't mean to bump you! BOB: Think nothing of it.* □ *JANE: I hope I didn't hurt your feelings when I said you were too loud. BILL: Don't give it a second thought. I was too loud.*

thinking out loud Go to (I'm) (just) thinking out loud.

This doesn't quite suit me. AND **It doesn't quite suit me.** This is not quite what I want.; This does not please me. (Compare to (It) suits me (fine).) □ *CLERK: How do you like this one? MARY: It doesn't quite suit me.* □ *BOB: This doesn't quite suit me. Let me see something a little darker. CLERK: How's this? BOB: Better.*

This is it! I have discovered the right thing!; This is the one! □ *"This is it!" shouted the scientist, holding a test tube in the air.* □ Sue: *This is it! This is the book that has all the shrimp recipes.* Mary: *I never saw anybody get so happy about shrimp!*

This is my floor. a phrase said by someone at the back of an elevator suggesting that people make way for an exit at a particular floor. □ *Mary said, "This is my floor," and everyone made room for her to get out of the elevator.* □ *"Out, please," said Tom loudly. "This is my floor!"*

This is someone. Go to Speaking.

This is where I came in. I have heard all this before. (When someone begins watching a film after it has begun, this phrase is said when the second showing of the film reaches familiar scenes.) □ *John sat through a few minutes of the argument, and when Tom and Alice kept saying the same thing over and over, John said, "This is where I came in," and he left the room.* □ *The speaker stood up and asked again for a new vote on the proposal. "This is where I came in," muttered Jane as she headed for the door.*

This isn't happening. Go to (Tell me) this isn't happening.

This one's on me. I will pay for the treat this time. (Usually said in reference to buying drinks. Compare to It's on me.) □ *As the waiter set down the glasses, Fred said, "This one's on me."* □ John: *Check, please.* Bill: *No, this one's on me.*

This taken? Go to (Is) this (seat) taken?

Those were the days. The days we have been referring to were the greatest of times. □ *A: Ah, yes. The eighties. B: Those were the days!* □ *Those were the days. Back when people knew right from wrong.*

through no fault of someone's **own 1.** not because of someone's fault. □ *We ended up missing the entire ceremony through no fault of our own.* □ *Through no fault of his own, he failed third grade. His eyes were bad, and nobody caught it.* **2.** not because of someone's skill, luck, or planning; in spite of all the bad things that happened. (Irony. Here *fault* = skill, effort, planning.) □ *We got to the ceremony right on time—through no fault of our own.* □ *Through no fault of our own, we managed to amass a small fortune by the time we were each forty years old.*

throw the book at someone to give someone, especially a defendant in court, the maximum punishment. (As if a judge were to throw a law book at a defendant, thereby charging the defendant with all the crimes in the book.) □ *The judge was really angry and threw the book at the poor slob just because he kept interrupting.* □ *Wow, was my boss mad at me. He threw the book at me and said if I ever did it again, I'd be out of a job.*

Till later. Go to (Good-bye) until then.

Till next time. Go to Good-bye for now.

Till then. Go to (Good-bye) until then.

Till we meet again. Go to Good-bye for now.

Time for a change. Go to (It's) time for a change.

Time I left. Go to (It's) time I left.

Time (out)! Stop everything for just a minute! □ *"Hey, stop a minute! Time out!" yelled Mary as the argument grew in intensity.* □ *Right in the middle of the discussion, Alice said, "Time!" Then she announced that dinner was ready.*

Time to call it a day. It's time to quit for the day. □ JANE: *Well, I'm done. Time to call it a day.* SUE: *Yes, let's get out of here.* □ JANE: *Well, I've done too much work.* SUE: *Yes, it's late. Time to call it a day.*

Time to call it a night. It's time to quit one's activities for the night. (Can refer to work or partying.) □ BOB: *Wow, it's late! Time to call it a night.* MARY: *Yes, it's really dark! Good night.* □ FRED: *Gee, I'm tired. Look at the time!* JANE: *Yes, it's time to call it a night.*

Time to go. Go to (It's) time to go.

Time to hit the road. Go to (It's) time to hit the road.

Time to move along. Go to (It's) time to run.

Time to move on. Go to (It's) time to move on.

Time to push along. Go to (It's) time to run.

Time to push off. Go to (It's) time to run.

Time to run. Go to (It's) time to run.

Time to shove off. Go to (I) have to shove off.

Time to split. Go to (It's) time to run.

Time we were going. Go to (It's) time we were going.

Times are changing. Things are changing rapidly and in amazing ways. □ SUE: *They paid nearly five hundred thousand for their first house!* RACHEL: *Well, I shouldn't be so surprised. Times are changing, I guess.* □ *"Times are changing," warned Mary. "You can't expect the world to stand still."*

(To) hell with that! I reject that! □ MARY: *I think we ought to go to the dance Friday night.* TOM: *To hell with that!* □ FRED: *Don't you want to drive me down to school?* JOHN: *To hell with that!*

to put it another way AND **put another way** a phrase introducing a restatement of what someone, usually the speaker, has just said. □ FATHER: *You're still very young, Tom. To put it another way, you don't have any idea about what you're getting into.* TOM: *But I still want to get married, so can I borrow fifty dollars?* □ JOHN: *Could you go back to your own room now, Tom? I have to study.* TOM: *(no answer)* JOHN: *Put another way, get out of here!* TOM: *Okay, okay. Don't get your bowels in an uproar!*

to the best of my knowledge Go to (as) far as I know.

Too bad. Go to (That's) too bad.

too good to be true almost unbelievable; so good as to be unbelievable. □ *The news was too good to be true.* □ *When I finally got a big raise, it was too good to be true.*

too little, too late not enough of something, delivered or performed too late. (See also a **day late and a dollar short.**) □ ANDY: *Your help with the picnic was appreciated, but it was too little, too late. By the time we got there, it was raining.* HELEN: *Sorry.* □ *It was a great speech, but the damage had already been done. It was just too little, too late.*

too much, too soon too much of something, such as power, wealth, or responsibility, too soon. □ *He really wasn't ready to lead the entire squad. He's clever, but it's too much, too soon.* □ DAN: *Should we promote him now or later?* IDA: *Later, I think. Promotion would be too much, too soon.*

Toodle-oo. AND **Ta-ta.; Toodles.** Good-bye. □ FRED: *Bye, you guys. See you.* SALLY: *It's been. Really it has. Toodle-oo.* □ MARY: *See ya, bye-bye.* SUE: *Ta-ta.*

Toodles. Go to Toodle-oo.

Took the words right out of my mouth. Go to (You) took the words right out of my mouth.

Trust me! I am telling you the truth. Please believe me. □ *Tom said with great conviction, "Trust me! I know exactly what to do!"* □ *MARY: Do you really think we can keep this party a secret until Thursday? SALLY: Trust me! I know how to plan a surprise party.*

try as I may a phrase that introduces an expression of regret or failure. □ *BILL: Try as I may, I cannot get this thing put together right. ANDREW: Did you read the instructions?* □ *RACHEL: Wow! This place is a mess! MOTHER: Try as I may, I can't get Andrew to clean up after himself.*

Try to catch you later. Go to (I'll) try to catch you some other time.

Try to catch you some other time. Go to (I'll) try to catch you some other time.

Tsup? What's up? (Slang.) □ *BILL: Tsup? TOM: Nothing. What's new with you? BILL: Nothing.* □ *BOB: Tsup? FRED: I'm getting a new car. BOB: Excellent!*

turn things around to reorganize and improve something. □ *They've just hired a really energetic new CEO who did very well at her last post. They're hoping she can really turn things around.* □ *As far as future profits go, another quarter of high earnings will turn things around.*

twist someone's **words (around)** to restate someone's words inaccurately when quoting them or trying to understand them. □ *Stop twisting my words around! Listen to what I am telling you!* □ *You are twisting my words again. That is not what I said!*

Under no circumstances. AND **Not under any circumstances.**
never. □ ANDREW: *Under no circumstances will I ever go back there again!* RACHEL: *Why? What happened?* □ SUE: *Can I talk you into serving as a referee again?* MARY: *Heavens, no! Not under any circumstances!*

under normal circumstances normally; usually; typically. □ *"We'd be able to keep the dog at home under normal circumstances," said Mary to the vet.* □ *"Under normal circumstances you'd be able to return to work in a week," explained the doctor.*

under oath bound by an oath; having taken an oath. □ *You must tell the truth because you are under oath.* □ *I was placed under oath before I could testify in the trial.*

Until later. Go to (Good-bye) until then.

Until next time. Go to Good-bye for now.

Until then. Go to (Good-bye) until then.

Until we meet again. Go to Good-bye for now.

Use your head! Start thinking!; Use your brain! □ TOM: *I just don't know what to do.* MARY: *Use your head! You'll figure out something.* □ ANDREW: *Come on, John, you can figure it out. A kindergartner could do it. Use your head!* JOHN: *I'm doing my best.*

used to do something to have done something [customarily] in the past. □ *We used to go swimming in the lake before it became polluted.* □ *I used to eat nuts, but then I became allergic to them.*

Vamoose! Get out!; Go away! (From Spanish *vamos,* "let's go.") □ *Bob: Go on. Get out of here! Vamoose! Bill: I'm going! I'm going!* □ *Bob: Go away! Bill: What? Bob: Vamoose! Scram! Beat it! Bill: Why? Bob: Because you're a pain.*

Very glad to meet you. Go to (I'm) (very) glad to meet you.

Very good. 1. It is good. □ *John: How do you like your lobster? Alice: Mmm. Very good.* □ *Jane: What did you think of the movie? Fred: Very good. Jane: Is that all? Fred: Yeah.* **2. As you say.**; Thank you for your instructions. (Typically said by someone in a serving role, such as a clerk, waiter, waitress, butler, maid, etc.) □ *Waiter: What are you drinking, madam? Sue: It's just soda. No more, thanks. Waiter: Very good.* □ *Mary: Would you charge this to my account? Clerk: Very good.*

Wait a minute. Go to Just a minute.

Wait a sec(ond). Go to Just a minute.

Wait up (a minute)! Wait for me while I catch up with you! □ *Tom, who was following Mary down the street, said, "Wait up a minute! I need to talk to you."* □ *JOHN: Hey, Sally! Wait up! SALLY: What's happening?*

walk something **back** to attempt to retract one's words by careful argument, restatement, and explanation. □ *Be careful how you state it. It will look very weak and amateurish if you have to walk it back afterward.* □ *He spent twenty minutes in a news conference walking back the assertion he made in the news conference yesterday.*

Want to know something? Go to (Do you) want to know something?

Want to make something of it? Go to (Do you) want to make something of it?

Watch! Go to (You) (just) watch!

Watch it! 1. Be careful. □ *RACHEL: Watch it! There's a broken stair there. JANE: Gee, thanks.* □ *MARY: Watch it! There's a pothole in the street. BOB: Thanks.* **2.** Do not act or talk that way. □ *SALLY: I really hate John! SUE: Watch it! He's my brother!* □ *BILL: You girls always seem to take so long to do a simple thing like getting dressed. MARY: Watch it!*

Watch out! Go to Look out!

Watch your mouth! Go to Watch your tongue!

Watch your tongue! AND **Watch your mouth!** Do not talk like that!; Do not say those things!; Do not say those bad words! □ *ANDREW: Don't talk to me like that! Watch your tongue! BILL: I'll talk to you any way I want.* □ *"Watch your mouth!" warned Sue. "I will not listen to any more of this slime!"*

the **way I see it** Go to from my perspective.

(way) over there in a place some distance away. □ *I see a house way over there in the field.* □ *My hat is over there on the table.*

Way to go! Go to (That's the) way to go!

We aim to please. We are happy to try to please you. (Usually a commercial slogan, but can be said in jest by one person, often in response to **Thank you.**) □ MARY: *This meal is absolutely delicious!* WAITER: *We aim to please.* □ TOM: *Well, Sue, here's the laundry detergent you wanted from the store.* SUE: *Oh, thanks loads. You saved me a trip.* TOM: *We aim to please.*

We all gotta go sometime. Death is inevitable. (A way to make light of death. Never said in sympathy. See also **When you('ve) gotta go, you gotta go.**) □ BOB: *I was very surprised to hear of Fred's death.* JAN: *Yes, it was so sudden.* BOB: *Well, we all gotta go sometime.* □ ANN: *Careful, Tom, you'll fall and kill yourself!* TOM: *So? We all gotta go sometime.*

(We) don't see you much around here anymore. AND **(We) don't see you around here much anymore.** We haven't seen you for a long time. (The *we* can be replaced with *I.*) □ BILL: *Hello, Tom. Long time no see.* TOM: *Yes, Bill. We don't see you much around here anymore.* □ *"We don't see you around here much anymore," said the old pharmacist to John, who had just come home from college.*

We had a lovely time. Go to I had a lovely time.

We must do this again (sometime). Go to Let's do this again (sometime).

We need to talk about something. an expression inviting someone to discuss something. □ BILL: *Can I come over tonight? We need to talk about something.* MARY: *I guess so.* □ *"Mr. Franklin," said Bill's boss sort of sternly, "I want to see you in my office for a minute. We need to talk about something."*

We were just talking about you. a phrase said when a person being discussed appears on the scene. (Compare to **Speak of the devil.**) □ TOM: *Speak of the devil, here comes Bill.* MARY: *We were just talking about you, Bill.* □ SALLY (approaching Tom and Bill): *Hi, Tom. Hi, Bill. What's new?* BILL: *Oh, Sally! We were just talking about you.*

Welcome. Come into this place. You are welcome here. □ *MARY: Welcome. Please come in. TOM: Thank you so much.* □ *BILL: I'm glad you could make it. Come in. Welcome. MARY: Thanks. My, what a nice place you have here.*

Welcome to our house. an expression said by a host or hostess when greeting guests and bringing them into the house. □ *ANDREW: Hello, Sally. Welcome to our house. Come on in. SALLY: Thanks. It's good to be here.* □ *TOM: Welcome to our house. Make yourself at home. HENRY: Thanks, I'm really tired.*

Welcome to the club! Go to Join the club!

well a sentence opener having no specific meaning, sometimes expressing reservation or indecision. (Words such as this often use intonation to convey the connotation of the sentence that is to follow. The brief intonation pattern accompanying the word may indicate sarcasm, disagreement, caution, consolation, sternness, etc.) □ *SALLY: Can you take this downtown for me? ANDREW: Well, I don't know.* □ *"Well, I guess," answered Tom, sort of unsure of himself.* □ *"Well, if you think you can treat me that way, you've got another think coming," raged Betty.* □ *BILL: What do you think about my haircut? JANE: Well, it looks okay to me.* □ *SUE: I've decided to sell my car. MARY: Well, if that's what you want.* □ *"Well, hello," smiled Kate.*

Well done! You did that nicely! □ *SALLY: Well done, Tom. Excellent speech. TOM: Thanks.* □ *In the lobby after the play, Tom was met with a chorus of well-wishers saying, "Well done, Tom!"*

We('ll) have to do lunch sometime. AND **Let's do lunch (sometime).** We must have lunch together sometime. (A vague statement that may lead to lunch plans.) □ *RACHEL: Nice to talk to you, Tom. We have to do lunch sometime. TOM: Yes, good to see you. I'll give you a ring.* □ *TOM: Can't talk to you now. Catch you later. MARY: We'll have to do lunch sometime.* □ *JOHN: Good to see you, Tom. TOM: Right. Let's do lunch sometime. JOHN: Good idea. I'll call you. Bye. TOM: Right. Bye.* □ *MARY: Catch you later. SUE: Sure. Let's do lunch. MARY: Okay. Call me. Bye.*

(Well,) I never! 1. I have never been so insulted! □ *BILL: Just pack up your things and get out! JANE: Well, I never!* □ *TOM: Look, your manners with the customers are atrocious! JANE: Well, I never!* **2.** I've never heard of such a thing. □ *TOM: Now they have machines* *that will do all those things at the press of a button. SALLY: Well, I never! I had no idea! □ JOHN: Would you believe I have a whole computer in this pocket? ALICE: I never!*

Well said. You said that very well, and I agree. □ *As Sally sat down, Mary complimented her, "Well said, Sally. You made your point very well." □ JOHN: And I for one will never stand for this kind of encroachment on my rights again! MARY: Well said! BOB: Well said, John! FRED: Yes, well said.*

We'll try again some other time. Go to Maybe some other time.

(Well,) what do you know! I am surprised to hear or learn that! (No answer is expected or desired.) □ *ANDREW: Well, what do you know! Here's a brand-new shirt in this old trunk. BOB: I wonder how it got there. □ TOM: These two things fit together like this. JOHN: Well, what do you know!*

We're all (standing) behind you. AND **Everyone is (standing) behind you.** Everyone is supporting you and is on your side. □ *I know that things are going badly for you, but you have our support. We're all standing behind you. □ Everyone is behind you on this, Fred. We hope you will press on and win in the long run. □ We are all standing behind you, no matter what.*

(We're) delighted to have you. Go to (I'm) delighted to have you (here).

(We're) glad you could come. Go to (I'm) glad you could come.

(We're) glad you could drop by. Go to (I'm) glad you could drop by.

(We're) glad you could stop by. Go to (I'm) glad you could drop by.

Were you born in a barn? an expression chiding someone who has left a door open or who is disorderly. □ *ANDREW: Close the door! Were you born in a barn? BOB: Sorry. □ FRED: Can't you clean this place up a little? Were you born in a barn? BOB: I call it the messy look.*

We've had a lovely time. Go to I've had a lovely time.

What (a) nerve! AND **Of all the nerve!** How rude! □ *BOB: Lady, get the devil out of my way! MARY: What a nerve! □ JANE: You can't have that one! I saw it first! SUE: Of all the nerve! I can too have it!*

What a pity! AND **What a shame!** an expression of consolation meaning That's too bad. (Can also be used sarcastically.) □ *BILL:*

I'm sorry to tell you that the cat died today. MARY: *What a pity!* □ MARY: *The cake is ruined!* SALLY: *What a shame!*

What a shame! Go to What a pity!

What about it? So what?; Do you want to argue about it? (Contentious.) □ BILL: *I heard you were the one accused of breaking the window.* TOM: *Yeah? So, what about it?* □ MARY: *Your piece of cake is bigger than mine.* SUE: *What about it?*

What about you? 1. What is your choice? (Compare to How about you?) □ TOM: *I'm having the pot roast and a cup of coffee. What about you?* MARY: *I want something fattening and unhealthy.* □ SALLY: *I prefer reds and purple for this room. What about you?* MARY: *Well, purple's okay, but reds are a little warm for this room.* **2.** What will happen to you? □ MARY: *My parents are taking my brothers to the circus.* SUE: *What about you?* MARY: *I have a piano lesson.* □ MARY: *All my friends have been accepted to colleges.* SUE: *What about you?* MARY: *Oh, I'm accepted too.*

What are you drinking? 1. a phrase inquiring what someone is already drinking so that the person who asks the question can offer another drink of the same thing. □ BILL: *Hi, Tom. Nice to see you. What are you drinking?* TOM: *Scotch and water.* BILL: *Waiter, another scotch and water and a martini.* TOM: *Thanks, Bill.* □ WAITER: *What are you drinking, madam?* SUE: *It's just soda. No more, thanks.* WAITER: *Very good.* **2.** a phrase inquiring what is being drunk at a particular gathering so that the person asking can request the same drink. (A way of finding out what drinks are available.) □ MARY: *Do you want a drink?* SUE: *Yes, thanks. Say, that looks good. What are you drinking?* MARY: *It's just ginger ale.* □ BILL: *Can I get you something to drink?* JANE: *What are you drinking?* BILL: *I'm having gin and tonic.* JANE: *I'll have that too, thanks.*

What are you having? What food or drink are you planning to order? (Either part of a conversation or a request made by food service personnel. In a restaurant, sometimes the waiter or waitress will signal to a guest to order first by saying this. Sometimes asked of the person paying for the food or drink to determine the appropriate price range.) □ WAITER: *Would you care to order now?* TOM: *What are you having, Mary?* MARY: *You order. I haven't made up my mind.* □ WAITER: *May I help you?* TOM: *What are you hav-*

ing, Pop? FATHER: I'll have the roast chicken, I think, with fries. TOM: I'll have the same.

What brings you here? What is your reason for being here? □ *TOM: Hello, Mary. What brings you here? MARY: I was invited, just like you.* □ *DOCTOR: Well, John, what brings you here? JOHN: I've had this cough for nearly a month, and I think it needs looking into.*

What can I do you for? Go to How may I help you?

What can I say? I have no explanation or excuse. What do you expect me to say? (See also **What do you want me to say?**) □ *BILL: Why on earth did you lose that big order? SALLY: What can I say? I'm sorry!* □ *BOB: You're going to have to act more aggressively if you want to make sales. You're just too timid. TOM: What can I say? I am what I am.*

What can I tell you? 1. What kind of information do you want? □ *BILL: I have a question. BOB: What can I tell you? BILL: When do we arrive at Chicago?* □ *MARY: I would like to ask a question about the quiz tomorrow. BILL: What can I tell you? MARY: The answers, if you know them.* **2.** I haven't any idea of what to say. (Compare to **What can I say?**) □ *JOHN: Why on earth did you do a dumb thing like that? BILL: What can I tell you? I just did it, that's all.* □ *MARY: I'm so disappointed with you, Fred. FRED: What can I tell you? I am too.*

What do you expect? Isn't this just the kind of thing you would expect? (Said with sarcastic resignation.) □ *Yeah, the IRS will squeeze every single dollar out of you. What do you expect?* □ *What do you expect? Cats scratch people. It's in their job description.*

What do you know? a typical greeting inquiry. (Informal. A specific answer is not expected. Often pronounced Wha-da-ya know?) □ *BOB: Hey, Tom! What do you know? TOM: Look who's here! Hi, Bob!* □ *JOHN: What do you know? MARY: Nothing. How are you? JOHN: Okay.*

What do you know for sure? How are you?; What do you know? (Familiar. An elaboration of **What do you know?** Does not require a direct answer.) □ *TOM: Hey, man! What do you know for sure? BILL: Howdy, Tom. What's new?* □ *JOHN: How are you doing, old buddy? BILL: Great, you ugly beast! JOHN: What do you know for sure? BILL: Nothing.*

What do you say? 1. Hello, how are you? (Informal.) □ *Bob: What do you say, Tom? Tom: Hey, man. How are you doing?* □ *Bill: What do you say, man? Fred: What's the good word, you old so-and-so?* **2.** What is your answer or decision? □ *Bill: I need an answer from you now. What do you say? Bob: Don't rush me!* □ *Sue: I can offer you seven hundred dollars for your old car. What do you say? Bob: I'll take it!* **3.** an expression urging a child to say **Thank you** or **please**. □ *When Aunt Sally gave Billy some candy, his mother said to Billy, "What do you say?" "Thank you," said Billy.* □ *Mother: Here's a nice glass of milk. Child: Good. Mother: What do you say? Child: Very good. Mother: No. What do you say? Child: Thank you.*

What do you think? What is your opinion? □ *Mary: This is our new company stationery. What do you think? Bill: Stunning. Simply stunning.* □ *Mary: We're considering moving out into the country. What do you think? Sue: Sounds good to me.*

What do you think about that? Go to What do you think of that?

What do you think of that? AND **What do you think about that?** Isn't that remarkable?; What is your opinion of that? □ *Bob: I'm leaving tomorrow and taking all these books with me. What do you think of that? Mary: Not much.* □ *Sue: I'm going to start taking cooking lessons. What do you think about that? Bill: I'm overjoyed! John: Thank heavens! Mary: Fortune has smiled on us, indeed!*

What do you think of this weather? a question used to open a conversation with someone, often someone one has just met. □ *Sue: Glad to meet you, Mary. Mary: What do you think about this weather? Sue: I've seen better.* □ *Bill: What do you think about this weather? Jane: Lovely weather for ducks.*

What do you think you are doing here? Why are you in this place? (Stern and threatening.) □ *John: Mary! Mary: John! John: What do you think you're doing here?* □ *"What do you think you're doing here?" said Fred to a frightened rabbit trapped in the garage.*

What do you want me to say? I have no response.; I have no answer. Do you have one for me to say? (Almost the same as **What can I say?; What can I tell you?**) □ *Tom: You've really made a mess of all of this! Bill: Sorry. What do you want me to say?* □ *Bob: All of these problems should have been settled some time ago. Why are they still plaguing us? Tom: What do you want me to say?*

What does that prove? So what?; That does not mean anything. (A defensive expression. The heaviest stress is on *that*. Often with *so*, as in the examples.) □ *Tom: It seems that you were in the apartment the same night that it was robbed. Bob: So, what does that prove? Tom: Nothing, really. It's just something we need to keep in mind.* □ *Rachel: You're late again on your car payment. Jane: What does that prove? Rachel: Simply that you can't afford the car, and we are going to repossess it.*

What else can I do? Go to What more can I do?

What else can I do for you? In what other way can I serve you? (Said by shopkeepers, clerks, and service personnel.) □ *Bill: What else can I do for you? Bob: Please check the oil.* □ *"Here's your prescription. What else can I do for you?" said the pharmacist.*

What else is new? Go to (So,) what else is new?

What for? Why?; For what reason? □ *A: I want you to clean your room. B: What for? It's clean enough.* □ *A: You need to leave now. B: What for? Did I do something wrong?*

What gives? What happened?; What went wrong?; What's the problem? □ *Bill: Hi, you guys. What gives? Bob: Nothing, just a little misunderstanding. Tom's a little angry.* □ *Bob: Where's my wallet? What gives? Tom: I think one of those roughnecks who just walked by us has borrowed it for a little while.*

What goes around, comes around. The results of things that one has done will someday come back to bother one. □ *So, he finally gets to see the results of his activities. Whatever goes around, comes around.* □ *Now he is the victim of his own policies. Whatever goes around comes around.*

What happened? What went wrong here? □ *Bob (approaching a crowd): What happened? Tom (with Bob): What's wrong? Bystander: Just a little mix-up. A car wanted to drive on the sidewalk, that's all.* □ *There was a terrible noise, an explosion that shook the house. Bob looked at Jane and said, "What happened?"*

What (have) you been up to? a greeting inquiry. (A detailed answer may be expected.) □ *Mary: Hello, Jane. What have you been up to? Jane: Been up to no good. What about you? Mary: Yeah. Me, too.* □ *John: Bill, baby! What you been up to? Bill: Nothing really. What about you? John: The same, I guess.*

What he's having. I would like to have the same as he ordered. (A response to a waiter or bartender. Also in other persons.) □ BOB: *I think I'd like a cup of coffee with cream.* WAITER: *And you, sir?* TOM: *What he's having.* □ *Q: Can I get you something to drink? A: A lemonade would be nice. No. I changed my mind. What he's having.*

What I wouldn't give for a something**!** I would give almost anything for something, especially food or drink.; I would really like to have something. □ *I am so thirsty. It's really hot. What I wouldn't give for a cold glass of tea!* □ ANDY: *Hey, Don, would you like a can of soda?* DON: *I guess, but what I wouldn't give for a nice cold beer!*

What if I do? Does it matter to you if I do it?; What difference does it make if I do it? (Saucy and colloquial.) □ TOM: *Are you really going to sell your leather coat?* BOB: *What if I do?* □ JANE: *You're not going to go out dressed like that, are you?* SUE: *So, what if I do?*

What if I don't? Does it matter to you if I do not do it?; What difference does it make if I do not do it? (Saucy and colloquial.) □ BOB: *You're certainly going to tidy up a bit before going out, aren't you?* TOM: *What if I don't?* □ FATHER: *You are going to get in by midnight tonight or you're grounded.* FRED: *So what if I don't?* FATHER: *That's enough! You're grounded as of this minute!*

What is it? What do you want from me?; Why do you want to get my attention? (There is also a literal meaning.) □ TOM: *John, can I talk to you for a minute?* JOHN: *What is it?* □ SUE: *Jane?* JANE: *What is it?* SUE: *Close the door, please.*

What makes you think so? 1. Why do you think that?; What is your evidence for that conclusion? □ TOM: *This bread may be a little old.* ALICE: *What makes you think so?* TOM: *The green spots on the edges.* □ BOB: *Congress is in session again.* TOM: *What makes you think so?* BOB: *My wallet's empty.* **2.** Is that not totally obvious? (Sarcastic.) □ JOHN: *I think I'm putting on a little weight.* MARY: *Oh, yeah? What makes you think so?* □ MARY (shivering): *Gee, I think it's going to be winter soon.* ALICE (also shivering): *Yeah? What makes you think so?*

What more can I do? AND **What else can I do?** I am at a loss to know what else to do.; Is there anything else I can do? (An expression of desperation, not an inquiry.) □ *Bob: Did you hear about the death in the Wilson family. Bill: Yes. I feel so helpless. I sent flowers. What more can I do?* □ *Bill: Is your child still sick? Mary: Yes. I'm giving her the medicine the doctor sent over. What more can I do?*

What now? Go to Now what?

What number are you calling? an expression used when one suspects that a telephone caller may have gotten the wrong number. □ *Bob (on the telephone): Hello? Mary: Hello, is Sally there? Bob: Uh, what number are you calling? Mary: I guess I have the wrong number. Sorry. Bob: No problem. Good-bye.* □ *When the receptionist asked, "What number are you calling?" I realized I had made a mistake.*

What of it? What does it matter?; Why treat it as if it were important?; Why do you think that this is any of your business? (Colloquial and a bit contentious.) □ *John: I hear you've been having a little trouble at the office. Bob: What of it?* □ *Sue: You missed a spot shaving. Fred: What of it?*

What say? What did you say? □ *Tom: My coat is there on the chair. Could you hand it to me? Bob: What say? Tom (pointing): Could you hand me my coat?* □ *Sue: Here's your paper. Fred: What say? Sue (louder): Here is your newspaper!*

What someone **said.** I agree with what someone else just said. (Sometimes used when a previous utterance is too difficult to repeat.) □ *Q: Bob stated his position quite clearly, though not concisely. What's your opinion, Andy? A: What Bob said.* □ *Q: With regard to the current economic malaise, do you think, as I do, that Keynesian economics, properly applied, of course, holds our only hope? A: What you said.*

What was the name again? Please tell me your name again. (More typical of a clerk than of someone just introduced.) □ *Clerk: What was the name again? Bill: Bill Smith.* □ *"What was the name again? I didn't write it down," confessed Fred.*

What would you like to drink? an offer to prepare an alcoholic drink. □ BILL: *Come in and sit down. What would you like to drink?* ANDREW: *Nothing, thanks. I just need to relax a moment.* □ WAITER: *What would you like to drink?* ALICE: *Do you have any grape soda?* WAITER: *I'll bring you some ginger ale, if that's all right.* ALICE: *Well, okay. I guess.*

What would you say if I did something**?** How would you feel or think about my doing something? (Also in other persons.) □ BILL: *What would you say if I ate the last piece of cake?* BOB: *Go ahead. I don't care.* □ MARY: *What would you say if we left a little early?* SALLY: *It's okay with me.*

What you been up to? Go to What (have) you been up to?

What you see is what you get. Nothing additional is concealed or available.; What is in front of you is all you get. □ Q: *Are there any red or green ones available?* A: *Sorry. What you see is what you get.* □ DIRECTOR: *Could we get a little more excitement in your face when you say the lines?* ACTOR: *Not today. I'm too upset. What you see is what you get.*

Whatever. Anything—it doesn't matter.; Either one. □ BOB: *Which do you want, red or green?* TOM: *Whatever.* □ MARY: *Do you want to go with me to the seashore or stay here?* JANE: *Whatever.*

Whatever turns you on. 1. If doing that pleases or excites you, then do it. □ MARY: *Do you mind if I buy some of these flowers?* BILL: *Whatever turns you on.* □ MARY: *I just love to hear a raucous saxophone play some smooth jazz.* BOB: *Whatever turns you on, baby.* **2.** If that kind of thing excites you, enjoy it. (Essentially sarcastic.) □ BOB: *I just go wild whenever I see pink gloves on a woman. I don't understand it.* BILL: *Whatever turns you on.* □ JANE: *You see, I never told anybody this, but whenever I see dirty snow at the side of the road, I just go sort of wild inside.* SUE: *Weird, Jane, weird. But, whatever turns you on.*

What'll it be? AND **Name your poison.; What'll you have?; What's yours?** What do you want to drink?; What do you want?; How can I serve you? (Typically said by a bartender or bar waiter or waitress.) □ TOM: *What'll it be, friend?* BILL: *I'll just have a Coke, if you don't mind.* □ WAITRESS: *What'll you have?* BOB: *Nothing, thanks.*

What'll you have? Go to What'll it be?

What's coming off? AND **What's going down?** What is happening here?; What is going to happen? (Slang. Also a greeting inquiry.) ☐ *BILL: Hey, man! What's coming off? TOM: Oh, nothing, just a little car fire.* ☐ *BOB: Hey, we just got here! What's going down? BILL: What does it look like? This is a party, dude!*

What's cooking? What is happening?; How are you? (Colloquial or slang.) ☐ *BOB: Hi, Fred! What's cooking? FRED: How are you doing, Bob?* ☐ *BOB: Hi, Bill! What's cooking? BILL: Nothing. Anything happening with you?*

What's eating someone**?** What is bothering someone? (Slang.) ☐ *TOM: Go away! BOB: Gee, Tom, what's eating you?* ☐ *BILL: Tom's so grouchy lately. What's eating him? BOB: Beats me!*

What's going down? Go to What's coming off?

What's going on (around here)? What is happening in this place?; What is the explanation for the strange things that are happening here? ☐ *BILL: There was an accident in the factory this morning. BOB: That's the second one this week. What's going on around here?* ☐ *MARY: What's all the noise? What's going on? SUE: We're just having a little party.*

What's happening? a general and vague greeting inquiry. (Colloquial.) ☐ *BOB: Hey, man! What's happening? BILL: Nothing. How you be?* ☐ *BILL: Hi, Tom. TOM: Hi, Bill. What's happening? BILL: Nothing much.*

What's in it for me? What is the benefit for me in this scheme? ☐ *BOB: Now, that plan is just what is needed. BILL: What's in it for me? What do I get out of it?* ☐ *SUE: We signed the Wilson contract yesterday. MARY: That's great! What's in it for me?*

What's it to you? Why does it matter to you?; It's none of your business. (Colloquial and a bit contentious.) ☐ *TOM: Where are you going? JANE: What's it to you?* ☐ *MARY: Bill's pants don't match his shirt. JANE: Does it matter? What's it to you?*

What's keeping someone**?** What is delaying someone? (The *someone* is replaced by a person's name or a pronoun.) ☐ *BOB: Wasn't Mary supposed to be here? BILL: I thought so. BOB: Well, what's keeping her? BILL: How should I know?* ☐ *BILL: I've been waiting here for an hour for Sally. SUE: What's keeping her?*

What's new? What things have happened since we last met? □ MARY: *Greetings, Jane. What's new?* JANE: *Nothing much.* □ BOB: *What's new?* TOM: *Not a whole lot.*

What's new with you? a typical response to **What's new?** □ MARY: *What's new?* SALLY: *Oh, nothing. What's new with you?* MARY: *The same.* □ FRED: *Hi, John! How you doing?* JOHN: *Great! What's new with you?*

What's not to love? Isn't it good?; Isn't that the best? □ *Yes, it's a great idea. What's not to love?* □ *Yeah. This is the best small car made. What's not to love?*

What's on tap for today? What is on the schedule for today?; What is going to happen today? (As a beer that is on tap and ready to be served.) □ TOM: *Good morning, Fred.* FRED: *Morning. What's on tap for today?* TOM: *Trouble in the morning and difficulty in the afternoon.* FRED: *So, nothing's new.* □ SALLY: *Can we have lunch today?* SUE: *I'll have to look at my schedule and see what's on tap for today.*

What's the (big) idea? What have you done?; Why did you do that? (Usually expressing a little anger.) □ *You knocked the book out of my hand. What's the big idea?* □ *What's the idea? You just about knocked me down! Watch where you're going!*

What's the catch? What is the drawback?; What are the negative factors? (Colloquial.) □ BILL: *How would you like to have these seven books for your very own?* SALLY: *What's the catch?* BILL: *There's no catch. You have to pay for them, but there's no catch.* □ BOB: *Here, take this dollar bill.* SUE: *So, what's the catch?* BOB: *No catch. It's counterfeit.*

What's the damage? What are the charges?; How much is the bill? (Slang.) □ BILL: *That was delicious. Waiter, what's the damage?* WAITER: *I'll get your check, sir.* □ WAITER: *Your check, sir.* TOM: *Thanks.* BILL: *What's the damage, Tom? Let me pay my share.* TOM: *Nonsense, I'll get it.* BILL: *Okay this time, but I owe you one.*

What's the deal? What's going on?; Why are you doing this? □ MARY: *What's the deal?* SUE: *Oh, hi, Mary. We're just cleaning out the closet.* □ BILL: *Hi, you guys. What's the deal?* BOB: *Nothing, just a little misunderstanding between Fred and Jane.*

What's the drill? 1. What is the assignment?; What am I meant to do? □ *BILL: I just came in. What's the drill? TOM: We have to carry all this stuff out to the truck.* □ *"What's the drill?" asked Mary. "Why are all these people sitting around like this?"* **2.** What are the rules and procedures for doing this? □ *BILL: I need to apply for new license plates. What's the drill? Is there a lot of paperwork? CLERK: Yes, there is.* □ *BILL: I have to get my computer repaired. Who do I talk to? What's the drill? BOB: You have to get a purchase order from Fred.*

What's the good word? a vague greeting inquiry. (Colloquial and familiar. A direct answer is not expected.) □ *BOB: Hey, Tom! What's the good word? TOM: Hi, Bob! How are you doing?* □ *SUE: What's happening? JANE: Hi, Sue. What's the good word?*

What's the matter (with you)? 1. Is there something wrong with you?; Are you ill? □ *BILL: What's the matter with you? FRED: I have this funny feeling in my chest. BILL: Sounds serious.* □ *BOB: I have to stay home again today. BILL: What's the matter with you? Have you seen a doctor?* □ *MARY: Oh, I'm so miserable! SUE: What's the matter? MARY: I lost my contact lenses and my glasses.* □ *JOHN: Ouch! ALICE: What's the matter? JOHN: I bit my tongue.* **2.** How very stupid of you! How can you be so stupid? (Usually said in anger.) □ *As Fred stumbled over the step and dumped the birthday cake on the floor, Jane screamed, "What's the matter with you? The party is in fifteen minutes and we have no cake!"* □ *MARY: I think I just lost the Wilson account. SUE: What! What's the matter with you? That account pays your salary!*

What's the problem? 1. What problem are you presenting to me? □ *BILL (coming in): I need to talk to you about something. TOM: What's the problem, Bill?* □ *"What's the problem?" said Mary, peering at her secretary over her glasses.* **2.** a question asking what the problem is and implying that there should not be a problem. □ *CHILD (crying): He hit me! FATHER: What's the problem? CHILD: He hit me! FATHER: Are you hurt? CHILD: No. FATHER: Then, stop crying.*

What's the scam? What's happening around here? (Slang.) □ *TOM: Hey, man! What's the scam? BILL: Greetings, oh ugly one! What's happening? TOM: Not much. Want to order a pizza? BILL: Always.* □ *John burst into the room and shouted, "Yo! What's the scam?" It took the prayer meeting a little time to get reorganized.*

What's the scoop? What is the news?; What's new with you? (Slang.) □ *Bob: Did you hear about Tom? Mary: No, what's the scoop?* □ *"Hi, you guys!" beamed John's little brother. "What's the scoop?"*

What's the world coming to? AND **What's this world coming to?** Things seem to be getting worse, and people are becoming more rude and inconsiderate all the time. (Perhaps a little old-fashioned.) □ *Doesn't anybody stop at a stop sign these days? What's the world coming to?* □ *Helen: Did you see what she was wearing! What's this world coming to?*

What's (there) to know? This doesn't require any special knowledge—so what are you talking about? □ *Bill: Do you know how to wind a watch? Bob: Wind a watch? What's there to know?* □ *Sue: We must find someone who knows how to repair a broken lawn mower. Tom: What's to know? Just a little tightening here and there. That's all it needs.*

What's this world coming to? Go to What's the world coming to?

What's to know? Go to What's (there) to know?

What's up? What is happening?; What are you doing lately? □ *Bob: Hi, Bill. What's up? Bill: Yo, Bob! Nothing going on around here.* □ *Tom (answering the telephone): Hello? Bill: Hi, this is Bill. Tom: What's up? Bill: You want to go camping? Tom: Sure.*

What's with someone or something**?** Why is someone or something in that condition?; What's going on with someone or something? □ *Mary: What's with Tom? He looks depressed. Bill: He broke up with Sally.* □ *"What's with this stupid coffeepot? It won't get hot!" groused Alice.*

What's wrong? There is something wrong here.; What has happened? □ *Mary: Oh, good grief! Bill: What's wrong? Mary: I forgot to feed the cat.* □ *Sue (crying): Hello, Sally? Sally: Sue, what's wrong? Sally: Oh, nothing. Tom left me.*

What's your deal? What's your problem?; What's wrong with you? □ *Ida: What's the matter? What's your deal? Dan: Nothing. I'm just tired.* □ *What's your deal, dude? That's one really bad mood.*

What's yours? Go to What'll it be?

when all is said and done AND **when everything is said and done** when it is all over (See also at the end of the day.) □ *When all is said and done, we probably would have been better off paying* *cash rather than taking out another loan.* □ *A: Looking back on things, I am pretty sure we made the right decision. B: But when everything is said and done, it's six of one and half a dozen of the other.*

When do we eat? What time is the next meal served? (Familiar. The speaker is hungry.) □ BILL: *This is a lovely view, and your apartment is great. When do we eat?* MARY: *We've already eaten. Weren't you just leaving?* BILL: *I guess I was.* □ ANDREW: *Wow! Something really smells good! When do we eat?* RACHEL: *Oh, mind your manners.*

when everything is said and done Go to when all is said and done.

When I'm good and ready. Not until I want to and no sooner. (A bit contentious.) □ MARY: *When are you going to rake the leaves?* FATHER: *When I'm good and ready.* □ BOB: *When are you going to help me move this piano?* FRED: *When I'm good and ready and not a minute before.*

When pigs can fly. Never!; Only when the impossible becomes possible! (Sarcastic.) □ *Q: When are you going to get this television mounted on the wall? A: When pigs can fly! It's just too heavy.* □ *Sure I can do the long list of things you just gave me. When pigs can fly! Do you really expect me to spend every waking hour working for peanuts?*

when you get a chance Go to when you get a minute.

when you get a minute AND **when you get a chance** a phrase introducing or concluding a request. □ BILL: *Tom?* TOM: *Yes?* BILL: *When you get a minute, I'd like to have a word with you.* □ *"Please drop over for a chat when you get a chance," said Fred to Bill.*

When you('ve) gotta go, you gotta go. 1. When one feels the urge to go to the toilet, it is expected that one should go take care of it. □ *A: Excuse me. I have to leave the room. B: When you gotta go, you gotta go.* □ HELEN: *Sorry, she's away from her desk.* DAN: *Yup, I know. When you gotta go, you gotta go.* **2.** When it is one's time to die, one simply dies. (Only jocular. See also **We all gotta go sometime.**) □ *Yes, Fred was young. But when you gotta go, you gotta go.* □ *I don't fret about death. When you've gotta go, you gotta go.*

Whenever. At whatever time you want.; At whatever time it happens—it really doesn't matter. □ BILL: *When should I pick you up?* SUE: *Oh, whenever. I don't care. Just come on over, and we'll take it from there.* □ MARY: *Well, Uncle Harry, how nice to have you for a visit. We need to book your return flight. When will you be leaving?* UNCLE: *Oh, whenever.*

Where can I wash up? AND **Is there some place I can wash up?** a way of asking where the toilet or bathroom is without referring to one's need to use it. (Of course, this is also appropriate to ask where one can wash one's hands.) □ *The minute Joe got to the house, he asked Fred, "Where can I wash up?"* □ FRED: *Welcome. Come in.* BILL: *Oh, is there someplace I can wash up?*

Where have you been all my life? an expression of admiration usually said to a lover. □ MARY: *I feel very happy when I'm with you.* JOHN: *Oh, Mary, where have you been all my life?* □ *John, who always seemed to sound like a paperback novel, grasped Alice's hand, stared directly at her left ear, and stuttered, "Where have you been all my life?"*

Where have you been hiding yourself? Hello, I haven't seen you in a long time. □ *I haven't seen you in a long time. Where've you been hiding yourself?* □ A: *Remember Bob?* B: *Where has he been hiding himself? We missed him at the meeting.*

Where (have) you been keeping yourself? I haven't seen you for a long time. Where have you been? □ BILL: *Hi, Alice! Where you been keeping yourself?* ALICE: *Oh, I've been around. How are you doing?* BILL: *Okay.* □ JOHN: *Tsup?* BILL: *Hi, man. Where you been keeping yourself?* JOHN: *Oh, I've been busy.*

Where is the rest room? the appropriate way of asking for the toilet in a public building. □ BOB: *'Scuse me.* WAITER: *Yes, sir.* BOB: *Where is the rest room?* WAITER: *To your left, sir.* □ MARY: *Where is the rest room, please?* CLERK: *Behind the elevators, ma'am.*

Where is your powder room? Go to Could I use your powder room?

Where there's smoke, there's fire. Wherever there are signs of a problem, the problem almost certainly exists. □ Q: *Should we investigate the complaints of rude remarks on the production line?* A: *Of course. Where there is smoke, there's fire.* □ ANDY: *He thinks his wife is seeing someone.* DAN: *Well, where there's smoke, there's fire.*

Where will I find you? Please give me directions for finding you. (Said when people are arranging to meet somewhere.) □ SUE: *Where will I find you?* BOB: *I'll be sitting in the third row somewhere.* □ TOM: *We'll get to the farm about noon. Where will we find you?* SALLY: *Probably in the barn. If you can't find me, just go up to the house and make yourself comfortable on the porch.*

Where's the fire? Where are you going in such a hurry? (Typically said by a police officer to a speeding driver.) □ OFFICER: *Okay, where's the fire?* MARY: *Was I going a little fast?* □ *"Where's the fire?" Bob called ahead to Sue, who had gotten well ahead of him in her excitement.*

which brings me to the (main) point a transitional phrase that introduces the main point of a discussion. □ BILL: *Keeping safe at times like this is very important—which brings me to the main point. Does your house have an adequate burglar alarm?* SALLY: *I knew you were trying to sell me something! Out!* □ LECTURER: *. . . which brings me to the point.* JOHN *(whispering): Thank heavens! I knew there was a point to all this.*

Who cares? Does anyone really care?; It is of no consequence. □ JOHN: *I have some advice for you. It will make things easier for you.* BOB: *Who cares?* JOHN: *You might.* □ SUE: *You missed a spot shaving.* FRED: *Who cares?*

Who do you think you are? Why do you think you can lord it over people that way?; Why are you so arrogant? (Usually said in anger.) □ TOM: *Just a minute! Who do you think you are? You can't talk to me that way!* BOB: *Says who?* □ *"Who do you think you are, bursting in here like that?" sputtered the doorman as Fred bolted into the club lobby.*

Who do you think you're kidding? 1. You aren't fooling anyone.; Surely, you do not think you can fool me, do you? □ BILL: *I must pull down about eighty thou a year.* BOB: *You? Who do you think you're kidding?* □ MARY: *This carpet was made in Persia by children.* TOM: *Who do you think you're kidding?*

Who do you think you're talking to? Why do you think you can address me in that manner?; You can't talk to me that way! □ *Tom: Get out of the way! Sue: Who do you think you're talking to? Tom: Then move please.* □ *Clerk: Look, take it or leave it. Isn't it good enough for you? Sue: Who do you think you're talking to? I want to see the manager!*

Who do you want to speak to? Go to Who do you want (to talk to)?

Who do you want (to talk to)? AND **Who do you want to speak to?; Who do you wish to speak to?; Who do you wish to talk to?** Who do you want to speak to over the telephone? (All these questions can also begin with *whom.* Compare to With whom do you wish to speak?) □ *Sue: Wilson residence. Who do you want to speak to? Bill: Hi, Sue. I want to talk to you.* □ *Tom (answering the phone): Hello? Sue: Hello, who is this? Tom: Who do you wish to speak to? Sue: Is Sally there? Tom: Just a minute.*

Who do you wish to speak to? Go to Who do you want (to talk to)?

Who do you wish to talk to? Go to Who do you want (to talk to)?

Who is it? Go to Who's there?

Who is this? Who is making this telephone call?; Who is on the other end of this telephone line? □ *Tom (answering the phone): Hello? Fred: Hello. Do you have any fresh turkeys? Tom: Who is this? Fred: Isn't this the Harrison Poultry Shop? Tom: No. Fred: I guess I have the wrong number.* □ *Mary (answering the phone): Hello? Sue: Hello, who is this? Mary: Well, who did you want? Sue: I want Grandma. Mary: I'm sorry, I think you have the wrong number.*

Who knows? I don't know who knows the answer to that question. □ *Tom: When will this train get in? Rachel: Who knows?* □ *Andrew: Why can't someone put this stuff away? Rachel: Who knows? Why don't you put it away?*

Who was it? Who called on the telephone or who was at the door? (Assumes that the caller or visitor is not waiting on the telephone or at the door.) □ *Sue (as Mary hangs up the telephone): Who was it? Mary: None of your business.* □ *Bill (as he leaves the door): What a pest! Sue: Who was it? Bill: Some silly survey.*

Who could have thought? Go to Who would have thought?

Who would 'a thunk? Go to Who would have thought?

Who would have thought? AND **Who could have thought?; Who would 'a thunk?; Who'd 'a thunk?** Who could have imagined (that such a thing could be)? (*Thunk* is an imaginary past participle of *think*, as in *think, thank, thunk. Thunk* is used only in this expression. The *'a* can also be represented in print as *a.*) □ *Tom's not only a race car driver but an accomplished saxophone player. Who'd 'a thunk?* □ *A: The boss's secretary turns out to be an escaped convict who is wanted in three states. B: Wow! Who would have thought?*

Whoa! Stop! (An instruction—ordering a horse to stop—said to a person.) □ *Bob: First, slip the disk into this slot, and then do a directory command to see what's on it. John: Whoa! You lost me back at "slip the disk . . ."* □ *"Whoa!" shouted Tom at Bill. "Don't move any more in that direction. The floor is rotten there."*

Who'd 'a thunk? Go to Who would have thought?

Whoops! a phrase indicating that an error has been made by someone. □ *"Whoops! I think you meant flout, not flaunt," corrected Sally.* □ *"Whoops! I meant to say mature, not old," said Kate.*

Who's calling(, please)? Who is this making this telephone call? □ *Rachel: Yes, Tom is here. Who's calling, please? Tom: Who is it? Rachel: It's Fred.* □ *Fred (answering the phone): Hello? Tom: Hello, is Bill there? Fred: Who's calling, please? Tom: This is Tom Wilson returning his call.*

Who's on the line? Go to Who's on the phone?

Who's on the phone? AND **Who's on the line?** Who is on the telephone line now?; Who just now called on the telephone? (The caller may still be waiting.) □ *Bill was on the telephone, and Mary walked by. "Who's on the phone?" asked Mary, hoping the call was for her.* □ *Tom asked, "Who's on the line?" Mary covered the receiver and said, "None of your business!"*

Who's there? AND **Who is it?** a question asking who is on the other side of a door or concealed from the speaker. □ *Hearing a noise, Tom called out in the darkness, "Who's there?"* □ *Hearing a knock, Mary went to the door and said, "Who is it?"*

Who's your friend? Who is that following along behind you? □ JOHN: *Hi, Tom. Who's your friend?* TOM: *Oh, this is my little brother, Willie.* JOHN: *Hi, Willie.* □ *Looking at the little dog almost glued to Bob's pants cuff, Sally asked, "Who's your friend?"*

why a sentence opener expressing surprise. (*Why* is pronounced like the name of the letter *Y*.) □ *"Why, it's just a little boy!" said the old sea captain.* □ BOB: *Why, what are you doing here?* MARY: *I was going to ask you the same thing.* □ MARY: *Why, your hair has turned white!* ANDREW: *No, I'm in the school play. This is just temporary.* □ RACHEL: *Why, this page is torn!* ANDREW: *I didn't do it!*

why don't you? a question that can be added to the end of a command. □ ANDREW: *Make a lap, why don't you?* BOB: *Okay. Sorry. I didn't know I was in the way.* □ *"Just keep bugging me, why don't you?" threatened Wally.* □ ANDREW: *Try it again, why don't you?* SUE: *I hope I get it right this time.*

Why not? 1. Please explain your negative answer. □ MARY: *No, you can't.* JANE: *Why not?* □ SUE: *Could I have another piece of cake?* MARY: *No.* SUE: *Why not?* MARY: *I want it.* **2.** I cannot think of a reason not to, so yes. □ BOB: *You want to go to see a movie next Friday?* JANE: *Why not?* □ FRED: *Do you feel like wandering over to the bowling alley?* TOM: *Why not?*

will be here any time Go to **should be here any** time.

Will I see you again? a question asked toward the end of a date implying that further dating would please the speaker if it would please the other party. (This question seeks to find out if there is interest in another date, leaving it open to the other party to confirm that the interest is mutual by requesting a further date. Compare to **Could I see you again?**) □ TOM: *I had a wonderful time tonight, Mary. Good night.* MARY: *Will I see you again?* TOM: *That would be nice. Can I call you tomorrow?* MARY: *That would be nice.* □ *"Will I see you again?" asked Sally, cautiously and hopefully.*

(Will there be) anything else? AND **Is that everything?; Is there anything else?; Will that be all?** Is there anything else you want?; Is there any other matter you wish to discuss?; Is there any other request? (These phrases are used by shopkeepers, clerks, and food service personnel to find out if the customer wants anything more.) □ CLERK: *Here's the roast you ordered. Will there be anything else?* RACHEL: *No, that's all.* □ WAITER: *Anything else?* BILL: *Just coffee.* □ *The clerk rang up the last item and asked, "Anything else?"* □ WAITER: *Anything else?* JANE: *No, that's everything.*

Will you be joining us? Will you be eating, drinking, meeting, or conversing with us? (A vague invitation to participate with a group of other people. See also (Would you) care to join us?) □ *We're going to have a bite to eat. Will you be joining us?* □ *Will you be joining us for drinks this evening?*

Will you excuse us, please? Go to Could you excuse us, please?

Will you hold? Go to Could you hold?

Win a few, lose a few. Sometimes one succeeds, and sometimes one fails. □ TOM: *Well, I lost out on that Wilson contract, but I got the Jones job.* SALLY: *That's life. Win a few, lose a few.* □ *"Win a few, lose a few," said Fred, staring at yesterday's stock prices.*

a **win-win situation** when almost any choice is a good choice. □ *Whether he pitches or you pitch, the batter will strike out, so it's a win-win situation.* □ *Whether they buy a stock or sell it, it's fine with me. I'm a broker, so it's a win-win situation for me.*

With my blessings. a phrase expressing consent or agreement; yes. □ BOB: *Can I take this old coat down to the rummage sale?* SUE: *With my blessing.* □ MARY: *Shall I drive Uncle Tom to the airport a few hours early?* SUE: *Oh, yes! With my blessing!*

with one's **tail between** one's **legs** appearing frightened or cowardly, like a frightened or defeated dog; appearing threatened or humiliated. □ *John seems to lack courage. When people criticize him unjustly, he just goes away with his tail between his legs and doesn't tell them that they're wrong.* □ *The frightened dog ran away with its tail between its legs when the bigger dog growled.*

With pleasure. a phrase indicating eager consent to do something. □ FRED: *Would you please take this note over to the woman in the red dress?* WAITER: *With pleasure, sir.* □ SUE: *Would you kindly bring in the champagne now?* JANE: *With pleasure.*

With whom do you wish to speak? a polite phrase used by telephone answerers to find out whom the caller wants to speak to. (Compare to **Who do you want (to talk to)?**) □ *John answered the telephone and then said, "With whom do you wish to speak?"* □ Tom *(answering the phone): Good morning, Acme Air Products. With whom do you wish to speak?* Sue: *Sorry, I have the wrong number.* Tom: *That's perfectly all right. Have a nice day.*

With you in a minute. Go to (Someone will) be with you in a minute.

within walking distance close enough to walk to. □ *Is the train station within walking distance?* □ *My office is within walking distance from here.*

without a doubt a phrase expressing certainty or agreement; yes. □ John: *This cheese is as hard as a rock. It must have been in the fridge for weeks.* Fred: *It's spoiled, without a doubt.* □ Mary: *Taxes will surely go up before I retire.* Jane: *Without a doubt!*

without further ado without any further words of introduction. (Often said when concluding a public introduction of someone.) □ *And without further ado, here is your friend and mine, Wally Wimple.* □ *Without further ado, I give you Mayor La Trivia!*

wonder if Go to (I) wonder if.

Won't bother me any. Go to (It) won't bother me any.

Won't breathe a word (of it). Go to (I) won't breathe a word (of it).

Won't tell a soul. Go to (I) won't breathe a word (of it).

Won't you come in? a standard way of inviting someone into one's home or office. □ Bill: *Won't you come in?* Mary: *I hope I'm not early.* □ *Tom stood in the doorway of Mr. Franklin's office for a moment. "Won't you come in?" said Mr. Franklin without looking up.*

Works for me. Go to (It) works for me.

Would if I could(, but I can't). Go to (I) would if I could(, but I can't).

Would you believe! Isn't that unbelievable?; How shocking! □ Tom: *Jane has run off and married Fred!* Sally: *Would you believe!* □ Jane: *Then the manager came out and asked us to leave. Would you believe?* Mary: *It sounds just awful. I'd sue.*

(Would you) care for another (one)? Do you want another drink or serving? □ *Tom stood there with an almost empty glass. Bill said, "Would you care for another one?"* □ WAITER: *Care for another one, madam?* SUE: *No, thank you.*

(Would you) care to dance? Do you want to dance with me?; Would you please dance with me? □ JOHN: *Would you care to dance?* MARY: *I don't dance, but thank you for asking.* □ *"Care to dance?" asked Bill, politely, hoping desperately that the answer would be no.*

(Would you) care to (do something**)?** Would you like to do something? (A polite invitation.) □ JOHN: *Would you care to step out for some air?* JANE: *Oh, I'd love it.* □ SUE: *Care to go for a swim?* MARY: *Not now, thanks.*

(Would you) care to join us? Do you want to join us? □ *Tom and Mary saw Fred and Sally sitting at another table in the restaurant. Tom went over to them and asked, "Would you care to join us?"* □ MARY: *Isn't that Bill and Sue over there?* JOHN: *Yes, it is. Shall I ask them to join us?* MARY: *Why not?* JOHN (after reaching the other table): *Hi, you guys! Care to join us?* BILL: *Love to, but Sue's mom is going to be along any minute. Thanks anyway.*

Would you excuse me? 1. a polite question that essentially announces one's departure. (Compare to **Could I be excused?**; **Excuse me.**) □ JANE: *Would you excuse me? I have to get home now.* ANDREW: *Oh, sure. I'll see you to the door.* □ *Rising to leave, Jane said, "Would you excuse me?" and left by the rear door.* **2.** a polite way of requesting passage through or by a group of people; a way of requesting space to exit an elevator. □ *There were two people talking in the corridor, blocking it. Tom said, "Would you excuse me?" They smiled and stepped aside.* □ FRED: *Would you excuse me? This is my floor.* SALLY: *Sure. It's mine too.*

Would you excuse us, please? Go to Could you excuse us, please?

Would you please? a phrase that agrees that what was offered to be done should be done. □ BILL: *Do you want me to take this over to the bank?* MARY: *Would you please?* □ TOM: *Can I take your coat?* SALLY: *Would you please?*

Wouldn't bet on it. Go to (I) wouldn't bet on it.

Wouldn't count on it. Go to (I) wouldn't bet on it.

Wouldn't if I were you. Go to (I) wouldn't if I were you.

Wouldn't know. Go to (I) wouldn't know.

Wow! an exclamation of surprise and amazement. □ *"Wow! A real shark!" said Billy.* □ SALLY: *Wow! I won the contest! What do I get?* RACHEL: *A stuffed doll.* SALLY: *Oh, goodie.* □ JANE: *Wow! I just made it. I thought I would miss this flight for sure.* SUE: *Well, you almost did.*

Ye gods (and little fishes)! Good grief! Wow! (A mild oath.) □ *Q: Can I have the car tonight. A: Ye gods, no! You never fill the gas tank!* □ *Ye gods and little fishes! You broke my cell phone!*

Yeah, sure. You just think so.; Not possible. (Sarcastic and cheeky.) □ *A: I know we can count on you to be here on time and work diligently until the end of the day. B: Yeah, sure.* □ *TEACHER: You are probably the most helpful little boy in my entire class. DONNY: Yeah, sure.*

Yes siree(, Bob)! Absolutely!; Without a doubt! (Not necessarily said to a male or anyone named Bob.) □ *MARY: Do you want some more cake? TOM: Yes siree, Bob!* □ *"That was a fine turkey dinner. Yes siree!" said Uncle Henry.*

Yesterday wouldn't be too soon. an answer to the question "When do you want this?" □ *MARY: Mr. Franklin, when do you want this? FRED: Well, yesterday wouldn't be too soon.* □ *ALICE: When am I supposed to have this finished? SUE: Yesterday wouldn't be too soon.*

yo a word used to get someone's attention or signal that the speaker is in a particular location. □ *ANDREW: Yo, Tom. I'm over here! TOM: I can't see you. Oh, there you are!* □ *BOB: Let's see who's here. I'll call the roll. Bill Franklin. BILL: Yo!*

You ain't just whistling Dixie. You are not just doing or saying something pointless. (The *ain't* is colloquial.) □ *ANDY: The price of gas is just too doggone high! HELEN: You ain't just whistling Dixie!* □ *When you keep talking about too many speeders on our street, you ain't just whistling Dixie.*

You ain't seen nothing yet! The best, most exciting, or cleverest part is yet to come! (The use of *ain't* is a fixed part of this idiomatic expression.) □ *ALICE: Well, the first act was simply divine.*

SUE: *Stick around. You ain't seen nothing yet!* □ MARY: *This part of the city is really beautiful.* BILL: *You ain't seen nothing yet!*

You all right? Go to You okay?

You (always) give up too eas(il)y. You don't stand up for your rights.; You give up without a fight. □ BILL: *Well, I guess she was right.* BOB: *No, she was wrong. You always give up too easily.* □ BOB: *I asked her to go out with me Friday, but she said she thought she was busy.* TOM: *Ask her again. You give up too easy.*

You and me both. AND **You and me too.** I am of the same opinion as you.; I am in the same condition as you. □ ANDY: *I'm really tired!* HELEN: *You and me both.* □ DAN: *I'm starved.* IDA: *You and me too.*

You and me too. Go to You and me both.

You and what army? Go to You and who else?

You and who else? AND **You and what army?** a phrase that responds to a threat by implying that the threat is a weak one. □ BILL: *I'm going to punch you in the nose!* BOB: *Yeah? You and who else?* □ TOM: *Our team is going to slaughter your team.* BILL: *You and what army?* □ BILL: *If you don't stop doing that, I'm going to hit you.* TOM: *You and who else?*

You are something else (again)! You are amazing or entertaining! □ *After Sally finished telling her joke, everyone laughed, and someone said, "Oh, Sally, you are something else!"* □ *"You are something else again," said Fred, admiring Sue's dynamic presentation.*

You asked for it! 1. You are getting what you requested! □ *The waiter set a huge bowl of ice cream, strawberries, and whipped cream in front of Mary, saying apologetically, "You asked for it!"* □ BILL: *Gee, this escargot stuff is gross!* MARY: *You asked for it!* **2.** You are getting the punishment you deserve! □ BILL: *The tax people just ordered me to pay a big fine.* BOB: *The careless way you do your tax forms caused it. You asked for it!* □ MOTHER: *I'm sorry to have to punish you in this fashion, but you asked for it!* BILL: *I did not!*

You been keeping busy? Go to (Have you) been keeping busy?

You been keeping cool? Go to (Have you) been keeping cool?

You been keeping out of trouble? Go to (Have you) been keeping out of trouble?

You been okay? Go to (Have you) been okay?

You bet. AND **You betcha.** Yes.; You can be quite certain. □ *BILL: Can I take one of these apples? BOB: You bet.* □ *BILL: Do you like this movie? TOM: You betcha.*

You bet your boots! Go to You bet your (sweet) life!

You bet your life! Go to You bet your (sweet) life!

You bet your (sweet) life! AND **You bet your boots!; You bet your life!; You bet your (sweet) bippy.** You can be absolutely certain of something! (Informal and colloquial.) □ *MARY: Will I need a coat today? BILL: You bet your sweet life! It's colder than an iceberg out there.* □ *BILL: Will you be at the game Saturday? TOM: You bet your boots!*

You betcha. Go to You bet.

You called? 1. a phrase used when one is returning a telephone call, meaning "What did you want to talk about when you called before?" □ *BILL (answering the phone): Hello? BOB: This is Bob. You called?* □ *TOM: It's Tom. You called? MARY: Hi, Tom. Yes, I wanted to ask you about these estimates.* **2.** a phrase said by someone who has been summoned into a person's presence. (Often used in jest, in the way a servant might answer an employer.) □ *MARY: Oh, Tom. Come over here a minute. TOM (coming to where Mary is standing): You called?* □ *TOM: Bill! Bill! Over here, Bill, across the street. BILL (panting from running and with mock deference): You called?*

You can bank on it. Go to You can take it to the bank.

(You can) call me name. My first name is *my name.* □ *My name is Wallace, but you can call me Wally.* □ *You can call me Fred. Everyone else does.*

You can say that again! That is so true or so insightful that it bears repeating. □ *BILL: Gee, it's cold today! MARY: You can say that again!* □ *BILL: This cake sure is good. FATHER: You can say that again.*

You can take it to the bank. AND **You can bank on it.** You are able to depend on the truthfulness of my statement: it is not counterfeit or bogus. (Also in other persons.) □ *Believe me. What I am telling you is the truth. You can take it to the bank.* □ *This information is as good as gold. Your client can bank on it.*

(You) can't! AND **(You) cannot!** You are wrong, you cannot!; Don't say you can, because you cannot. (The second form is the typical response to **(I) can too.**) □ BILL: *Don't tell me I can't, because I can!* BOB: *Cannot!* BILL: *Can too!* BOB: *Cannot!* BILL: *Can too!* □ TOM: *I want to go to the rock concert. Bill can go and so can I, can't I?* MOTHER: *No, you can't!*

(You) can't beat that. AND **(You) can't top that.** No one can do better than that. (The *you* represents both personal and impersonal antecedents. That is, it means second person singular or plural, and *anyone*.) □ MARY: *Wow! Look at the size of that lobster! It looks yummy!* BILL: *Yeah. You can't beat that. I wonder what it's going to cost.* □ *"What a view! Nothing like it anywhere! You can't top that!" said Jeff, admiring the view he was paying two hundred dollars a night for.*

You can't expect me to believe that. AND **You don't expect me to believe that.** That is so outrageous that no one could believe it. □ BILL: *My father is running for president.* BOB: *You can't expect me to believe that.* □ JANE: *Everyone in our family has one extra toe.* MARY: *You don't expect me to believe that!*

(You) can't fight city hall. There is no way to win in a battle against a bureaucracy. □ BILL: *I guess I'll go ahead and pay the tax bill.* BOB: *Might as well. You can't fight city hall.* □ MARY: *How did things go at your meeting with the zoning board?* SALLY: *I gave up. Can't fight city hall. Better things to do.*

(You) can't get there from here. a catchphrase said jokingly when someone asks directions to get to a place that can be reached only by a circuitous route. □ BILL: *How far is it to Adamsville?* TOM: *Adamsville? Oh, that's too bad. You can't get there from here.* □ *"Galesburg? Galesburg, you say?" said the farmer. "By golly, you can't get there from here!"*

You can't mean that! Surely you do not mean what you said! □ BILL: *I hate you! I hate you! I hate you!* MARY: *You can't mean that.* □ SALLY: *The cake burned, and there's no time to start another before the party.* MARY: *You can't mean that!*

(You) can't take it with you. Since you cannot take your wealth with you when you die, you ought to enjoy it while you're alive. (A proverb.) □ JANE: *Go ahead, enjoy it while you've got it. You can't take it with you.* ANDREW: *I love logic like that.* □ HENRY: *Sure, I* *spent a fortune on this car. Can't take it with you, you know.* RACHEL: *And this way, you can share it with your friends.*

(You) can't top that. Go to (You) can't beat that.

(You) can't win them all. AND **(You) can't win 'em all.** a catchphrase said when someone, including the speaker, has lost in a contest or failed at something. (The *you* is impersonal, meaning *one, anyone.* The apostrophe on *'em* is not always used.) □ MARY: *Gee, I came in last again!* JANE: *Oh, well. You can't win them all.* □ *"Can't win 'em all," muttered Alice as she left the boss's office with nothing accomplished.*

You changed your mind? Go to (Have you) changed your mind?

You clean up good. Go to You clean up well.

You clean up well. AND **You clean up good.; You scrub up well.; You scrub up good.** appears decent and well-groomed after a little effort. (Jocular. A parody of what a country person might use as a compliment for someone who looks neat and tidy, as for a date. Also in other persons.) □ *Hey, you scrub up good, Maude!* □ *Q: How do I look? A: You scrub up pretty well, Travis.* □ *Zeke is no great fashion plate, but he cleans up well.*

(You) could have fooled me. I would have thought otherwise.; I would have thought the opposite. □ HENRY: *Did you know that this land is among the most productive in the entire state?* JANE: *You could have fooled me. It looks quite barren.* □ JOHN: *I really do like Mary.* ANDREW: *Could have fooled me. You treat her rather badly sometimes.*

You could have knocked me over with a feather. I was extremely surprised.; I was so surprised that I was disoriented and could have been knocked over easily. □ ANDREW: *When she told me she was going to get married, you could have knocked me over with a feather.* SALLY: *I can see why.* □ JOHN: *Did you hear that they are going to tear down city hall and build a new one—price tag twelve million dollars?* SALLY: *Yes, and when I did, you could have knocked me over with a feather.*

You couldn't (do that)! AND **You wouldn't (do that)!** an indication of disbelief that someone might do something. □ BILL: *I'm going to run away from home!* JANE: *You couldn't!* □ BILL: *I get so mad at my brother, I could just strangle him.* TOM: *You couldn't do that!*

You do the math. The conclusion is clear and simple, and you can figure it out by yourself.; It's a monetary decision and an easy one at that. □ *A new one is $400 and I can get a reconditioned one for $150. You do the math.* □ *It's as big a car as we can afford. You do the math!*

You doing okay? Go to (Are you) doing okay?

You don't expect me to believe that. Go to You can't expect me to believe that.

You don't know the half of it. You really don't know how bad it is.; You might think that what you have heard is bad, but you do not know the whole story. □ *MARY: They say you've been having a bad time at home. SALLY: You don't know the half of it.* □ *SALLY: The company has no cash, they are losing orders right and left, and the comptroller is cooking the books. MARY: Sounds bad. SALLY: You don't know the half of it.*

You don't know where it's been. It may be dirty, so do not touch it or put it in your mouth, because you do not know where it has been and what kind of dirt it has picked up. (Most often said to children.) □ *MOTHER: Don't put that money in your mouth. You don't know where it's been. BILL: Okay.* □ *FATHER: Take that stick out of your mouth. You don't know where it's been. BOB: It's been on the ground.*

You don't say. 1. a general response to something that someone has said. (Expresses a little polite surprise or interest, but not disbelief.) □ *BILL: I'm starting work on a new job next Monday. BOB: You don't say.* □ *SALLY: The Jones boys are keeping a pet snake. ALICE: You don't say.* **2.** You have just said something that everybody already knows. □ *BILL: I think I'm beginning to put on a little weight. JANE: You don't say.* □ *JOHN: My goodness, prices are getting high. SUE: You don't say.*

You first. an invitation for someone to precede the speaker. □ *BILL: Let's try some of this goose liver stuff. JANE: You first.* □ *BILL: The water sure looks cold. Let's jump in. BOB: You first.*

(You) getting any? Are you having any luck in the sexual realm? (Low. Male to male. Offensive and tacky in contemporary, urban discourse.) □ *Q: Hey, Max. Getting any? A: Yeah. Sure.* □ *Good grief! Are losers like you still saying "You getting any?" instead of "Hello"?*

You go to your church, and I'll go to mine. You do it your way, and I'll do it mine. (Has nothing to do with church attendance.) □ *Yes, you are faster, but I am more exact. You go to your church, and I'll go to mine.* □ *Q: Don't you think you ought to follow my example on this matter? I am certain that my way is the best way. A: I'm doing just fine. You go to your church, and I'll go to mine.*

You got it! 1. Good, you understand it!; Finally, you understand it! □ *BILL: Does that mean I can't have the car tonight? FATHER: You got it!* □ *BOB: The ax has fallen. You're fired! You don't work here any longer! There are no more paychecks coming to you! BILL: In other words, I'm out of a job. BOB: You got it!* **2.** Here is what you asked for!; You will get what you request! □ *DON: Can I have a cheeseburger and fries? ANDREW: You got it!* □ *HANNA: I'd like weekends off and a higher salary. ISABEL: You got it!*

You got me beat. Go to (It) beats me.

You got me there. I do not know the answer to your question. □ *Q: What is this thing? A: You got me there. I don't know.* □ *Q: How much butter do I need in this recipe? A: You got me there. I have no idea what the answer is.*

You hear? Go to (Do) you hear?

You heard someone. Don't argue. You heard your instructions from someone. (The *someone* can be a person's name, a title, or a pronoun.) □ *ANDREW: You heard the man. Get moving. HENRY: Don't rush me!* □ *BILL: What makes her think she can tell me what to do? BOB: She's the boss. Do it! You heard her!*

You just don't get it! You really don't understand what people are trying to tell you! □ *Everyone tells you that you are a bore, but you just don't get it!* □ *You just don't get it! People avoid you because you offend them.*

(You) (just) gotta love it! It is just so ideal!; It's perfect! □ *It's so cute! You just gotta love it!* □ *Great song. I keep singing it in my head. Gotta love it!*

You (just) wait (and see)! AND **Just (you) wait (and see)!** Wait and see what will happen.; If you wait, you will see that what I predict will be true. □ *JOHN: You'll get what you deserve! Just you wait! JANE: Mind your own business.* □ *BILL: Things will get better. Just wait! SUE: Sure, but when?*

(You) (just) watch! Just pay attention to what I do, and you will see that what I said is true! □ *RACHEL: I'll get her to change! You just watch! ANDREW: Good luck!* □ *ANDREW: You watch! You'll see I'm right. SALLY: Sure, you are.* □ *BOB: Watch! This is the way it's done. BILL: You don't know what you're doing. BOB: Just watch!*

You know? Go to (Do you) know what I'm saying?

you know an expression occurring at the beginning or the end of a statement for emphasis. (This expression is often overused, in which case it is meaningless and irritating. Almost the same as You know? but with no expectation of an answer.) □ *ANDREW: Sure, I spent a fortune on this car. Can't take it with you, you know. RACHEL: But there are better things to do with it here and now.* □ *BILL: Do you always lock your door? TOM: Usually. There's a lot of theft around here, you know.* □ *You know, I think people don't really pay attention to—you know—what they say.*

You know what? Go to (Do you) know what?

You know what I mean? Go to (Do you) know what I'm saying?

You know (what I'm saying)? Go to (Do you) know what I'm saying?

You leaving so soon? Go to (Are you) leaving so soon?

You make me laugh! What you said is totally ridiculous.; You are totally ridiculous. (Compare to Don't make me laugh!) □ *BILL: I have this plan to make electricity from garbage. SALLY: What a dumb idea! You make me laugh!* □ *BILL: I'm really sorry. Give me another chance. I'll never do it again! JANE: You make me laugh!*

You mean to say something**?** Go to (Do) you mean to say something?

You mean to tell me something**?** Go to (Do) you mean to say something?

You okay? AND **You all right?** (Are you) doing okay? (A polite inquiry into someone's current state of well-being. Sometimes said when a person is acting a little crazy.) □ *Q: Hey, Fred. You just poured your drink on the floor. You okay? A: Sure.* □ *You look a little pale. You all right?*

You (really) said a mouthful. You said exactly what needed to be said.; What you said was very meaningful and had great impact. (Colloquial and folksy.) □ *BILL: Did you hear what I said to her? JANE: Yes. You said a mouthful. Was she mad?* □ *BILL: This is the*

worst food I have ever eaten. It is either stale, wilted, dry, or soggy!
TOM: *You said a mouthful!*

You said a mouthful. Go to You (really) said a mouthful.

You said it! I agree with you entirely! (There is a stress on both *you* and *said*.) □ BILL: *Wow, it's really hot in here!* BOB: *You said it!* □ MARY: *Let's get out of here! I can't stand this movie.* SALLY: *You said it!*

You scrub up good. Go to You clean up well.

You scrub up well. Go to You clean up well.

You think you're so smart! You act as if you know far more than you do. □ A: *I know more about it than you do.* B: *You think you're so smart! You don't know anything!* □ *Boy! He thinks he's so smart!*

You too. Go to (The) same to you.

(You) took the words right out of my mouth. You said exactly what I meant to say before I had a chance to say it, and, therefore, I agree with you very much. □ BILL: *I think she's old enough to know better.* TOM: *You took the words right out of my mouth.* □ MARY: *This movie is going to put me to sleep.* JANE (yawning): *You took the words right out of my mouth.*

You wait! Go to You (just) wait (and see)!

You want to know something? Go to (Do you) want to know something?

You want to make something of it? Go to (Do you) want to make something of it?

You want to step outside? Go to (Do) you want to step outside?

You watch! Go to (You) (just) watch!

You wish! Go to (Don't) you wish!

You wouldn't be trying to kid me, would you? You are not lying, are you? □ BILL: *There's a mouse sitting on the toe of your shoe.* TOM: *You wouldn't try to kid me, would you?* □ BILL: *The history final examination was changed to yesterday. Did they tell you?* BOB: *You wouldn't be trying to kid me, would you?*

You wouldn't dare ((to) do something**)!** an exclamation that shows disbelief about something that the speaker has threatened to do.

□ *Bill: I'm going to leave school. Tom: You wouldn't dare leave!*
□ *Bill: Be quiet or I'll slap you. Jane: You wouldn't dare!*

You wouldn't (do that)! Go to You couldn't (do that)!

You('d) better believe it! a way of emphasizing a previous statement. □ *Bill: Man, you're the best goalie this team has ever had! Tom: You better believe it!* □ *Bill: This food is so bad. It will probably stunt my growth. Tom: You'd better believe it!*

(You'd) better get moving. an expression encouraging someone to leave. □ *Jane: It's nearly dark. Better get moving. Mary: Okay. I'm leaving right now.* □ *Bob: I'm off. Good night. Bill: Yes, it's late. You'd better get moving.*

(You'd) better mind your Ps and Qs. You have to pay attention to details, especially of etiquette. (Older. There are numerous attempts to explain the origin of this phrase, and none is conclusive.) □ *When you go to the party, mind your Ps and Qs.* □ *Q: Aunt Clara is such a stickler for manners, isn't she? A: Yes. You really have to mind your Ps and Qs when you're around her.*

You'll be sorry you asked. The answer to the question you just asked is so bad that you will be sorry you asked it. (Compare to **(Are you) sorry you asked?**) □ *Father: What are your grades going to be like this semester? Sally: You'll be sorry you asked.* □ *Mary: How much did you pay for that lamp? Jane: You'll be sorry you asked.*

You'll be the death of me (yet). You and your problems may, in fact, kill me. (An exaggeration, of course.) □ *Henry: You'll be the death of me yet. Why can't you ever do anything right? Andrew: I got a talent for it, I guess.* □ *Bill: Mom, the teacher says you have to go to school again for a conference. Mother: Oh, Billy, you'll be the death of me.*

You'll get onto it. Don't worry. You will become more comfortable with this situation soon.; You will catch the spirit of the situation soon. □ *Bill: I just can't seem to do this right. Bob: You'll get onto it.* □ *Mary: How long does it take to learn to work this computer? Jane: Don't fret. You'll get onto it.*

You'll get the hang of it. Don't worry. You will learn soon how it is done. □ *Mary: It's harder than I thought to glue these things together. Tom: You'll get the hang of it.* □ *Bill: I can't seem to swing* *this club the way you showed me.* SALLY: *You'll get the hang of it. Don't worry. Golf is easy.*

You'll never get away with it. You will never succeed with that illegal or outrageous plan. □ BILL: *I have a plan to cheat on the exam.* MARY: *You'll never get away with it.* □ JANE: *I think I can trick everybody into walking out on the performance.* MARY: *That's awful. You'll never get away with it.*

Your guess is as good as mine. I really do not know.; You know as well as I do. □ MARY: *What time do we eat around here?* BOB: *Your guess is as good as mine.* □ BILL: *Why would anyone build a house like that way out here in the woods?* BOB: *Your guess is as good as mine.*

Your place or mine? an expression asking whose dwelling should be the site of a rendezvous. (Often associated with a sudden or spontaneous sexual encounter.) □ BILL: *So, do you want to go somewhere?* MARY: *Your place or mine?* □ BILL: *I was thinking of a movie. What's this "You're place or mine?"* MARY: *Okay, I'll rent the movie and we'll watch it at your place.*

Your secret is safe with me. I will not tell your secret to anyone. □ *Don't worry. I won't tell. Your secret's safe with me.* □ *Your secret is safe with me. I will carry it to my grave.*

You're dern tootin'! You are absolutely right! (Colloquial and folksy. Never the full form *tooting*.) □ TOM: *Are you really going to take up boxing?* BOB: *You're dern tootin'!* □ FATHER: *Do you really want to buy that droopy-looking puppy?* BILL: *You're dern tootin'!*

You're excused. 1. You may leave the room, the table, etc. (Said in response to **Could I be excused?**) □ MOTHER: *Are you finished, Tom?* TOM: *Yes, ma'am.* MOTHER: *You're excused.* □ BILL *(raising his hand): Can I leave the room? I have to go get my books off my bike.* TEACHER: *You're excused.* BILL: *Thanks.* **2.** You must leave the room or the premises. (Typically said at the end of a scolding.) □ FATHER: *I've heard quite enough of this nonsense, Tom. You're excused.* TOM: *Sorry.* □ ANDREW: *That is the end of this conversation. You're excused.* BOB: *But, there's more.* **3.** You are forgiven for belching or for some other breach of strict etiquette. (Said in response to **Excuse me.**) □ TOM *(after belching): Excuse me.* FATHER: *You're excused.* □ SALLY: *Excuse me for being so noisy.* MOTHER: *You're excused.*

You're (just) wasting my time. What you have to say is of no interest to me. □ RACHEL: *I've heard enough. You're just wasting my time. Good-bye.* MARY: *If that's the way you feel about it, good-bye.* □ BILL: *Come on, Bill. I'll show you what I mean.* BILL: *No, you're wasting my time.*

You're on! Your bet, challenge, or invitation is accepted. □ Q: *What about a few beers at the club?* A: *You're on!* □ Q: *I think we can do it. Want to try?* A: *You're on!*

You're only young once. You only have a limited period to behave like a young, and perhaps foolish, person. □ IDA: *Sorry we made so much noise last night.* DAN: *It's okay. You're only young once.* □ *I really hope you are learning something through all your mistakes. Thank heavens you're only young once.*

You're out of your mind! AND **You've got to be out of your mind!** You must be crazy for saying or doing that! (Said to someone who has said or done something silly or stupid.) □ ANDREW: *Go to the Amazon? You're out of your mind!* JANE: *Maybe so, but doesn't it sound like fun?* □ MARY: *Come on, Jane. Let's go swimming in the river.* JANE: *Look at that filthy water. Swim in it? You've got to be out of your mind!*

You're telling me! I know all too well the truth of what you are saying. □ TOM: *Man, it's hot today!* BOB: *You're telling me!* □ JANE: *This food is really terrible.* SALLY: *Wow! You're telling me!*

You're the doctor. You are in a position to tell me what to do.; I yield to you and your knowledge of this matter. (The person being addressed is most likely not a physician.) □ BILL: *Eat your dinner, then you'll feel more like playing ball. Get some energy!* TOM: *Okay, you're the doctor.* □ TEACHER: *You'd better study the first two chapters more thoroughly.* BOB: *You're the doctor.*

You're too much! 1. You are too much of a problem for me. □ ANDREW: *You're too much! I'm going to report you to the head office!* BOB: *Go ahead. See if I care.* □ BOB: *Get out! Just go home! You're too much!* ANDREW: *What did I do?* BOB: *You're a pest!* **2.** You are just too funny, clever, entertaining, etc. □ ALICE: *Oh, Fred, that was really funny. You're too much!* FRED: *I do my best.* □ SALLY: *What a clever thing to say! You're too much!* ANDREW: *Actually, I didn't make it up myself.*

You're welcome. The polite response to **Thanks** or **Thank you**. (Made emphatic and more gracious with an adjective, such as *quite* or *very*.) □ FATHER: *Thank you.* MOTHER: *You're welcome.* □ BOB: *We all thank you very much.* SALLY: *You're quite welcome.*

Yourself? Go to And you?

You've got another think coming. You will have to rethink your position. (The second part of an expression something like, "If you think that, then **you've got another think coming.**" Also with *thing* rather than *think*.) □ RACHEL: *If you think I'm going to stand here and listen to your complaining all day, you've got another think coming!* BILL: *Frankly, I don't care what you do.* □ ANDREW: *If you think you can get away with it, you've got another think coming!* BOB: *Get away with what? I didn't do anything!*

(You've) got me stumped. I can't possibly figure out the answer to your question. □ BILL: *How long is the Amazon River?* JANE: *You've got me stumped.* □ BOB: *Do you know of a book that would interest a retired sea captain?* SALLY: *You've got me stumped.*

You've got to be kidding! This cannot be the truth. Surely you are kidding me! □ BOB: *Sally is getting married. Did you hear?* MARY: *You've got to be kidding!* □ BILL: *I think I swallowed my gold tooth!* MOTHER: *You've got to be kidding!*

You've got to be out of your mind! Go to You're out of your mind!

Yup. Yes. (Colloquial and folksy. Considered rude or disrespectful in some situations, such as a child speaking to an adult.) □ BILL: *Want some more?* TOM: *Yup.* □ MARY: *Tired?* JANE: *Yup.*

Z

Zip it up! Go to Zip (up) your lip!

Zip (up) your lip! AND **Zip it up!** Be quiet!; Close your mouth and be quiet! (Slang and slightly rude.) □ *"I've heard enough. Zip your lip!" hollered the coach.* □ ANDREW: *All right, you guys. Shut up! Zip it up!* BOB: *Sorry.* BILL: *Be quiet.* ANDREW: *That's better.*

Key Word Index

Use this index to find an expression that you want to look up in the Dictionary. First, pick out any major word in the expression you are seeking. Second, look that word up in this index to find the form of the expression used in the Dictionary. Third, look up the phrase in the Dictionary. Entries that are single words should be looked up in the Dictionary directly.

This index provides a convenient way to find an expression using one or more of the words that follow the first word in an entry head. Without the index, there would be no way to find phrases by these "included" words.

Function words, such as pronouns, conjunctions, and prepositions, are not indexed.

Hints

1. When you are trying to find an expression in this index, look up a noun first, if there is one.

2. When you are looking for a noun, try first to find the singular form or the simplest form of the noun.

3. When you are looking for a verb, try first to find the present-tense form or the simplest form of the verb.

4. In most expressions with a noun or pronoun as a variable part of an expression, it will be represented by the word "someone" or "something" (or both) in the form of the expression used in the Dictionary. If you do not find the noun you want in the index, it may, in fact, be a variable word.

5. Use the index as a thematic or topical index by scanning the groups of dictionary entries at each index entry word.

able Able to sit up and take (a little) nourishment.

able (I'm) able to sit up and take (a little) nourishment.

absolutely Absolutely not!

accept I can accept that.

accept I can't accept that.

acquaintance Delighted to make your acquaintance.

acquaintance (I'm) delighted to make your acquaintance.

act Act your age!

ado without further ado

afraid Afraid not.

afraid Afraid so.

afraid 'Fraid not.

afraid 'Fraid so.

afraid (I'm) afraid not.

afraid (I'm) afraid so.

afternoon (Good) afternoon.

again Again(, please).

again Call again.

again Come again.

again Could I see you again?

again Do we have to go through all that again?

again Don't make me say it again!

again Don't make me tell you again!

again Good to see you (again).

again Here we go again.

again Hope to see you again (sometime).

again How's that again?

again (I) hope to see you again (sometime).

again (It's) good to see you (again).

again Let's do this again (sometime).

again Let's not go through all that again.

again Not again!

again Run it by (me) again.

again Run that by (me) again.

again Till we meet again.

again Until we meet again.

again We must do this again (sometime).

again We'll try again some other time.

again What was the name again?

again Will I see you again?

again You are something else (again)!

again You can say that again!

age Act your age!

age Age before beauty.

age in this day and age

ahead Go ahead.

ahead (Go ahead,) make my day!

aim We aim to please.

ain't Ain't it the truth?

ain't That ain't the way I heard it.

ain't You ain't just whistling Dixie.

ain't You ain't seen nothing yet!

alarm I don't want to alarm you, but

alive alive and kicking

alive alive and well

alive (Goodness) sakes alive!

alive Look alive!

alive Sakes alive!

all after all

all all in all

all All is not lost.

all all over

all All right.

all All right already!

all All systems are go.

all All the best to someone.

all all the more reason for doing something

all all things considered

all Are you (all) set?

all By all means.

all Can't win them all.

all Did you order all this weather?

all Do we have to go through all that again?

all Doesn't bother me at all.

all Don't spend it all in one place.

all Everything will work out (all right).

all Everything's going to be all right.

all first of all

all for all intents and purposes

all Haven't got all day.

all (I) haven't got all day.

all I was up all night with a sick friend.

all If that don't beat all!

all I'm all ears.

all (It) doesn't bother me at all.

all It takes all kinds (of people) (to make a world).

all (It) won't bother me at all.

all It'll all come out in the wash.

all It's all someone needs.

all It's written all over one's face.

all know where all the bodies are buried

all Let's not go through all that again.

all Not at all.

all Of all the nerve!

all Of all things!

all once and for all

all The shame of it (all)!

all That (all) depends.

all That's all folks.

all That's all someone needs.

all Things will work out (all right).

all We all gotta go sometime.

all We're all (standing) behind you.

all when all is said and done

all Where have you been all my life?

all You all right?

all (You) can't win them all.

alligator Later, alligator.

anything Don't do anything I wouldn't do.

anything If there's anything you need, don't hesitate to ask.

anything (Is) anything going on?

anything Is there anything else?

anything (Will there be) anything else?

anytime Anytime you are ready.

anytime Come back anytime.

anywhere Put it anywhere.

approach Take a shotgun approach to the problem.

argue Can't argue with that.

argue (I) can't argue with that.

army You and what army?

aside Step aside.

ask (Are you) sorry you asked?

ask Couldn't ask for more.

ask Doesn't hurt to ask.

ask Don't ask.

ask Don't ask me.

ask (I) couldn't ask for more.

ask I couldn't ask you to do that.

ask if I might ask

ask If there's anything you need, don't hesitate to ask.

ask If you don't see what you want, please ask (for it).

ask (I'm) sorry you asked (that).

ask (It) doesn't hurt to ask.

ask (It) never hurts to ask.

ask Never hurts to ask.

ask Sorry (that) I asked.

ask Sorry you asked.

ask You asked for it!

ask You'll be sorry you asked.

away Don't stay away so long.

away Fire away!

away Go away!

away right away

away You'll never get away with it.

awfully Thanks awfully.

back Come back and see us.

back Come back anytime.

back Come back when you can stay longer.

back Get back to me (on this).

back Get off my back!

back I'll call back later.

back I'll get back to you (on that).

back keep something on the back burner

back Let me get back to you (on that).

back push back (against someone or something)

back Right back at you.

back walk something back

bad (It's) not half bad.

bad My bad.

bad Not bad.

bad Not half bad.

bad (That's) too bad.

bad Too bad.

balance on balance

best Everything will work out for the best.

best Give it your best shot.

best Give my best to someone.

best Things will work out for the best.

best to the best of my knowledge

bet Don't bet on it!

bet (I) wouldn't bet on it.

bet I('ll) bet

bet Wouldn't bet on it.

bet You bet.

bet You bet your boots!

bet You bet your life!

bet You bet your (sweet) life!

bet You betcha.

betcha You betcha.

better Better be going.

better Better be off.

better Better get moving.

better Better get on my horse.

better Better hit the road.

better Better keep quiet about it.

better Better keep still about it.

better Better late than never.

better better left unsaid

better Better luck next time.

better Better mind your Ps and Qs.

better Better safe than sorry.

better Better than nothing.

better Better things to do.

better Could be better.

better Couldn't be better.

better do someone one better

better go someone one better

better Got better things to do.

better (I) could be better.

better (I) couldn't be better.

better I have better things to do.

better (I'd) better be going.

better (I'd) better be off.

better (I'd) better get moving.

better (I'd) better get on my horse.

better (I'd) better hit the road.

better (It) couldn't be better.

better (It's) better than nothing.

better (I've) (got) better things to do.

better (I've) never been better.

better (I've) never felt better.

better (I've) seen better.

better Might be better.

better Never been better.

better Never felt better.

better Seen better.

better So much the better.

better (Someone had) better keep quiet about it.

better (Someone had) better keep still about it.

better The sooner the better.

better (Things) could be better.

better (Things) might be better.

better You('d) better believe it!

better (You'd) better get moving.

better (You'd) better mind your Ps and Qs.

beware Let the buyer beware.

big Like it's such a big deal!

big No big deal!

big What's the (big) idea?

bill Could I have the bill?

bit bit by bit

bit quite a bit

bite Bite your tongue!

bite grab a bite (to eat)

bite I'll bite.

black in black and white

blank Fill in the blanks.

blessing Be thankful for small blessings.

blessing With my blessing(s).

blood curdle someone's blood

blood Hell's bells (and buckets of blood)!

blow It blows my mind!

board Are you on board?

body know where all the bodies are buried

body Over my dead body!

book Not in my book.

book throw the book at someone

boot You bet your boots!

born Were you born in a barn?

both You and me both.

bother Doesn't bother me any.

bother Doesn't bother me at all.

bother Don't bother.

bother Don't bother me!

bother Don't bother me none.

bother (It) doesn't bother me any.

bother (It) doesn't bother me at all.

bother (It) don't bother me none.

bother (It) won't bother me any.

bother (It) won't bother me at all.

bother Won't bother me any.

bottom Bottoms up.

bounce That's the way the ball bounces.

bowel Don't get your bowels in an uproar!

boy Boy howdy!

boy Boy, oh boy!

boy Boys will be boys.

boy How's my boy?

boy How's the boy?

boy Oh, boy.

break Break a leg!

break break a sweat

break Break it up!

break Give me a break!

break sound like a broken record

breath Don't hold your breath.

breath Don't waste your breath.

breath I don't have time to catch my breath.

call Call me name.

call Could I call you?

call Could I have someone call you?

call Could I tell someone who's calling?

call Don't call us, we'll call you.

call Give me a call.

call Good call!

call I'll call back later.

call issue a call for something

call Let's call it a day.

call (Most) folks (around here) call me name.

call Nice call!

call Thank you for calling.

call Time to call it a day.

call Time to call it a night.

call What number are you calling?

call Who's calling(, please)?

call You called?

call (You can) call me name.

came This is where I came in.

candidly speaking (quite) candidly

cap put a cap on something

card Cash or credit (card)?

care As if (I cared)!

care Care for another?

care Care if I join you?

care Care to dance?

care Care to (do something)?

care Care to join us?

care Could(n't) care less.

care (Do you) care if I join you?

care (I) could(n't) care less.

care I don't care.

care (Just) taking care of business.

care Like I care!

care See if I care!

care Take care (of yourself).

care Taking care of business.

care Who cares?

care (Would you) care for another (one)?

care (Would you) care to dance?

care (Would you) care to (do something)?

care (Would you) care to join us?

careful Be careful.

case be the case

case in any case

cash Cash or credit (card)?

cat Look (at) what the cat dragged in!

cat Looks like something the cat dragged in.

cat (Someone) looks like something the cat dragged in.

cat There's more than one way to skin a cat.

catch Catch me later.

catch Catch me some other time.

catch Catch you later.

catch Good catch!

catch I didn't catch the name.

day That'll be the day!

day There aren't enough hours in the day.

day Those were the days.

day Time to call it a day.

dead Over my dead body!

deal deal someone in

deal Like it's such a big deal!

deal No big deal!

deal What's the deal?

deal What's your deal?

dear Dear me!

death You'll be the death of me (yet).

declare I (do) declare!

definitely Definitely!

definitely Definitely not!

delighted Delighted to have you.

delighted Delighted to make your acquaintance.

delighted (I'm) delighted to have you (here).

delighted (I'm) delighted to make your acquaintance.

delighted (We're) delighted to have you.

denial in denial

depend That (all) depends.

dern You're dern tootin'!

devil Speak of the devil.

die I'm (just) dying to know.

difference (It) makes me no difference.

difference (It) makes no difference to me.

difference Makes me no difference.

difference Makes no difference to me.

dig Dig in!

dig Dig up!

diggety Hot diggety (dog)!

dinner Dinner is served.

distance within walking distance

Dixie You ain't just whistling Dixie.

doctor You're the doctor.

dog Hot diggety (dog)!

dog Hot dog!

dollar a day late and a dollar short

door check something at the door

doubt I doubt it.

doubt I doubt that.

doubt no doubt

doubt No doubt about it.

doubt (There is) no doubt about it.

doubt without a doubt

down Anything new down your way?

down (Are) things getting you down?

down Come in and sit down.

down Do sit down.

down Don't let someone or something get you down.

ever if I ever saw one

ever more than you('ll ever) know

every every other person or thing

every How's every little thing?

everyone Everyone is (standing) behind you.

everything drop everything

everything everything humanly possible

everything Everything okay?

everything Everything will work out (all right).

everything Everything will work out for the best.

everything Everything's coming up roses.

everything Everything's going to be all right.

everything Hold everything!

everything (Is) everything okay?

everything Is that everything?

everything That beats everything!

everything when everything is said and done

evil the lesser of two evils

exactly My sentiments exactly.

excuse Can you excuse us, please?

excuse Could I be excused?

excuse Could you excuse us, please?

excuse Excuse me.

excuse Excuse me?

excuse Excuse, please.

excuse 'Scuse (me).

excuse 'Scuse me?

excuse 'Scuse, please.

excuse Will you excuse us, please?

excuse Would you excuse me?

excuse Would you excuse us, please?

excuse You're excused.

expect As I expected.

expect Do you expect me to believe that?

expect I expect.

expect I expect not.

expect I expect (so).

expect (Just) as I expected.

expect What do you expect?

expect You can't expect me to believe that.

expect You don't expect me to believe that.

extra go the extra mile

eye Here's mud in your eye.

face Get out of my face!

face have some face time with someone

face in someone's face

face It's written all over one's face.

face Shut your face!

face take someone or something at face value

fair Fair to middling.

fair No fair!

family How's the family?

family How's your family?

fancy Fancy meeting you here!

fancy Fancy that!

far (as) far as I know

far (as) far as I'm concerned

far far as I know

far far as I'm concerned

fast Make it fast.

fat fat chance

fault through no fault of someone's **own**

favor Thank God for small favors.

feather You could have knocked me over with a feather.

fed I'm (really) fed up (with someone or something).

feedback I'd like some feedback on something.

feel (I've) never felt better.

feel Never felt better.

feeling (Are you) feeling okay?

feeling Feeling okay.

feeling How (are) you feeling?

feeling How you feeling?

feeling I just have this feeling

feeling (I'm) feeling okay.

feet Come in and take a load off your feet.

felicitation Greetings and felicitations!

felt (I've) never felt better.

felt Never felt better.

few I have to wash a few things out.

few Win a few, lose a few.

field come out of left field

field field questions

field level the playing field

fight Can't fight city hall.

fight Don't give up without a fight!

fight I won't give up without a fight.

fight Them's fighting words!

fight (You) can't fight city hall.

figure Go figure!

fill Fill in the blanks.

final one final thing

final one final word

find Where will I find you?

fine Fine by me.

fine Fine with me.

fine (It) suits me (fine).

fine not to put too fine a point on it

fine Suits me (fine).

fine (That's) fine by me.

fine (That's) fine with me.

finger have one's finger in too many pies

finish I'm not finished with you.

fire Fire away!

fire Where there's smoke, there's fire.

fire Where's the fire?

first first of all

first in the first place

first Ladies first.

first Not if I see you first.

first You first.

fish Ye gods (and little fishes)!

five Give me five!

five Slip me five!

flattery Flattery will get you nowhere.

flight Have a nice flight.

floor Floor it!

floor This is my floor.

flop That's the way the mop flops.

fly Go fly a kite!

fly Got to fly.

fly How time flies.

fly It'll never fly!

fly (I've) got to fly.

fly (My,) how time flies.

fly off to a flying start

fly When pigs can fly.

folks (Most) folks (around here) call me name.

folks That's all folks.

follow Do you follow?

fool Could have fooled me.

fool (You) could have fooled me.

foolishness Enough (of this) foolishness!

foolishness (That's) enough (of this) foolishness!

foot Come in and take a load off your feet.

foot I wouldn't touch something with a ten-foot pole.

forbid God forbid!

forget Don't forget to write.

forget Forget (about) it!

forth and so forth

frankly quite frankly

frankly (speaking) (quite) frankly

free for free

free get off scot-free

free No such thing as a free lunch.

free (There's) no such thing as a free lunch.

French Pardon my French.

fret Fret not!

friend Any friend of someone('s) (is a friend of mine).

friend I was up all night with a sick friend.

friend Who's your friend?

fruit pick the low-hanging fruit

fun Have fun.

funeral It's your funeral.

funny Cut the funny stuff!

funny That's funny.

further without further ado

gain No pain, no gain.

game have a chip in the game

game have some skin in the game

gas Now you're cooking (with gas)!

general in general

head Can't make heads or tails of something.

head Heads up!

head (I) can't make heads or tails of something.

head need something like a hole in the head

head off the top of one's head

head (right) off the top of one's head

head Use your head!

hear did you hear?

hear (Do) you hear?

hear Glad to hear it.

hear Good to hear your voice.

hear have you heard?

hear I hear what you're saying.

hear I hear you.

hear (I) never heard of such a thing!

hear (I'm) glad to hear it.

hear (I'm) sorry to hear that.

hear (It's) good to hear your voice.

hear I've heard so much about you.

hear like to hear oneself talk

hear Never heard of such a thing.

hear Sorry to hear that.

hear That ain't the way I heard it.

hear You hear?

hear You heard someone.

heart Have a heart!

heart Take heart.

heartbeat do something in a heartbeat

heaven (Good) heavens!

heaven Heavens!

heaven (My) heavens!

heaven Thank heavens!

hell hell on earth

hell Hell with that!

hell Hell's bells (and buckets of blood)!

hell There will be hell to pay.

hell (To) hell with that!

hello Say hello to someone (for me).

help Can't be helped.

help Can't help it.

help Could I help you?

help Couldn't be helped.

help Couldn't help it.

help Help me (out) with this.

help Help me understand this.

help Help yourself.

help How can I help you?

help How may I help you?

help (I) can't help it.

help (I) couldn't help it.

help (It) can't be helped.

help (It) couldn't be helped.

help May I help you?

hesitate If there's anything you need, don't hesitate to ask.

hide Where have you been hiding yourself?

high leave someone high and dry

highway (It's) my way or the highway.

highway My way or the highway.

history The rest is history.

hit Better hit the road.

hit Got to hit the road.

hit (I'd) better hit the road.

hit (It's) time to hit the road.

hit (I've) got to hit the road.

hit Time to hit the road.

hold Can you hold?

hold Could you hold?

hold Don't hold your breath.

hold Hold everything!

hold Hold it!

hold Hold on (a minute)!

hold Hold, please.

hold Hold the line(, please).

hold Hold the wire(, please).

hold Hold your horses!

hold Hold your tongue!

hold Please hold.

hold Will you hold?

hole need something like a hole in the head

home Come in and make yourself at home.

home drive something home

home Got to go home and get my beauty sleep.

home (I've) got to go home and get my beauty sleep.

home Make yourself at home.

hood look under the hood

hook hook up with someone

hop Hop to it!

hope Hope not.

hope Hope so.

hope Hope to see you again (sometime).

hope (I) hope not.

hope (I) hope so.

hope (I) hope to see you again (sometime).

hopefully hopefully

horse Better get on my horse.

horse Hold your horses!

horse I could eat a horse!

horse (I'd) better get on my horse.

horse (I'm so hungry) I could eat a horse!

horsefeathers Horsefeathers!

hot Hot diggety (dog)!

hot Hot dog!

hot Hot enough for you?

hot Hot ziggety!

hot (Is it) hot enough for you?

hotcakes selling like hotcakes

hour There aren't enough hours in the day.

house My house is your house.

house Our house is your house.

house Welcome to our house.

howdy Boy howdy!

howdy Howdy(-do).

humanly everything humanly possible

humble in my humble opinion

just I'm (just) dying to know.

just (I'm) just getting by.

just (I'm) just looking.

just (I'm just) minding my own business.

just (I'm) (just) plugging along.

just (I'm) (just) thinking out loud.

just (It) just goes to show (you) (something).

just (It's) just what you need.

just Just a minute.

just Just a moment.

just Just a second.

just (Just) as I expected.

just Just getting by.

just Just goes to show (you).

just (Just) gotta love it!

just just let me say

just just like that

just Just looking.

just Just plugging along.

just (Just) taking care of business.

just Just thinking out loud.

just Just wait!

just Just want(ed) to (do something).

just Just watch!

just Just what you need.

just Just wondering.

just Just (you) wait (and see)!

just let me (just) say

just (Let's) just move on.

just Some people (just) don't know when to give up.

just Some people (just) don't know when to quit.

just That's (just) too much!

just That's just what you need.

just We were just talking about you.

just You ain't just whistling Dixie.

just You just don't get it!

just (You) (just) gotta love it!

just You (just) wait (and see)!

just (You) (just) watch!

just You're (just) wasting my time.

keep Been keeping busy.

keep Been keeping cool.

keep Been keeping out of trouble.

keep Better keep quiet about it.

keep Better keep still about it.

keep Could you keep a secret?

keep (Have you) been keeping busy?

keep (Have you) been keeping cool?

keep (Have you) been keeping out of trouble?

keep I'll thank you to keep your opinions to yourself.

keep (I've) been keeping busy.

keep (I've) been keeping cool.

keep (I've) been keeping out of trouble.

know (Do you) know what I'm saying?

know (Do you) want to know something?

know Don't I know it!

know Don't I know you from somewhere?

know Don't you know?

know Don't you know it!

know far as I know

know God only knows!

know How do you know?

know How do you know someone?

know How should I know?

know How will I know you?

know I don't know.

know I know (just) what you mean.

know (I) wouldn't know.

know if you know what's good for you

know I'm (just) dying to know.

know Know something?

know Know what?

know Know what I mean?

know Know what I'm saying?

know know when one is not wanted

know know where all the bodies are buried

know Lord knows I've tried.

know more than you('ll ever) know

know Some people (just) don't know when to give up.

know Some people (just) don't know when to quit.

know Want to know something?

know (Well,) what do you know!

know What do you know?

know What do you know for sure?

know What's (there) to know?

know What's to know?

know Who knows?

know Wouldn't know.

know You don't know the half of it.

know You don't know where it's been.

know You know?

know you know

know You know what?

know You know what I mean?

know You know (what I'm saying)?

know You want to know something?

knowledge to the best of my knowledge

lady Ladies first.

lake Go jump in the lake!

lap Make a lap.

last I didn't (quite) catch that (last) remark.

last That's the last straw!

late Better late than never.

let Let's get out of here.

let Let's get together (sometime).

let Let's go somewhere where it's (more) quiet.

let Let's have it!

let (Let's) just move on.

let Let's not go through all that again.

let Let's shake on it.

let Let's talk (about it).

level Are you leveling with me?

level level the playing field

lie No lie?

life Having the time of my life.

life (I'm) having the time of my life.

life Life's been good (to me).

life Not in this life!

life Not on your life!

life That's the story of my life.

life Where have you been all my life?

life You bet your life!

life You bet your (sweet) life!

lift (Could I) give you a lift?

lift Could I have a lift?

lift Give you a lift?

lift How about a lift?

lift Thanks for the lift.

like Don't even look like something!

like How do you like it here?

like How do you like school?

like How do you like that?

like How do you like this weather?

like I don't want to sound like a busybody, but

like I would like (for) you to meet someone.

like I would like to introduce you to someone.

like I'd like some feedback on something.

like I'd like some input about something.

like I'd like (to have) a word with you.

like I'd like to speak to someone, please.

like I'm like you.

like (It) sounds like a plan.

like just like that

like Like I care!

like like I said

like like I was saying

like Like it or lump it!

like Like it's such a big deal!

like like to hear oneself talk

like like you say

like Looks like something the cat dragged in.

like need something like a hole in the head

like selling like hotcakes

like (Someone) looks like something the cat dragged in.

like sound like a broken record

like Sounds like a plan.

look Look who's talking!

look Looking good.

look Looks like something the cat dragged in.

look (Someone) looks like something the cat dragged in.

loop keep someone in the loop

loose Loose lips sink ships.

lord Lord knows I've tried.

lose lose one's train of thought

lose Win a few, lose a few.

lost All is not lost.

lost almost lost it

lost Get lost!

lot Lots of luck!

lot Thank you a lot.

lot Thanks (a lot).

loud For crying out loud!

loud (I) read you loud and clear.

loud (I'm) (just) thinking out loud.

loud Just thinking out loud.

loud Read you loud and clear.

loud thinking out loud

love Don't you just love it?

love Gotta love it!

love I don't love something

love (I) love it!

love (Just) gotta love it!

love Love it!

love Not for love nor money.

love What's not to love?

love (You) (just) gotta love it!

lovely I had a lovely time.

lovely I've had a lovely time.

lovely Lovely weather for ducks.

lovely Thank you for a lovely evening.

lovely Thank you for a lovely time.

lovely We had a lovely time.

lovely We've had a lovely time.

low pick the low-hanging fruit

luck (The) best of luck (to you).

luck Better luck next time.

luck Good luck!

luck Lots of luck!

luck No such luck.

lucky lucky for you

lull lull before the storm

lump Like it or lump it!

lunch Let's do lunch (sometime).

lunch No such thing as a free lunch.

lunch (There's) no such thing as a free lunch.

lunch We('ll) have to do lunch sometime.

mad so mad I could scream

made Have I made myself clear?

main in the main

main That brings me to the (main) point.

main which brings me to the (main) point

make Can't make heads or tails of something.

make Come in and make yourself at home.

make Delighted to make your acquaintance.

make Do I make myself (perfectly) clear?

make (Do you) want to make something of it?

make Don't make me laugh!

make Don't make me no nevermind.

make Don't make me say it again!

make Don't make me tell you again!

make Don't make yourself a stranger!

make (Go ahead,) make my day!

make Have I made myself clear?

make (I) can't make heads or tails of something.

make (I'm) delighted to make your acquaintance.

make (It) don't make me no nevermind.

make (It) makes me no difference.

make (It) makes no difference to me.

make It takes all kinds (of people) (to make a world).

make kiss and make up

make Make a lap.

make Make it fast.

make Make it snappy!

make make it (to something)

make Make it two.

make Make mine something.

make Make my day!

make Make no mistake (about it)!

make Make up your mind.

make Make your mind up.

make Make yourself at home.

make Makes me no difference.

make Makes me no nevermind.

make Makes no difference to me.

make Makes no nevermind to me.

make need to make a pit stop

make That makes two of us.

make They (just) don't make them like they used to.

make Want to make something of it?

make What makes you think so?

make You make me laugh!

make You want to make something of it?

man man up

manner in a manner of speaking

manners Mind your manners.

manners Remember your manners.

many How many times do I have to tell you?

math You do the math.

matter Doesn't matter to me.

matter (It) (really) doesn't matter to me.

matter Really doesn't matter to me.

matter What's the matter (with you)?

maybe I don't mean maybe!

maybe Maybe some other time.

meal Enjoy your meal.

mean By all means.

mean (Do you) know what I mean?

mean (Do) you mean to say something?

mean (Do) you mean to tell me something?

mean I don't mean maybe!

mean I know (just) what you mean.

mean Know what I mean?

mean No offense meant.

mean You can't mean that!

mean You know what I mean?

mean You mean to say something?

mean You mean to tell me something?

meantime in the meantime

meet Fancy meeting you here!

meet Glad to meet you.

meet Have you met someone?

meet Haven't we met before?

meet I believe we've met.

meet I don't think we've met.

meet I would like (for) you to meet someone.

meet I'm glad to meet you.

meet (I'm) pleased to meet you.

meet (I'm) (very) glad to meet you.

meet (It's) nice to meet you.

meet Nice to meet you.

meet Pleased to meet you.

meet Till we meet again.

meet Until we meet again.

meet Very glad to meet you.

memory jog someone's memory

mention not to mention someone or something

mention not worth mentioning

message Could I leave a message?

message Could I take a message?

message (Do you) get the message?

message Get the message?

middling Fair to middling.

might if I might ask

might might as well (do something)

might Might be better.

might (Things) might be better.

mile Give one an inch, and one will take a mile.

mile Give people an inch, and they will take a mile.

mile go the extra mile

million Thanks a million.

mind Better mind your Ps and Qs.

mind Changed my mind.

mind Changed your mind?

mind Do you mind?

mind (Do you) mind if I do something?

mind (Do you) mind if I join you?

mind Don't mind if I do.

mind Don't mind me.

mind (Have you) changed your mind?

mind (I) changed my mind.

mind (I) don't mind if I do.

mind If you don't mind.

mind I'll thank you to mind your own business.

mind (I'm just) minding my own business.

mind It blows my mind!

mind keep in mind that

mind keep (it) in mind that

mind Make up your mind.

mind Make your mind up.

mind Mind if I do something?

mind Mind if I join you?

mind Mind your manners.

mind Mind your own business.

mind Minding my own business.

mind Never mind!

mind You changed your mind?

mind (You'd) better mind your Ps and Qs.

mind You're out of your mind!

mind You've got to be out of your mind!

mine Any friend of someone('s) (is a friend of mine).

mine Make mine something.

mine You go to your church, and I'll go to mine.

mine Your guess is as good as mine.

mine Your place or mine?

minute Be with you in a minute.

minute Hang on (a minute).

minute Hold on (a minute)!

minute Just a minute.

minute (Someone will) be with you in a minute.

minute Wait a minute.

minute Wait up (a minute)!

minute when you get a minute

minute With you in a minute.

mistake Make no mistake (about it)!

moment Hang on a moment.

moment Just a moment.

moment One moment, please.

money Not for love nor money.

money Not for my money.

monkey I'll be a monkey's uncle!

month Haven't seen you in a month of Sundays.

month (I) haven't seen you in a month of Sundays.

mop That's the way the mop flops.

nevermind (It) don't make me no nevermind.

nevermind Makes me no nevermind.

nevermind Makes no nevermind to me.

new Anything new down your way?

new (So) what else is new?

new That's a new one on me!

new What else is new?

new What's new?

new What's new with you?

news No news is good news.

news That's news to me.

next Better luck next time.

next (Good-bye) until next time.

next (I'll) see you next year.

next Next question.

next See you next year.

next Till next time.

next Until next time.

nice Had a nice time.

nice Have a nice day.

nice Have a nice flight.

nice Have a nice trip.

nice (I) had a nice time.

nice (It's been) nice talking to you.

nice It's nice to be here.

nice It's nice to have you here.

nice (It's) nice to meet you.

nice (It's) nice to see you.

nice Nice call!

nice Nice going!

nice Nice job!

nice Nice place you have here.

nice Nice talking to you.

nice Nice to be here.

nice Nice to have you here.

nice Nice to meet you.

nice Nice to see you.

nice Nice weather we're having.

nick in the nick of time

night Good night.

night I must say good night.

night I was up all night with a sick friend.

night I'll be saying good night.

night Nighty-night.

night Time to call it a night.

none bar none

none Don't bother me none.

none (It) don't bother me none.

none (It's) none of your business!

none None of your business!

none None of your lip!

normal under normal circumstances

nose Get your nose out of my business.

nose Keep your nose out of my business.

nose No skin off my nose.

nose put someone's nose out of joint

nose (That's) no skin off my nose.

note Drop me a note.

nothing Better than nothing.

nothing for nothing

nothing Here goes nothing.

nothing (I have) nothing to complain about.

nothing (It's) better than nothing.

nothing Nothing doing!

nothing Nothing for me, thanks.

nothing Nothing much.

nothing Nothing to complain about.

nothing Nothing to it!

nothing (There's) nothing to it!

nothing Think nothing of it.

nothing You ain't seen nothing yet!

nourishment Able to sit up and take (a little) nourishment.

nourishment (I'm) able to sit up and take (a little) nourishment.

now Could I take your order (now)?

now from now on

now Good-bye for now.

now Have to go now.

now (I) have to go now.

now Not right now, thanks.

now now, now

now now then

now Now what?

now (Now,) where was I?

now Now you're cooking (with gas)!

now Now you're talking!

now right now

now That's enough for now.

now What now?

nowhere Flattery will get you nowhere.

number What number are you calling?

oath under oath

oblige Much obliged.

offense No offense meant.

offense No offense taken.

office Could I see you in my office?

okay (Are you) doing okay?

okay (Are you) feeling okay?

okay Been okay.

okay Doing okay.

okay Everything okay?

okay Feeling okay.

okay (Have you) been okay?

okay (I'm) doing okay.

okay (I'm) feeling okay.

okay (Is) everything okay?

okay (I've) been okay.

okay Okay by me.

okay Okay with me.

okay (That's) okay by me.

okay (That's) okay with me.

okay You been okay?

okay You doing okay?

okay You okay?

old from the old school

old the good old days

old That's old school.

once If I've told you once, I've told you a thousand times.

once once and for all

once once more

once You're only young once.

one do someone one better

one Don't spend it all in one place.

one from day one

one go someone one better

one Have a good one.

one I owe you one.

one if I ever saw one

one I'm with you on that (one).

one It's six of one and half a dozen of another.

one It's six of one and half a dozen of the other.

one my one and only

one the one and only, someone

one one final thing

one one final word

one One moment, please.

one one more thing

one one more time

one one way or another

one Tell me another (one)!

one That's a new one on me!

one There's more than one way to skin a cat.

one This one's on me.

one (Would you) care for another (one)?

only God only knows!

only I'm only looking.

only my one and only

only the one and only, someone

only You're only young once.

open open a conversation

opener for openers

opinion I'll thank you to keep your opinions to yourself.

opinion in my humble opinion

opinion in my opinion

opinion keep one's opinions to oneself

opinion Keep your opinions to yourself!

order (Are you) ready to order?

order Could I take your order (now)?

order Did you order all this weather?

order Ready to order?

other Catch me some other time.

other every other person or thing

other (I'll) try to catch you some other time.

other in other words

other It's six of one and half a dozen of the other.

other Maybe some other time.

other on the other hand

other Try to catch you some other time.

other We'll try again some other time.

outside (Do) you want to step outside?

outside You want to step outside?

owe I owe you one.

owe owing to something

own I'll thank you to mind your own business.

own (I'm just) minding my own business.

own Mind your own business.

own Minding my own business.

own through no fault of someone's own

pain No pain, no gain.

pain share someone's pain

paint Do I have to paint (you) a picture?

parade rain on someone's parade

pardon Beg pardon.

pardon Beg your pardon.

pardon beg your pardon, but

pardon begging your pardon, but

pardon (I) beg your pardon.

pardon (I) beg your pardon, but

pardon Pardon (me).

pardon Pardon me for living!

pardon Pardon my French.

part take someone's part

pass let something pass

past a thing of the past

pay There will be hell to pay.

people It takes all kinds (of people) (to make a world).

people Some people (just) don't know when to give up.

people Some people (just) don't know when to quit.

perfect Do I make myself (perfectly) clear?

perhaps Perhaps a little later.

permit Permit me.

person every other person or thing

personally take something personally

perspective from my perspective

Pete For Pete('s) sake(s)!

phone Who's on the phone?

pick pick and choose

pick pick the low-hanging fruit

picky Don't be so picky!

picky I'm not picky.

picture Do I have to paint (you) a picture?

picture (Do you) get the picture?

picture Get the picture?

pie have one's finger in too many pies

pig When pigs can fly.

pit need to make a pit stop

pity For pity('s) sake(s)!

pity What a pity!

place Don't spend it all in one place.

place in the first place

place in the wrong place at the wrong time

place Is there some place I can wash up?

quit Some people (just) don't know when to quit.

quite Having quite a time.

quite I didn't (quite) catch that (last) remark.

quite I'm having quite a time.

quite It doesn't quite suit me.

quite quite a bit

quite quite frankly

quite speaking (quite) candidly

quite (speaking) (quite) frankly

quite This doesn't quite suit me.

rain rain on someone's parade

raise raised in a barn

rampant run rampant

reach Reach out to someone.

read Do you read me?

read (I) read you loud and clear.

read Read you loud and clear.

ready Anytime you are ready.

ready (Are you) ready for this?

ready (Are you) ready to order?

ready Ready for this?

ready Ready to order?

ready When I'm good and ready.

real (I'll) see you (real) soon.

real See you (real) soon.

really (I) really must go.

really I'm (really) fed up (with someone or something).

really (It) (really) doesn't matter to me.

really Really doesn't matter to me.

really Really must go.

really That (really) burns me (up)!

really You (really) said a mouthful.

reason all the more reason for doing something

recognize How will I recognize you?

record sound like a broken record

religious religious about doing something

remark I didn't (quite) catch that (last) remark.

remember Remember me to someone.

remember Remember to write.

remember Remember your manners.

remind need I remind you that

rest Give it a rest.

rest Give something a rest.

rest No rest for the wicked.

rest The rest is history.

rest (There's) no rest for the wicked.

rest Where is the rest room?

riddance Good-bye and good riddance.

ride Thanks for the ride.

right All right.

right All right already!

right Am I right?

right Be right there.

say That's easy for you to say.

say That's what I say.

say Well said.

say What can I say?

say What do you say?

say What do you want me to say?

say What say?

say What someone said.

say What would you say if I did something?

say when all is said and done

say when everything is said and done

say You can say that again!

say You don't say.

say You know (what I'm saying)?

say You mean to say something?

say You (really) said a mouthful.

say You said a mouthful.

say You said it!

scam What's the scam?

scare scared silly

scenery a change of scenery

school from the old school

school How do you like school?

school That's old school.

scoop What's the scoop?

scot get off scot-free

Scott Great Scott!

scream so mad I could scream

scrub You scrub up good.

scrub You scrub up well.

seal My lips are sealed.

search Search me.

seat (Is) this (seat) taken?

second Don't give it a (second) thought.

second Hang on a second.

second Just a second.

second Wait a sec(ond).

secret Could you keep a secret?

secret keep a secret

secret Your secret is safe with me.

see Am I glad to see you!

see as I see it

see Be seeing you.

see Come back and see us.

see Could I see you again?

see Could I see you in my office?

see Don't see you much around here anymore.

see (Don't you) see?

see Good to see you (again).

see Haven't I seen you somewhere before?

see Haven't seen you in a long time.

see Haven't seen you in a month of Sundays.

see Hope to see you again (sometime).

see (I) haven't seen you in a long time.

see (I) haven't seen you in a month of Sundays.

sit Do sit down.

sit (I'm) able to sit up and take (a little) nourishment.

situation a win-win situation

six It's six of one and half a dozen of another.

six It's six of one and half a dozen of the other.

size That's about the size of it.

skin by the skin of someone's teeth

skin Give me (some) skin!

skin have some skin in the game

skin No skin off my nose.

skin No skin off my teeth.

skin Skin me!

skin Slip me some skin!

skin (That's) no skin off my nose.

skin There's more than one way to skin a cat.

skip Skip it!

slack Cut me a little slack.

slack Cut me some slack.

sleep Got to go home and get my beauty sleep.

sleep (I've) got to go home and get my beauty sleep.

slip Slip me five!

slip Slip me some skin!

slow slow going

slow slower and slower

small Be thankful for small blessings.

small Don't sweat the small stuff.

small Thank God for small favors.

smart You think you're so smart!

smile Keep smiling.

smile Smile when you say that.

smoke Where there's smoke, there's fire.

snap Snap it up!

snap Snap to it!

snappy Make it snappy!

sock Stuff a sock in it!

some and then some

some Catch me some other time.

some Cut me some slack.

some (Do) have some more.

some Give me (some) skin!

some have some face time with someone

some Have some more.

some have some skin in the game

some I'd like some feedback on something.

some I'd like some input about something.

some (I'll) try to catch you some other time.

some Is there some place I can wash up?

some Maybe some other time.

sorry Sorry to hear that.

sorry Sorry you asked.

sorry You'll be sorry you asked.

sort Sort of.

soul Don't tell a soul.

soul (I) won't tell a soul.

soul Won't tell a soul.

sound I don't want to sound like a busybody, but

sound (It) sounds like a plan.

sound let out a sound

sound safe and sound

sound sound like a broken record

sound Sounds like a plan.

soup Soup's on!

spare spare someone something

speak as we speak

speak Can I speak to someone?

speak Could I speak to someone?

speak Don't speak too soon.

speak I'd like to speak to someone, please.

speak in a manner of speaking

speak May I speak to someone?

speak so to speak

speak speak ill of someone

speak Speak of the devil.

speak Speak up.

speak Speaking.

speak speaking (quite) candidly

speak (speaking) (quite) frankly

speak Who do you want to speak to?

speak Who do you wish to speak to?

speak With whom do you wish to speak?

speechless I'm speechless.

spell Come in and sit a spell.

spell Do I have to spell it out (for you)?

spend Don't spend it all in one place.

spend spend (some) quality time with someone

spin put a spin on something

spin spin a yarn

split Got to split.

split (It's) time to split.

split (I've) got to split.

split Time to split.

spoke I spoke out of turn.

spoke I spoke too soon.

square Be there or be square.

stand Don't stand on ceremony.

stand Everyone is (standing) behind you.

stand from where I stand

stand stand up and be counted

stand We're all (standing) behind you.

start for starters

start off to a flying start

stay Come back when you can stay longer.

stay Don't stay away so long.

stay Stay out of my way.

stay Stay out of this!

stay Stay with me.

step (Do) you want to step outside?

step Step aside.

step You want to step outside?

stick Stick with it.

still Better keep still about it.

still Keep still.

still Keep still about it.

still (Someone had) better keep still about it.

stop Glad you could stop by.

stop I'll put a stop to that.

stop (I'm) glad you could stop by.

stop need to make a pit stop

stop Stop the music!

stop Stop the presses!

stop (We're) glad you could stop by.

storm lull before the storm

story That's the story of my life.

straight set someone straight

stranger Don't be a stranger!

stranger Don't make yourself a stranger!

straw That's the last straw!

strike it strikes me that

stuck (stuck) in a rut

stuck stuck in traffic

stuff Cut the funny stuff!

stuff Don't sweat the small stuff.

stuff Stuff a sock in it!

stuff That's the stuff!

stump Got me stumped.

stump (You've) got me stumped.

subject Drop the subject!

subject off the subject

such as such

such (I) never heard of such a thing!

such Like it's such a big deal!

such Never heard of such a thing.

such No such luck.

such No such thing as a free lunch.

such (There's) no such thing as a free lunch.

suit It doesn't quite suit me.

suit (It) suits me (fine).

suit Suit yourself.

suit Suits me (fine).

suit This doesn't quite suit me.

Sunday Haven't seen you in a month of Sundays.

Sunday (I) haven't seen you in a month of Sundays.

suppose I 'spose.

suppose I 'spose not.

suppose I 'spose (so).

suppose I suppose.

suppose I suppose not.

suppose I suppose (so).

suppose (It's) not supposed to.

suppose Not supposed to.

suppose (Someone or something is) supposed to do something.

suppose (Someone's) not supposed to.

suppose 'Spose not.

suppose 'Spose so.

suppose Suppose I do?

suppose Suppose I don't?

suppose Supposed to.

suppose Supposing I do?

suppose Supposing I don't?

sure Can't say for sure.

sure Charmed(, I'm sure).

sure Don't be too sure.

sure For sure.

sure (I) can't say for sure.

sure Likewise(, I'm sure).

sure Oh, sure (someone or something will)!

sure Sure as shooting!

sure Sure thing.

sure What do you know for sure?

sure Yeah, sure.

surprise come as no surprise

surprise I'm not surprised.

surprise take someone by surprise

suspect I suspect.

suspect I suspect not.

suspect I suspect (so).

swap swap something out

sweat break a sweat

sweat Don't sweat it!

sweat Don't sweat the small stuff.

sweat No sweat.

sweet You bet your (sweet) life!

system All systems are go.

table have a chair at the table

tail Can't make heads or tails of something.

tail Get off my tail!

tail (I) can't make heads or tails of something.

tail with one's tail between one's legs

take Able to sit up and take (a little) nourishment.

take Can't take it with you.

take Come in and take a load off your feet.

take Could I take a message?

take Could I take your order (now)?

take Give one an inch, and one will take a mile.

take Give people an inch, and they will take a mile.

take Got to take off.

take (I'm) able to sit up and take (a little) nourishment.

take (Is) this (seat) taken?

take It takes all kinds (of people) (to make a world).

take (I've) got to take off.

take (Just) taking care of business.

take No offense taken.

take take a potshot at someone or something

take Take a shotgun approach to the problem.

tell Don't make me tell you again!

tell Don't tell a soul.

tell Don't tell me what to do!

tell How many times do I have to tell you?

tell (I) won't tell a soul.

tell No way to tell.

tell Tell me another (one)!

tell Tell me more.

tell (Tell me) this isn't happening.

tell (There's) no way to tell.

tell What can I tell you?

tell Won't tell a soul.

tell You mean to tell me something?

tell You're telling me!

ten I wouldn't touch something with a ten-foot pole.

test put someone or something to the test

thank Can't thank you enough.

thank (I) can't thank you enough.

thank I'll thank you to keep your opinions to yourself.

thank I'll thank you to mind your own business.

thank No, thank you.

thank No, thanks.

thank No thanks to you.

thank Not right now, thanks.

thank Nothing for me, thanks.

thank Thank God for small favors.

thank Thank goodness!

thank Thank heavens!

thank Thank you.

thank Thank you a lot.

thank Thank you for a lovely evening.

thank Thank you for a lovely time.

thank Thank you for calling.

thank Thank you for inviting me.

thank Thank you for inviting us.

thank Thank you for sharing.

thank Thank you so much.

thank Thank you very much.

thank Thanks (a lot).

thank Thanks a million.

thank Thanks awfully.

thank Thanks, but no thanks.

thank Thanks for coming.

thank Thanks for having me.

thank Thanks for the lift.

thank Thanks for the ride.

thank Thanks loads.

thankful Be thankful for small blessings.

thing all things considered

thing (Are) things getting you down?

thing Better things to do.

thing Don't worry about a thing.

thing every other person or thing

thing Got better things to do.

thing How're things going?

think You've got another think coming.

thought Don't give it a (second) thought.

thought Don't give it another thought.

thought (I) never thought I'd see you here!

thought lose one's train of thought

thought Never thought I'd see you here!

thought Who could have thought?

thought Who would have thought?

thousand If I've told you once, I've told you a thousand times.

thousand Never in a thousand years!

thousand No, no, a thousand times no!

thousand Not in a thousand years!

through Coming through(, please).

through Do we have to go through all that again?

through Let's not go through all that again.

through talk through one's hat

through through no fault of someone's **own**

throw throw the book at someone

thunk Who would 'a thunk?

thunk Who'd 'a thunk?

ticket That's the ticket!

tie sever ties with someone

time About that time.

time at the present time

time Been a long time.

time Better luck next time.

time Catch me some other time.

time Don't waste my time.

time Don't waste your time.

time Give it time.

time (Good-bye) until next time.

time Had a nice time.

time Have a good time.

time have some face time with someone

time Haven't seen you in a long time.

time Having a wonderful time; wish you were here.

time Having quite a time.

time Having the time of my life.

time How many times do I have to tell you?

time How time flies.

time I don't have time to breathe.

time I don't have time to catch my breath.

time I had a lovely time.

time (I) had a nice time.

time (I) haven't seen you in a long time.

time If I've told you once, I've told you a thousand times.

time (I'll) try to catch you some other time.

time (I'm) having a wonderful time; wish you were here.

time I'm having quite a time.

time (I'm) having the time of my life.

time in the interest of saving time

time in the nick of time

time in the wrong place at the wrong time

time (It's) about that time.

time (It's) been a long time.

time It's that time.

time (It's) time for a change.

time (It's) time I left.

time (It's) time to go.

time (It's) time to hit the road.

time (It's) time to move along.

time (It's) time to move on.

time (It's) time to push along.

time (It's) time to run.

time (It's) time to shove off.

time (It's) time to split.

time It's time we should be going.

time (It's) time we were going.

time I've had a lovely time.

time Long time no see.

time Maybe some other time.

time (My,) how time flies.

time No, no, a thousand times no!

time one more time

time ought to be here any time

time should be here any time

time since time immemorial

time spend (some) quality time with someone

time Thank you for a lovely time.

time There's no time like the present.

time Till next time.

time Time for a change.

time Time I left.

time Time (out)!

time Time to call it a day.

time Time to call it a night.

time Time to go.

time Time to hit the road.

time Time to move along.

time Time to move on.

time Time to push along.

time Time to push off.

time Time to run.

time Time to shove off.

time Time to split.

time Time we were going.

time Times are changing.

time Try to catch you some other time.

time Until next time.

time We had a lovely time.

time We'll try again some other time.

word Could I have a word with you?

word Don't breathe a word of this to anyone.

word (I) won't breathe a word (of it).

word I'd like (to have) a word with you.

word in other words

word Mum's the word.

word My word!

word one final word

word or words to that effect

word Take my word for it.

word Them's fighting words!

word Took the words right out of my mouth.

word twist someone's words (around)

word What's the good word?

word Won't breathe a word (of it).

word (You) took the words right out of my mouth.

work Close enough for government work.

work Does it work for you?

work Don't work too hard.

work Everything will work out (all right).

work Everything will work out for the best.

work How's that working for you?

work How's that working (out)?

work How's that working out (for you)?

work (It) works for me.

work It'll never work!

work (It's) close enough for government work.

work I've got work to do.

work Keep up the good work.

work Things will work out (all right).

work Things will work out for the best.

work Works for me.

world How's the world (been) treating you?

world It takes all kinds (of people) (to make a world).

world Not for the world!

world What's the world coming to?

world What's this world coming to?

worry Don't worry.

worry Don't worry about a thing.

worry Not to worry.

worse Could be worse.

worse (I) could be worse.

worse (I've) seen worse.

worse Seen worse.

worse (Things) could be worse.

worth for what it's worth

worth It isn't worth it.

worth It isn't worth the trouble.